WILD WISDOM

WILD WISDOM

PRIMAL SKILLS TO SURVIVE IN NATURE

DONNY DUST

ILLUSTRATIONS BY BOB VENABLES

SIMON ELEMENT

NEW YORK LONDON TORONTO SYDNEY NEW DELHI

SIMON
ELEMENT

An Imprint of Simon & Schuster, LLC
1230 Avenue of the Americas
New York, NY 10020

This publication contains the opinions and ideas of its author. It is intended to provide helpful and informative material on the subjects addressed in the publication. It is sold with the understanding that the author and publisher are not engaged in rendering medical, health, or any other kind of personal professional services in the book. The reader should consult his or her medical, health, or other competent professional before adopting any of the suggestions in this book or drawing inferences from it.

The author and publisher specifically disclaim all responsibility for any liability, loss, or risk, personal or otherwise, that is incurred as a consequence, directly or indirectly, of the use and application of any of the contents of this book.

First Simon Element hardcover edition August 2024

SIMON ELEMENT is a trademark of Simon & Schuster, LLC

Simon & Schuster: Celebrating 100 Years of Publishing in 2024

For information about special discounts for bulk purchases, please contact Simon & Schuster Special Sales at 1-866-506-1949 or business@simonandschuster.com.

The Simon & Schuster Speakers Bureau can bring authors to your live event. For more information or to book an event, contact the Simon & Schuster Speakers Bureau at 1-866-248-3049 or visit our website at www.simonspeakers.com.

Interior design by Laura Levatino

Printed and Bound in the United Kingdom by CPI Group (UK) Ltd, Croydon, CR0 4YY

10 9 8 7 6 5 4 3 2 1

Library of Congress Cataloging-in-Publication Data has been applied for.

ISBN 978-1-6680-1343-4
ISBN 978-1-6680-1344-1 (ebook)

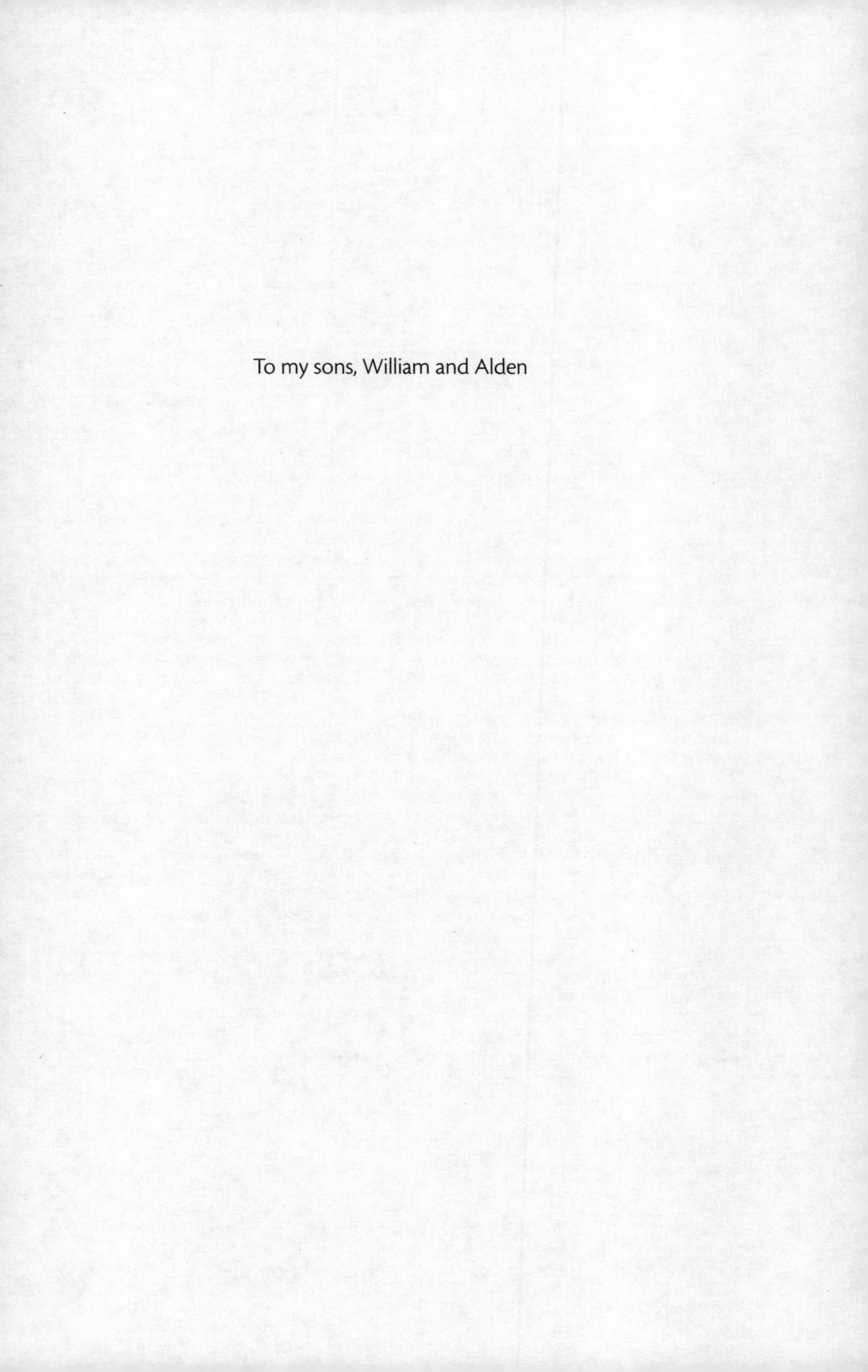

To my sons, William and Alden

CONTENTS

ACKNOWLEDGMENTS

Gary, thanks for teaching, coaching, and mentoring me in this adventure. Sometimes the teacher is the student.

William and Alden, thanks for always being amazing sons and supporting my not-so-normal approach to life. Remember your name.

Marissa, thanks for always being there in the late hours of the night and on cold mornings. May our adventures be endless!

David, thanks for coaching me in all stuff books. It's a different world.

Bob, I appreciate the time, effort, and energy in your drawings.

The team at Simon & Schuster—Justin, Ingrid, Gina, Jessica, Richard, and everyone else—thanks for the chance to share my Wild Wisdom with the world. You gave me a shot when others didn't.

INTRODUCTION

Our plan was simple. My kids and I would start in Boulder, Utah, and walk to Escalante, a town nearly thirty miles away. Southern Utah is the land of slickrock and canyons. At a little more than six thousand feet in elevation, the route would take us through a mixed bag of alpine meadows, pinyon pine, and Juniper forests. We'd welcome the shade offered by cottonwoods along the Escalante River. We'd crane our necks as sandstone walls rose into the brilliant blue skies the Southwest is so famous for and take breaks to admire the various rock formations: natural bridges and arches.

It was March, and crusty, patchy snowfields still dotted the mountainsides and frosted the edges of creek beds. The route we'd be taking roughly traced the Boulder Mail Trail, where Mormon settlers traversed this rugged land on horseback to (surprise!) deliver mail to the isolated outpost of Boulder. We used cairns—stacked rocks placed by those who first blazed the trail—as a rough guide, supplemented by an inaccurate topographic map my then eleven-year-old son used to assist himself with his terrain association navigation. As my backcountry experience has evolved over the last decade or so, I've relied less and less on having all the gear and more and more on having all the knowledge. This trek and others like it—either solo or with my sons, or leading wilderness survival classes—have evolved that ethos further. One fundamental principle underlies it all: there's no right or wrong in your approach to how much you pack out into the backcountry. What matters the most is you returning with an appreciation for what the natural world has to offer and can teach us about ourselves. For me and my kids, that meant only our sleeping bags, one change of clothes, a few snacks, and two one-liter bottles of water. This allowed plenty of room to carry back epic stories and insights from our experience together.

I'm enormously grateful to spend time like this with my kids. Not only do I get to share formative experiences with them but they also get a glimpse of my passion for ancient ways of living and surviving in the wild. I also get to pass on some of what I've learned about self-reliance and survival over the years. While this hike wasn't a full-on exploration and example of the more hard-core experiences I've had in emulating hunter-gatherer cultural practices, it does offer them the opportunity to do what more and more people across this country are craving: to stop immersing themselves in screens and images and exchange their virtual reality experiences for actual ones. We get out there and we do.

A part of our trek took us down into Death Hollow, nearly between our starting and ending points. Despite its name, this section teems with life. This tributary of the Escalante River is a permanent stream that meanders through a deep canyon, sometimes resting in quiet pools or quickening through cascades and small waterfalls. We were grateful to splash, play, and refill our water bottles. Once we were restored and rejuvenated, we reluctantly moved on. We shed that lingering desire to remain, and soon our curiosity drove us on. Eagerness to see what was beyond the next bend replaced any thoughts of what we were leaving behind. If nothing else, that's one insight I want to pass along to my kids, and what motivated my desire to write this book: curiosity about the natural world to discover beyond the next bend and what else life can offer to restore our mental, physical, and emotional well-being and reestablish our primal connections to nature.

What my kids are experiencing in southern Utah is a far cry from what lit my fire as a fourteen-year-old living in Middletown, New Jersey. With Asbury Park just down Route 35, I could have had rock and roll fantasies of being born to run like "the Boss," Bruce Springsteen, or harbored some other Jersey Shore dreams. Instead, my life changed one day wandering through the stalls of a flea market in town. I did see racks of records and more than a few surf-casting rigs, but what caught my eye was a copy of the *U.S. Army Survival Manual*. Its curled cover and dog-eared pages sat among stacks of other paperback copies of thrillers and romance novels. As I flipped through its pages, I saw photos of makeshift animal traps, shelters fabricated from found forest objects, and edible plants. I fell in love. I briefly thought about how it had made its way to a flea market, possibly from Fort Dix, but those thoughts of its origin were soon forgotten.

This book was a practical guide that needed to be put to use. While the name Middletown might conjure up images of a typical strip mall-infested suburb, its name is a bit of giveaway. While there is a commercial township center, the town sits in the middle of a vast network of woodlands and lowlands just miles from the Atlantic Ocean. Like veins, various waterways lead to the ocean. Numerous greenways, parks, and open spaces became my classroom and my proving ground. I guess I've always been a bit of a nonconformist, and I was drawn to life there rather than the haunts along the boardwalk. While my friends and classmates were scoping out attractive possible sexual partners or deciding between a white slice or a margherita slice, I was in the woodlands and wetlands, scoping out edible plants and mushrooms. For me, hooking up meant fashioning a means to catch a fish out of a rib bone from a long-dead rabbit. Rather than having my nostrils filled with the smell of frying foods, popped corn, and tanning oil, they were taking in the odor of leafy muck, mud, and sun-heated grasses. In truth, I was the one being hooked and reeled in by a force that I was inexplicably drawn to. Life outdoors fired

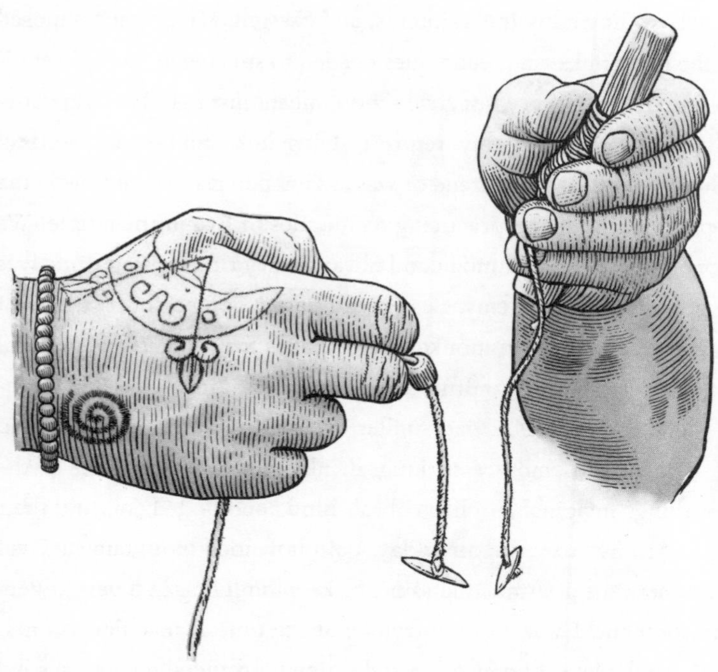

my curiosity and fed my desire to be creative. Still today those two driving forces dominate my life and are the backbone of most of what I have to share in this book. In time, those forces led me down another path that few of my classmates trod.

In 1999, I joined the United States Marine Corps and served for twelve years among the small percentage of Americans who raise their hands in response to the call of duty. The Corps is an organization that allows young men like me to find our place in the world and discover a sense of purpose. I was never really interested in getting a traditional education beyond high school, but I learned one hell of a lot serving. The military's ethos of embracing your strengths and building upon your weaknesses to convert them is very much a central part of my life. I firmly believe that anyone with enough knowledge can develop their fundamental skills to a level of expertise where they are able to not just survive but thrive in the outdoors.

While in the Marines, I attended various survival schools where I could narrow down my initial interest and passion. My training exposed me to the tips, tricks, and techniques needed to survive in multiple environments. In the military, survival school meant just that: keeping yourself alive to evade the enemy, return to friendlies, and resume fighting. Whether I volunteered to attend or was assigned to go, I spent time in the Philippines learning and practicing techniques to live in the jungle. We were operating in stealth mode and always wary of exposing ourselves to the presence of the enemy. I can recall living along a short stretch of beach and tracking down monkeys and snakes for food. I was grateful we could swallow a few handfuls of fresh water and fashion crude weapons to defend ourselves. I had similar experiences in Okinawa, Japan, where I learned to embrace sucking, drinking, and eating some of the nastiest things imaginable—like cobra's blood and boiled ants and their eggs—just to live to see another day. I also attended mountain survival schools where the goal was the same: to keep on living in a very different environment. I was an infantryman at the time, a machine gunner, and that grunt's level of education and training provided me with a solid foundation on which I could build.

Later, I advanced my career and attended various Marine Corps regimental schools where I learned about leadership. I also rappelled and fast-roped out of helicopters using a SPIE rig in special patrol insertion/extraction drills. You definitely wanted to survive those airborne experiences. Eventually, I was recruited into the Marines' counterintelligence/human intelligence field and embedded with various peoples in different environments. In that capacity, I had to provide my assets on the ground with the ability to survive by denying, detecting, and deceiving terrorism, espionage, sabotage, and subversion. If one hundred Marines got on a plane to fly into Iraq, the Philippines, Borneo, Indonesia, Malaysia, South Korea, or anywhere else I was serving downrange, my main goal was to ensure all one hundred of them survived.

I also served as an interrogator and as an intelligence collector. I learned a lot about people and their relationship with the biological imperative—the cellular level needed to exist in the face of multiple threats. Again, that was all survival at its most fundamental and primal. You may be aware of American psychologist Abraham Maslow and his hierarchy of needs. His work is often depicted as a pyramid of our basic survival needs: physiological and safety at the bottom, our psychological needs (belongingness and love) and esteem needs above them, and our higher-order needs, like self-actualization and creative expression, at the top. Much of my early training in survival and my understanding of human psychology, including my own, centered around those two categories at the bottom.

As my understanding, skills, and curiosity evolved, I became much more interested in what I call "thrival." Thriving in the outdoors means more than just merely getting by to see another cycle of sunrise and sunset. It means really enjoying being out in the bush and having all our needs met through nature. You don't just embrace the suck, endure the pain, and eke out a basic existence in your mental and physical pain cave. You also seek and find comfort, satisfy curiosity about yourself and the world, and express your creativity. You find your place mentally, physically, and primally aligned with the forces that helped shaped humanity. You transcend what most people in contemporary life experience in an age when technological advances have made us physically comfortable but often complacent, uncomfortable, and unhappy with our lives. In the pages that follow, I'll go into this transformative means of looking at what it means to thrive in the bush and the benefits we can all derive from doing so.

In the military, I learned a lot about the importance of having a plan and how it impacts the lower-level needs more than the higher-level needs. However, some believe otherwise. If you've got every one of your bases covered and you've got every bit of gear to make your way in the bush more comfortable, then you've got more time to focus on those higher-level growth needs like belonging, esteem, and self-actualization. That's a valid point. I started out as an infantryman and lugged a .50-caliber machine gun, humping my way many a mile. Having been there and done that, maybe that's why I've opted for a new approach. While I still believe you have to be prepared in nature, I've learned a couple of fundamental principles: Know more and carry less and nature provides all.

As you move through this book, you'll see in much greater detail how my thinking and means of surviving and thriving have evolved. I'll share stories behind those principles (and others) and how they liberated me from the tyranny of technology. They allowed me to better enjoy the pleasure of the primal and connect with our humanness, which dates back millennia. Reconnecting with how our human ancestors both survived and thrived has allowed me to grow in ways I would not have expected but am deeply grateful to have experienced.

Just as I took that trip to Utah with my kids, when I shared experiences and knowledge with them, I'm hoping this book can do the same. The saying that experience is the best teacher holds truth. Whether it's talking about my military experience, sharing what I learned from conversations and shared adventures with others in the field, or my fascination and admiration for what prior cultures and indigenous groups learned and taught, I hope that I can help reconnect you to nature.

It's often said that Mother Nature can be a cruel mistress. She can also bedevil us with her beauty. The past few years have been difficult for many people. We've seen the influence of a virus that has claimed lives and reinforced that a healthy, well-balanced lifestyle can sustain us. Our physical, emotional, and psychological selves were threatened and put to an enormous test. Out of all of that, along with the growing recognition that our intervention in the natural order has resulted in serious environmental consequences, I'm not as discouraged as you might think. As a result of being shut out of social interactions at restaurants, bars, schools, and places of work, and because of other aspects of social distancing, many people felt compelled to get outside and back into nature. Like me being drawn to the field survival manual and the resources it provided, Americans and others around the world found an outlet in the natural world. We saw this in many forms: for example, the sale of bicycles skyrocketed, and the parking areas of trailheads that once were barely populated overflowed with vehicles. We faced a challenge and seized an opportunity.

Something deep inside us called out. That voice could be heard when the streets of our cities and towns quieted and we paused to reflect on what really mattered and what we really wanted.

Maybe it was just out of sheer boredom or because our indoor interactions were so limited and so potentially dangerous that we had to get out. Maybe we felt a desire to escape restrictive rules and regulations that governed our social interactions. However, I don't think these are the only reasons. I believe that in the face of an existential crisis that few of us had ever experienced before, an alarm sounded in a primal part of our brain. Long-dormant cellular responses shrugged off years of disuse and keyed in a code for survival. When threatened, our flight-or-fight responses always kick in. Some retreated into binge watching and ordering takeout, and that's okay, but a large segment of the population either opted for, or combined that nesting instinct with, another aspect of our human/animal responses. In the face of this pathogen and the threat it created, many chose to fight the fear and get outdoors. Maybe it was simpler than that. Maybe, with no other outlets, we did what many mothers encourage their kids to do: go outside and play.

I know from personal experience that when our physical well-being is threatened, change is catalyzed. We reprioritize and engage in a perspective shift. This doesn't just happen when our survival literally hangs in the balance. When you serve in the military, you're on "active duty." I thrived in an active, kinetic environment where I was both physically and mentally engaged for most of the day. When it came time for me to leave the Marine Corps, I was faced with a tough transition. What kind of work could I find that would meet my needs and desires to be fully immersed in life like I had been while serving? How could I find a kinetic environment like the one I'd just been existing in for nearly all of my life to that point? Simply put: How could I continue to be happy?

When it comes down to it, what drew me then and draws me now to life outdoors and a primal connection with nature is fun. I'm happiest outside. I'm happiest when I'm moving and doing—both physically and mentally. The kind of thinking and problem-solving that is required when being outside is incredibly stimulating. The stakes don't have to be life-or-death. Even in facing lesser challenges, we experience what it really means to be alive and not just survive. For a lot of us, getting by and staying safe even when not engaged in outdoor pursuits poses a threat to our well-being. We fall into routines. We live mindlessly. We rely on devices to solve our problems and easily answer any questions we have, and in our search for a life of ease we've developed a dis-ease. Lurking in the shadows is this frequent thought: *If this whole thing falls apart, do I have what it takes to endure?*

In the pages that follow, I'll interrogate these questions. I offer both a look at how we got to this point and a practical how-to handbook for taking the next steps deeper into the backcountry. Part manifesto and part reference that updates what I learned from the *U.S. Army Survival Manual*, what I have to share works well for those who want to explore both their physical and mental limits. It's a guide for how to think and how to act to maximize your outdoor experiences while minimizing risk to your well-being. It will help you not just endure but enjoy. You'll not only survive but thrive in the outdoors.

I've been there and done that. I've gone deep into my body and soul and into nature and have come back with some hard-earned lessons and insights. My hope is that by letting both this book and curiosity be your guide, you'll get out there, dig deeper, go farther, have more fun, and learn more about yourself and the world you inhabit than ever before.

PART I

A SURVIVAL MANIFESTO

 CHAPTER 1 

OUR PRIMAL PAST

I'm thrilled that my adolescent fascination with survival has transformed into the way I make my living. Today, I operate a survival and wilderness self-reliance school in Colorado. I have clients who come from around the world. Thanks to my kids, I've managed not just to survive but to thrive in the social media world. They urged me to join the world of social media, and more than ten million people have made the choice to follow me and watch my survival-oriented videos. As a result of that media exposure, I've appeared on television and in other media, and in some quarters I've earned the reputation for being a "professional caveman." I appreciate all that recognition, but, more accurately, I'm passionate about remote primitive survival, ancient/historical technologies, and lithic arts. I'll explain those three things in greater detail down the line. For now, I'll sum me up by saying that I'm mainly interested in how we can all apply collective knowledge to live wild.

PUTTING A FINER EDGE ON THE STONE AGE

What I find most interesting about being dubbed a "caveman" is that I believe many people who use that term are using it as a compliment but with an unacknowledged edge. When people think of a caveman, they likely envision a gruff, inarticulate, blunt-headed, grunting, fur-clad protohuman whose savagery far outdistances his sagacity—his smarts. I don't view our ancestors that simplistically. I believe, as do most anthropologists, that the cavemen and cavewomen who preceded us and existed in the Stone Age outdistanced us in a number of ways. It took not just good fortune and the luck of the genetic draw to survive the planetary upheaval they experienced. I don't think we give enough credit to our earliest ancestors for their brains while concentrating too much on their brawn.

Similarly, I think that, for many of us, Darwin's theory of evolution has been reduced to an easy catchphrase: "survival of the fittest." Which species flourished and which ones floundered and died out came down to a kind of test of physical prowess or simply the roll of the genetic dice. In a lot of cases, then, species of all kinds, human and otherwise, were victims of a cosmic game of chance. I don't quite see it that way. I will admit that Darwinism—survival of the fittest—helps people develop a big-picture understanding of humans' past. However, that big picture is an incredibly complex one, and what did and didn't survive comes down to a large number of factors. Among them is the fact that human evolution and species survival relied a great deal on socialization. Our forming an ever-widening social circle has been both a boon and a bust—the latter because tribal conflicts persist to this day.

The same is true when we slap a label like "caveman" on our ancestors. I think most of us would recoil, if at some point in the future after some new evolutionary leap, that newly evolved species looked back at us humans and our fossil record and decided to name us based on where we laid our heads down at night. Those who study human history and evolution try to lend us a hand and give us scientific hooks on which we can hang our understanding of how different hominids (the family classification we belong to along with the great apes) were active and evolved. We've all seen charts that depict the ascent of man, and most of them show the progression in a straight line. That's not accurate; what really should be represented is a web, since there was interbreeding with other primates.

EARLY PROTO-HUMANS

What I think makes sense to consider is the point at which the first known species of the genus *Homo* came along. *Homo habilis* was one of our earliest human ancestors, and its Latin name means

"Handy Man." It got that name because, in 1964, scientists at the time thought that this species, which lived 2.4 to 1.5 million years ago, was the first to make tools. (Later studies showed that stone tools predate any of the beings in the genus *Homo*.) That's a tough call to make because there were other species of early humans, like *Australopithecus africanus*, also around at the time, and none of them had developed a patent office to keep track of who invented what and when. (There's also no record of who borrowed what tools from whom and failed to return them promptly, thus demonstrating one downside of primates becoming social beings.) Regardless of who was the first, the important thing to keep in mind is that some pre-human and human species were making tools a *long* time ago. And as far as we know, no other species apart from those in the genus *Homo* has fashioned tools to any great degree. They may use found objects to aid in some tasks, but that's not the same as truly making tools.

About 1.89 million years ago, another human species was active, *Homo erectus*, or "Upright Man." They had body proportions more like modern humans: longer legs and shorter arms than their predecessors. This indicates that they were better adapted to life on the ground. They lost some of their tree-climbing adaptations and were likely able to walk and run long distances. They also had a braincase that was larger in proportion to the size of their face. Skeletal remains that we've uncovered reveal that they looked similar to us. They were toolmakers as well, and one of their major innovations was crafting hand axes and cleavers—more sophisticated implements than the earliest stone types.

Their bigger brains—as much as 80 percent larger than their earlier ancestors' brains—and taller bodies meant they needed more energy to function than other species. This brain growth shows the human evolution from this species as the real starting point for modern humans. Being the toolmakers they were, their innovations helped process protein sources, especially meat but also fish, shellfish, and birds, along with plants and leaves to satisfy that bigger-brain energy requirement. As humans, 20 percent of our calorie consumption goes toward "feeding" our brains. They also seemed to have mastered the art and science of making fires and using them for cooking, warmth, and protection against large predators. Cooking was especially important because cooked food is easier for us to process as energy than raw food. Scientists also believe that those tools aided them in surviving during climate changes.

Their adaptability allowed them to survive in habitats in Southeast Asia and Africa. The species also managed to stick around for two million years, lasting until just over one hundred thousand years ago. By walking upright, they were able to cover long distances. As anyone who hikes or runs knows, muscle exertion produces heat. If your skin is covered with fur, you retain that heat, and you sweat and tire quickly. The species *Homo erectus* wasn't covered from head to toe with fur; therefore it literally ran cooler and could pursue its prey, including the big felines, over longer distances on foot. Once the prey was exhausted, *Homo erectus*, with its long arms, was able to throw rocks and spears a greater distance and with more accuracy than any other primate. Part of that rock throwing was the luck of the genetic draw, but also those early humans figured out how to use tools to aid their hunting. Along with the tools, they devised strategies to take advantage of their long arms. Brains and brawn worked together to help certain species outpace other members of their class.

Earliest proto-humans likely lived in pairs, but by the time *Homo erectus* arrived at its peak and thereafter, we lived in groups of around one hundred. Why that number? Scientists believe it is easy for us to keep track of and account for. As this species thrived, they likely exceeded that number and tensions and stresses arose, resource competition increased, and one group split off to form another group or moved to another area—including setting out on the water.

NOT THE ONLY GAME IN TOWN

Homo erectus wasn't the only early human species; there were also *Homo neanderthalensis*, or Neanderthals. They went extinct approximately forty thousand years ago, and the reason for their disappearance is the subject of great debate. What isn't up for debate is that

Neanderthals were quite advanced as they navigated the waters of the Mediterranean. In addition to making stone tools, creating fire, and having hearths, they used birch bark tar as an adhesive to make clothes and weave. They used medicinal plants to treat injuries and were capable of storing food. They were likely apex predators at the top of the food chain. They also had symbolic thoughts, made art and music, and were possibly capable of speaking. That makes them a pretty creative bunch. Physically, compared to us today, Neanderthals were shorter-limbed and stouter. Why that adaptation occurred isn't fully known, but some believe that because of the colder climate they inhabited, the closer their extremities were to their core, the better they were able to conserve body heat. Compared to other species, they were relatively few in number, and therefore genetic variation was low. That may explain, in part, why they went extinct.

What's of even greater debate is when the split between Neanderthals and modern humans occurred. When Neanderthals split from their ancestor, *Homo heidelbergensis*, is also unclear. But the fact is that they did become distinct species. And the question of why one species, modern humans, or *Homo sapiens*, came to enjoy such a dominant position is worth thinking more about. It's also interesting to note that for a long time Neanderthals suffered a bad reputation. One German scientist in the late nineteenth and early twentieth century created a primate family tree and labeled Neanderthals as *Homo stupidus*. I don't know for sure if that was the seed of the unthinking caveman stereotype that persists to a large degree today, but the fact that it has endured in popular culture for as long as it has troubles me. Yes, Neanderthals have had their reputation rehabilitated to some degree, but across the board I'd argue that not just them but all early humans deserve a lot more credit for what they accomplished than discredit for how "primitive" they were. That word is relative. Today, modern humans may be considered the pinnacle of evolution, supremely adaptive and intellectually powerful, but I still believe that we have a lot to learn from our ancestors and there's much to admire about their survivability.

A little more than a decade ago, a genome project revealed the possibility of interbreeding between Neanderthals and modern humans.

Starting a few years ago, people took genetic tests for a variety of reasons, including determining how much Neanderthal DNA they carried. If your ancestors came from Europe, Asia, or Australasia, you have at least some. In some quarters, the more Neanderthal DNA you had, the greater your bragging rights. Some liked the associations with the caveman brute stereotype, while others opted for the more "evolved" modern human/*Homo sapiens*–like view of them.

THE LONE SURVIVOR

All humans today are members of the *Homo sapiens* species. In other words, we are the only human species that hasn't gone extinct. *Homo sapiens* started three hundred thousand years ago, and modern *Homo sapiens* originated seventy-five thousand years ago. Relatively speaking, that seventy-five thousand years of existence for modern humans is fairly brief. Like the other species, early *Homo sapiens* made stone tools but eventually created smaller, more sophisticated and specialized ones including things like fishhooks, bows and arrows, and even sewing needles. I don't need to list all the technological advances we've created since, especially since some of you may be reading this on a tablet—and I'm not talking about the stone ones our not-so-distant relatives used. About sixty thousand years ago, *Homo sapiens* were able to outcompete every other early human species. What ended *Homo erectus*'s two-million-year run? In other words, what made *Homo sapiens* superior to all others, including Neanderthals? The most current thinking is that the members of *Homo sapiens* weren't necessarily more intelligent than other hominids. They were more social, and banding together to form strong social ties enabled them to move to different environments and increase in number. That may be true, but I also don't want to dismiss entirely the role that intelligence played in aiding the survival and development of all the various human species.

So why does this examination of evolutionary history matter? For me, it's not so much about remembering all these different Latin names of our ancestors; instead, it's about reconnecting not just with what these early humans did but with how they thought. Survival is always about solving a problem. And the problem is this: How do I continue to exist in the face of forces that act against that desire, often referred to as the biological imperative? All creatures feel the urge to persist, and some act programmatically to do so, but with our bigger brains came a bigger tool set we could use to figure out what we could do to continue living. And as I pointed out above, as we thrived and survived in greater numbers, we also produced social and environmental problems that needed to be solved. Heading out to a new location was just one possible solution. We managed to devise others. Traveling farther and wider meant encountering new forces—environmental, meteorological, and social—that resulted in more problems that needed to be solved. As our bigger brains were used to deal with those issues, they continued to grow. Going all the way back to *Homo habilis* and its becoming bipedal, their ability to manipulate their hands and fingers allowed them to gesture, one of the earliest forms of human-to-human communication. Of course, the evolution toward spoken and then written language also required a large amount of brainpower.

Bottom line, this brief tour through human evolution and what so-called cavemen were like is meant to point out a fundamental fact about survival: it isn't simply the strongest who survive but the smartest and the most adaptable. Yes, you must have some physical capabilities as a modern human to survive, but it's even more important to have high-quality gray matter than high-quality muscle mass. I should know. I've done some survival "competitions," and the mental mistakes and poor choices ultimately led me to drop out. The spirit was willing, but the thought processes were weak, which led to wreaking havoc on the body. Our earliest ancestors had to strike a balance among the physical, mental, and emotional aspects of self, as do we as modern humans.

TAKING CONTROL OF OUR PRIMAL HISTORY

Fortunately, there's a way to link what our primal ancestors did and thought to help us solve the problems we face in our natural world and in our artificial world. Survival courses like the ones I conduct—and, to a lesser extent, survival-based entertainment and information available on a wide variety of platforms—offer many insights and approaches to connect us to our past. It may sound as if it's as simple as getting back to basics, returning to a previous time, and living a simpler existence where the stakes were higher to master the same skills as Neanderthals and other early human species, but it's far more than that. It isn't so much about emulating what those people did as it's about solving the problems we face with the same set of thinking tools that they employed. In fashioning a tool like a hand axe or learning to make a fire or set a trap, we're relying primarily on our brains and then our bodies to survive in the natural world. We're using our brains to help build up a sense of security, develop a level of perseverance that exceeds any we've exhibited before. We're going to develop a toolbox of critical thinking skills and performative skills that we can take from our experiences out in the bush and bring back home. We can get in touch with our essential human self that isn't as far removed from us as we think. We need to think about curiosity, creativity, and critical thinking in a new way. All three are essential to success in our daily lives, in our careers or jobs, and in having control over our own personal evolution.

WHY MASTER PRIMAL SKILLS?

For most of us, our basic needs are more than met. We have easy access to food. We have a roof over our heads every night except when we choose to sleep under the stars. All our material needs are met. Yet, job satisfaction is at an all-time low. Satisfaction with or acceptance of our government, our elected officials, and those who differ with our points of view is trending seriously downward. For many, forced containment with those we're closest to exposed fault lines in those relationships. Being socially distant and sometimes having to mourn the loss of close personal connections possibly increased mental health problems among us. We've had to find other sources of personal fulfillment and a sense of satisfaction.

A return to nature and learning forms of survival is an opportunity for us to challenge ourselves and find a new form of satisfaction. In some ways, the pandemic highlighted our lack of connection to nature. As the pandemic shut us off from social gatherings indoors, many people fled to the outdoors. National parks, local parks, trailheads, walking and cycling paths, and nearly every form of outdoor activity saw an increase in participation. I'm not certain how it can be measured, but I do wonder what level of satisfaction that produced. What I don't have to wonder about is the fact the pandemic did result in a perspective shift. We recalibrated in a variety of ways. Many people questioned their relationship with work, with other people, and with nature.

As human evolution has progressed to this point, we've lost a connection to nature. We once lived seasonally. We once moved nomadically. We ate locally. We housed naturally. We "exercised" functionally. We slept "organically": without electricity, the rise and fall of the sun dictated when we slept and woke. At various times, we've seen movements that encouraged a move toward one or more of the above. Some groups returned to a life that encompasses all the things we've lost. Likely, the people who engaged and fostered that approach didn't think that what they were advocating for was a return to what it meant to be a caveman. But in my case I do think that what I offer is exactly that. I've reframed for myself, and I hope to for you, what it means to live like a caveman. They survived by solving problems; they used their brains and not just their brute physicality to endure. They thought it more than they toughed it.

I get that a "professional caveman" is a bit of an oxymoron. Our early human ancestors didn't earn a living by mastering a set of survival skills; they literally earned their existence. That's a pretty hard-core way to go about in the world. But when faced with that reality, they adopted and adapted, standing up to expand their understanding of taking and releasing control and when to think and act.

In studying them and our present incarnation, I think I offer some insights into tips and tricks that will help us individually and collectively to give those early humans a run for their longevity records. Records are made to be broken, after all.

HOW MY TRAINING SESSIONS WORK

Once we're deep into the environment, I ask my students to drop their packs and sit, look, listen, and smell. Essentially, I'm telling them to "freeze." Fainting isn't an optimal response, but freezing is. If you simply flee or fight before adequately assessing a situation, then you're basing your choice on either bad data or no data at all. For me, freezing is the essential first step in survival.

I frequently refer to the pattern of life. That pattern exists with variations in every environment. The key is to detect that pattern. Pattern recognition relies on observation. Observation in the wild relies on being attuned to our senses. (Prior to being out in that environment, we can do some reading and research, but the old line about experience being the best teacher really does apply here.) Whether you're in the jungle, desert, mountains, or tundra, you can discover a pattern of existence in that zone. For me, survival and thrival are intricately entwined in detecting that pattern and understanding the implications of it.

There are many nuances and intricacies that make up that pattern. Often, in baseline physiological and safety survival, detecting that pattern can help you meet your fundamental needs. You don't really become a part of the pattern; you understand and exploit it. When you're thriving in the natural world, you do become a part of that larger pattern. You live within it and you adapt and adopt your behaviors, attitudes, and thinking to connect with that particular place and time in the natural world. My goal when I travel to a particular place to be out in nature is to find pleasure in subsuming myself into that pattern. I've been on enough trails and moved past enough campsites to know that for some people that's not their end goal. Maybe you've experienced what I have when people are hiking and either carrying on a nearly nonstop conversation, listening to music—either having it broadcast from a device or hearing it privately on their headphones—or consulting their smartphones or snapping photos. It's hard to imagine that they've detected that natural pattern and blended in with it. In fact, it's quite the opposite from what

I intend. They're altering the landscape and soundscape. They're not adapting or adopting their behaviors to fit in. Instead, they are layering on a veneer they've brought with them from outside that environment onto the natural one that existed before they arrived.

That sounds judgy, and I run the risk of protesting too much by saying that it's fine for those people, but it's not what I want out of my time in nature. But that really is how I feel. I wish that they could use the well-intentioned statement of "leave no trace" that governs how we should conduct ourselves in public places where the natural world has been set aside for us. But I don't demand that they take the same approach that I do. When I say that nature provides us with everything we need, I'm not simply talking about things we can consume and utilize to meet our physical needs—food, water, shelter, and safety; I'm saying that nature provides us with all kinds of information that will help us locate those things, as well as stimuli that enable us to feel a sense of belonging and love. When we can identify the source of a sound—a bird's call, the branch-snap of a deer approaching—and have our senses confirmed, we can feel a sense of pride. When we use our critical thinking skills out in the bush to solve a problem, our cognitive needs are met in novel ways that truly matter. They may not be life-or-death-level problems, but the satisfaction that comes from finding a water source when lips are chapped and mouths are parched sure beats listening to the sound of our GPS voice leading us to a gas station when the low-fuel light is illuminated on our car's dashboard.

There isn't much that I can add to the notion that the natural world offers us an abundance of aesthetic delights. Through my explorations and adventures in nature, I enjoy its beauty and solve the problems inherent in being in a variety of environments. As a result, I have the kinds of peak experiences that lead to self-actualization and transcendence. I don't just survive; I thrive. I feel whole and at peace to a far greater degree out there in here (I'm patting my heart as I write this) than I do at most any other time in my life. And when I do it in the company of my family, those feelings of satisfaction are heightened even more. When I see a client lighting up with the same fire that burns in me, the intensity grows exponentially.

ANOTHER CAR ON THE "F" TRAIN

Unless we are cursed with a mental illness that compels us otherwise, we are all driven to survive. I believe we all want to thrive in whatever environment we exist in—out in nature and in "civilization." Some of us don't like to be challenged or pushed outside the limits of our comfort zone. I get it. Many people think that fear is real. Like I tell my kids: YOU SHOULD FEAR NOTHING.

Fear is a projection of events and circumstances that have not yet happened.

Fear is a projection of the unknown.

People ask me all the time if I carry a gun when I go out in the wild. I tell them no, never. They ask, "Aren't you afraid of bears or mountain lions?" I tell them I'm not because I'm not. It's not beneficial to my survival to expend valuable energy on something that hasn't happened and is very unlikely to happen. I live in Colorado, and the chances of me being attacked and killed by a mountain lion are, statistically, only slightly greater than my chances of being eaten alive by another human being. David Baron, in his excellent book *The Beast in the Garden: The True Story of a Predator's Deadly Return to Suburban America*, makes that claim. In 1991, a young man by the name of Scott Lancaster was attacked and killed by a mountain lion while running on a trail near Clear Creek High School in Idaho Springs. Six years later, another man was killed by a mountain lion in Rocky Mountain National Park. During the winter of 1874, a prospector and self-proclaimed wilderness guide by the name of Alferd Packer confessed to resorting to eating the flesh of dead members of his traveling party during an arduous trek through the San Juan Mountains in the depths of a harsh winter. I'll take my chances and carry less with no fear of encountering either of those two fates. I would never let fear dictate or prevent me from doing what I want to do. That's not to say I advocate for being reckless and endangering myself unnecessarily. I believe in being prepared and, even more so, developing the skills, abilities, and acquiring the knowledge to survive by risking and responding accordingly.

My military experience shaped a lot of my thinking about fear. When I was downrange while doing counterintelligence work in Iraq, for example, I accepted the fact that at some point I might very well fall victim to a sniper's bullet. I also understood that if a sniper took me out, I wouldn't even know it had happened. So, why fear it? I prepared for that eventuality and understood the environment in which I was operating. I figured that if it was a sniper or an improvised explosive device (IED), I couldn't let fear get in the way of me doing what I was tasked to do: gather human intelligence. My intelligence and my preparedness, I believed, would help tip the scales. So, if I got smart enough and if I got prepared enough, I was willing to accept the consequences of what fate had in store for me. I wasn't willing to accept the consequences for not being thoughtful enough or prepared enough that I'd get myself shot up or blown up. I wasn't willing to accept the consequences for being so preoccupied by fear that I allowed my situational awareness in that environment to slip.

Ultimately, it comes down to a kind of cost-benefit analysis, or risk and reward. Being out in the natural world and existing in as primal a state as possible does for me what nothing else in the world I've experienced has. And I've seen the same thing with many of my clients as they've enjoyed professional success. They may have great friendships and family relationships, but even after just a two-day course I'll see a certain look come over them. They'll tell me that they have never felt so good. We may not have been successful in catching fish for dinner the night before, but that didn't matter. That morning we caught one fish and cooked it up and shared it among the four of us. And it was the best damn fish we'd ever eaten. Everything felt right in the world. And that's because we were out there in Mother Nature, and though she can be harsh, she won't lie to you. She will not cheat and she will not steal. The natural world is 100 percent honest all the time. It is the purest thing that has ever existed.

And the connection that we feel to it is the same. As humans, we arose from the water, the land, and the air. Unfortunately, though, over the course of hundreds of years, we've distanced ourselves from those primal elements. In doing so, we've severed some of those connections; however, we can span that gap. When you're out in the bush and you're cold, you can bundle yourself up in a $500 high-end-brand jacket and capture the heat your body is losing, or you can build a fire and enjoy the warmth and comfort of knowing that you provided for your needs yourself. That feeling is 100 percent true and authentic. Even if you fail at making a fire, you can drop to the ground, do push-ups, spring back up, and do jumping jacks, and you'll be heated by your body's exertions. You can face a challenge and figure out a way to overcome it. You can develop resilience against hardship and apply those lessons about always finding a way through, around, or over any obstacle you might face in your life in the bush or in the burbs. And you'll develop a better perspective. Maybe your luggage is taking a lot longer to reach the carousel than you'd like or some other calamity like that will befall you. When you've faced even harsher consequences for failure or f***ups—your own or others'—your resilience will increase, as will your body of knowledge and your faith to rise above your circumstances. There's a real beauty in relying on your own brains and brawn.

CHAPTER 2

HAVE THE HEART TO MAKE CHANGES

The broad scope of human evolution is of great interest to me. This curiosity led me to flint-knapping and other primitive arts. In a very real way, I've regressed in my approach to my relationship with the outdoors. The fact that I now call what I strive to do "living wild" is indicative of that retrograde direction. So you might be wondering: How can you "evolve" by going backward? Well, like a lot of things in life, just because something is an apparent contradiction, that doesn't mean we can't derive some benefit from exploring those concepts. I believe that we can all benefit greatly by looking back at how our human ancestors lived and emulating some of their approaches to surviving and thriving. We can derive a lot of wisdom and enhance our lives when we decide to go wild.

THE NATURE OF THE MISSION

As I mentioned in the introduction, I developed a fascination with and an appreciation for living in nature early on. That continued when I served in the military, though it didn't take my preferred form: wandering free in the woods and taking in its sights and sounds and smells for the pure pleasure of it. Instead, my time in the Marine Corps was about learning survival skills to ensure that I lived to fight another day. It was a bare-bones approach with a clearly defined set of expectations/goals attached. Evade capture. Return to the unit. Continue to fight. And, at the time, those seemed to me to be reasonable, tangible, logical goals. They still are. But what's changed is the nature of the enterprise. In civilian life, I don't go out in the bush with a specific mission. Instead, capture, evasion—literal life-and-death struggles—figure prominently in my mind. Sure, I could come up against some baddies who want to do me harm—insects, animals, and even humans—and those threats do exist as potentialities, but they aren't the dominant forces against which I battle. I don't really think of living wild in terms of warfare or conquest.

I know that culturally, in particular in popular culture, we love the concept of struggling for survival. All you have to do is turn on your television and you'll see various iterations on that theme. I wasn't a great student when I was in school, but I do remember sitting in an English class where we talked about literature and the basic conflicts that drive it: man versus man, man versus society, and man versus nature. We'd read a story in our anthology, and one of the first questions the teacher would ask would be, "Which of the three main conflicts was the main one in this story?" Kids would shoot their arms up like arrows and then twist their hands trying to get the teacher's attention. I don't remember the name of the story, but we read about two factions of people living in the Carpathian Mountains. I remember that name because they sounded exotic. I wondered how different it might be from where I lived near the Rockies. The name tells you what to expect: rocks. With the Carpathians, I wasn't so sure but was curious to find out.

In any case, this story was about two guys, one from each of the clans that were in conflict, wandering through the woods on a wintry, stormy late afternoon shortly before sunset. A vague boundary existed in the heavily wooded mountainside. There'd been poachers from each side encroaching on the other's territory. The two dudes were out there armed and eager—if not to find suitable game to eat with winter bearing down on them, then to capture a poacher. As fate would have it, they came upon each other in the forest. The wind was howling, the snow was blowing, and both were brain cold and struggling to make sense of what they were encountering. They approached each other, post-holing through the deep snow, rifles cocked and ready. They got into it vocally, challenging the other's rights to be on the land and leveling threats. Before they could make good on those threats, they heard a crack above the roaring wind. It wasn't fire from weapons; instead, what they heard was the trunk of a spruce tree splintering. They both looked up and saw the tree falling toward them. In the deep snow, they stood little chance of escaping and they didn't. They lay there stunned while pinned to the ground by enormous branches of the spruce's canopy. Then reality hit them. Darkness had also fallen. Neither of them could move easily. In the fierce cold and without being able to move their limbs freely, hypothermia and death were real possibilities.

They had to do something.

In the end, they realized that the only way they'd survive was by cooperating. One of the men had a delimbing axe in addition to his rifle. He couldn't really swing it, but he could pass it on to the other man, whose arms were both free. After hours of effort, he was able to extricate himself. Now he faced a choice. Do I leave my sworn enemy to die and let nature take its course, or do I rescue him?

This was a junior high class, so you can guess that cooperating won out.

For a lot of reasons, I remember that story so well and saw that all three of those main conflicts played out in obvious ways in the plot. Instead of struggling with each other, working together was the way to survive. (There were lots of references to them thrashing around and trying to free themselves in order to reach their weapons and just making the situation worse.) They each had to figure out ways to not fight against the forces they faced but to use physics and things like leverage to get the trunk off the more seriously injured man.

IT'S NOT ABOUT DOMINATION

I could go on, but the main point I want to make in sharing that story is that it took me a relatively long time to get over the notion that living wild wasn't about dominating nature but cooperating with it. Nature wasn't the enemy that had to be defeated, but it offered me all the things I needed in order to survive and to thrive. Yes, I would sometimes be involved in a struggle, but those engagements were more about me solving a problem intellectually—and to a lesser degree physically—than it was sheer might against might. I've heard this said about aging athletes and their impending retirement and/or reduction in productivity. Father Time is undefeated. We can say much the same about Mother Nature. They are formidable foes, and woe to anyone who thinks that it's better to fight against them than to learn to work with them. One of my mantras is that Mother Nature offers everything we need to survive—and that's not just so that all our basic needs are met but so that our higher-order ones are as well.

A buddy of mine is a do-it-yourself fanatic. He had a tree on his property that threatened his home's roof and some power lines. He wanted some help in taking that bad boy down, and I assisted. (Spoiler alert: the two of us didn't get trapped by it.) He had a whole set of ratchet straps, ropes, a come-along, and a winch attached to his truck that he was going to use to make sure he felled the tree in the direction he wanted: away from the house and the power lines.

I don't know if it was the Pythagorean theorem or Avogadro's number he used to calculate all the angles, but it took nearly an hour to get all the lines intersected properly. By the time he fired up his chain saw, the only thing in doubt was whether the many lines attached to that lodgepole pine would be able to fall and not get hung up like a tent pole in our little three-ring circus. It didn't. The tree fell, and my buddy's look of glee was priceless. He was relieved that things had gone as planned. Over the years, he's taken down many more trees on his lot, and he's refined his game through experience. Unless there's a real possibility of property or personal damage, he goes minimal: just the right cut with the saw and no intricate ropes and pulleys. He's happier and more efficient. He's also said to me that he doesn't even like using his chain saw anymore. He lives in a mountain neighborhood that's pretty quiet, and the whining, raspy scream of a high-strung two-stroke engine, even when wearing ear protection, gets to be too annoying. He also said that he's found pleasure in swinging a nicely weighted Scandinavian-made felling axe and then bucking that tree with an equally well-made delimbing axe. Sure, those tools require him to keep the blades sharp, but he finds that relaxing and rewarding. He also enjoys the workout he gets by doing that task by hand. Man versus machine is one of those basic dramatic conflicts that we didn't talk about in my junior high English class, but we've all encountered that one. Oftentimes simpler is better. Blistering my hands instead of blistering my tongue cursing a balky machine is frequently my preferred option.

In my friend's tree-felling evolution and my relationship with living wild, the most obvious point is that we've gone back to basics. Where the two of us depart a bit is in the initial phases of our endeavors. The one thing that the military seemed to stress above all others was the need to be prepared and to have a specific, highly detailed, multilevel plan of action. In the Corps we talked about having a plan to have a plan. That's important in a very fluid endeavor where the stakes are high and there are multiple levels of authority and accountability in play.

THE BEST-LAID PLANS

Over time, and in response to several influences, I recalibrated on the planning and now very much prefer to keep a minimal objective in mind when I go out into the bush. My evolution wasn't prompted by a rejection of all the things the military taught me about operational effectiveness. Plans are good things, but they aren't the only things. As we grow in experience and wisdom, we find out that there are many more options available to us. I would imagine that anyone reading this who has spent time outdoors on multiday excursions has bumped up against the different planning styles of their fellow travelers. Group dynamics are an interesting phenomenon, but it's really beyond the scope of this book to get into them in great depth.

To be honest, I really prefer to be out in the bush alone or with a canine companion who can communicate without uttering a word. I've always enjoyed being out in the wilderness by myself and having no real plan in mind for the day besides getting a little bit farther along the journey from point A to point B, while allowing for, and seeking out, several detours along the way.

MAN PLANS AND THE UNIVERSE LAUGHS

One of the major events in my life occurred on February 3, 2017. It was 2:30 a.m.

Something is wrong. My chest is on fire. It hurts . . . It hurts so bad, I thought.

My mind was racing. I was thirty-seven years old. I was as healthy as could be. Now I'd been torched with a series of sensations unlike anything I'd ever felt before.

I was off to the ER to get checked out. After filling out the obligatory paperwork and having my pocketknife confiscated, I was administered a few doses of morphine. That likely explains my fragmented memories of what happened next. I do remember being wheeled into a room with bright lights and lots of monitoring equipment.

My next recollection was a young female doctor welcoming me back to the land of the conscious. She told me that I had suffered a massive heart attack. My left anterior descending (LAD) artery was 99 percent blocked. She was blunt about it. I should have been dead. I had survived what many refer to as a "widow-maker" blockage. I wasn't the typical candidate for an LAD blockage like the one I'd developed. I didn't eat unhealthily, wasn't a diabetic, obese, a smoker, or a sedentary guy. Rather, I was a loser in the genetic lottery. Having a family history of cardiac disorders predisposed me to a heart attack and arterial blockage. I was lucky I hadn't died. I would need six months of a cardiac recovery plan to recuperate from this.

So, the thing is I didn't buy into that genetics-only explanation. I tortured myself for quite a while thinking of all the dumb shit I'd done that could have stressed that artery. All the times I didn't do an extra ten repetitions or another mile or so of running. I was embarrassed that I thought of myself as a fit and healthy dude and I wasn't.

I tried to laugh my health scare off with buddies by saying, "Hey, I was a Marine; we're always getting issued shitty gear," while pointing to my heart.

What I did take seriously was the cardiac rehabilitation plan that I had to follow for the first six weeks post-attack. In a way, I was back in the Corps, doing basic training classes three days a week. Life became regimented and continued to be after those classes. I had to follow a strict regimen and a heart-healthy diet, stay active and keep my cardiovascular system strong, take my meds, keep positive and motivated, and maintain a stress-free lifestyle. Stress and depression were real threats to my well-being, and they were frequently like snipers, making their presence known only when it was too late. The military infused in us the importance of developing situational awareness. I'll get into that in more detail later, but basically it means staying alert and attuned and permanently checked into a room in the reality hotel. Post–heart attack, I did a quick assessment of my situation. I fine-tuned those observations and impressions throughout my recovery. As a result of observing and vigilant self-checking, I made these sobering judgments: I'd survived that first heart attack and could then look forward to living another fifty or more years. That is, of course, barring an accident or some other major health challenge. Even if I made it to eighty or so years, I'd likely have another heart attack, one that would most likely kill me. Understanding *how* I was likely to die was one thing; knowing *when* it would happen was another.

A SHIFT IN MY PERSPECTIVE ON PLANNING

I came to an understanding that we can develop all kinds of plans, but sometimes other forces intervene. No one plans to have a heart attack. I don't know of too many people who, when asked in a job interview or elsewhere about their five-year plan, account for a major health disruption. I'm not saying we should or we shouldn't, but I do know that plans have their place in our lives. My cardiac rehab plan was one that I took seriously. I continue to take my health seriously. That said, I've had my fill of overplanning. As a result of my heart crisis, I decided that I needed to make some additional changes. With the exception of having a few drinks now and then, I was doing everything to be healthy and avoid a heart attack and yet still had one. The old saying about an adventure not really beginning until the first thing goes wrong is true. I'd had plenty of things go wrong before, but this one was different on an entirely different scale. It was an epic, life-altering situation that turned out to be among the best things that ever happened to me. I decided to live life full-time in a way that sparked our very evolution thousands and thousands of years ago. I'd take chances, meet new people, and put myself out there to share and enjoy all that I could. That was the objective. The plan was to let go of the micro-planning. That has worked out for me, but I understand that it may not work for everyone.

I offer my plan-less plan as an option. One of the on-call nurses I spoke with the first night I was hospitalized told me that I was lucky and there was some reason I'd survived what most don't. It was on me, she said, to help people. I can't force a lifestyle or an approach to living wild on anyone. I know that it works for me, and I hope that in some ways, large and small, you can adapt and adopt what fits with your current and evolving state.

After having an LAD blockage known as a widow-maker at the age of thirty-seven and almost dying, I spent time reflecting on my life and what I could have done better, what I could have done differently, and ultimately what I could do to prevent it. I spent time thinking . . . lots of thinking. First in a hospital bed, then on short walks around my house, and then in caves next to roaring fires. My conclusion was simple: *Stop thinking about what happened and what you could have done different. Use what you know because it works. Just keep on living for today and tomorrow and live better.* I took this new outlook on my heart attack and buried all my pity, anger, humiliation, shame, and guilt deep in the mountains, never to unearth it but simply to let it rot away until it doesn't exist. I thought to myself that this is the only life I have and I need to dedicate it to my physical self, my mental longevity, my emotional well-being, and my primal instincts. I can't give my family everything if I'm not mentally, physically, emotionally, and primally on track. I began to think about what aspects of life, pre–heart attack, contributed to my physical, mental, and emotional health. That is when I created scavenging. I scavenged methods and applications from my past to feed my future recovery, as my pre–heart attack pattern of life was not wrong but needed to be modified or mended. I also scavenged concepts and ideas from other, new sources of information and applied them to aid in my recovery moving forward.

OWN THE EXPERIENCE

One of the main areas of my pre–heart attack life that needed to be modified was what I felt had become an overreliance on gear and technology. As much as the next person, I liked having and acquiring things—particularly those that would aid me in spending time in my favorite places out in the wilderness. In my desire to strip down and simplify what I brought with me into the bush, I was clearly bucking a trend. But I felt like if I was really going to experience the joy and freedom of doing as often as possible the thing that brought me the greatest joy, I needed to strip everything down to its essentials. Recent data from the US government's Bureau of Economic Activity shows that in 2020 the outdoor recreation economy accounted for $374.3 billion in sales, or 1.8 percent of the gross domestic product (GDP). In some states, like Montana, where the rugged outdoor life is given greater primacy, the outdoor recreation figure makes up 4.3 percent of the state GDP.

Over the years, I know that I contributed perhaps more than my fair share to keep that recreation industry booming. Though the figures aren't yet available, based on all that I've experienced and read in regard to more people getting outdoors during the pandemic, I would imagine those figures are even greater. As with much of what I have to say, my decision to cut back on the gear that I buy and bring with me is a matter of personal choice. There's no right or wrong answer, and what I present here is simply another option. It's one that works well for me and my desire to live as freely as possible from as many constraints as I can. A tent, a sleeping pad, a sleeping bag, a cookstove, base layers, mid-layers, outer layers, and all the rest of the gear on offer are often described as "essentials" by marketers and catalog copywriters. I don't want to spend too much time on this aspect of my evolution other than to say that when I took the time to reflect on my approach to living wild, I came to a realization.

I realized the gear didn't bring me joy. Yes, it gave me access and ease to enable me to experience moments of transcendence, but the thrill and pleasure of acquisition had diminished over the years. While in the military, despite my joking about the Marines always getting the shittiest gear, we were extremely well equipped for being out in various environments. Humping a ruck that weighed eighty pounds was the norm, and just about everyone I served with was a devout worshipper at the altar of the latest, greatest, most durable, lightest-weight gear. We would kneel down at that altar, but given how much all that stuff weighed, it was sometimes difficult to stand up again.

My more minimalist approach—one that brings me closer to living like our human ancestors did—gives me joy. On a pleasure-per-ounce scale, since I shed the weight of excess gear, my enjoyment has increased exponentially. I feel more in touch with my primal ancestors and my primal self when all I bring with me is a knife, a skin/hide, a pot to cook in, and a means to start a fire. Depending on the climate, I'll also take along a wool blanket. Over the years, I've come to understand and take enormous pleasure in knowing that nature can provide everything we need. Knowing how to take advantage of that bounty is also an enormous source of pride and satisfaction. Carrying those feelings around doesn't take much effort at all. They are also a good source of fuel to keep you going. Certainly, as any cyclist, runner, hiker, or outdoors enthusiast knows, you can go farther faster and have more fun when you travel light(er).

From that desire to have an even more direct connection to our primal existence, I developed an ethos that guides me and my personal approach to living wild: **Know more and carry less.** In the next chapter, I'm going to explore the first part of that in greater detail. In the second half of the book, I'll focus more specifically on physical items and how to use them and how to adjust your load to take a no-tech, low-tech, or high-tech approach to packing. What you're about to find out is that some of the most essential items you need to survive while living wild all fit in a pack smaller than your skull.

CHAPTER 3

THE CRITICAL THINKING/SURVIVAL CONNECTION

The most valuable piece of equipment you need to carry with you in order to live wild is one that you don't need to ever remind yourself to pack. You always have your brain with you. Of course, how you use your brain is crucial to your success in living wild. At least you don't have to pore over gear comparison articles in magazines, do a deep dive into the murky waters of internet forums, or spend hours picking the brain of someone you consider more experienced, knowledgeable, or skillful than you to find the most lightweight, efficient, and durable choice of cranial computers to suit your needs. You don't even need to purchase any adjunct processors or more memory to operate at full capacity. Each of us is born with an innate sense of creativity. And that skill is the most important thrival and survival skill of all. As I like to tell my students and remind myself, the hope is that you can walk into the wilds of the world with nothing and walk out with everything. And by "everything" I mean a real connection to the natural world through which we benefit mentally, physically, and emotionally. Living wild brings us back to the land and firmly plants in us a state of well-being.

MAKING SENSE(S) OF YOUR TIME IN THE WILD

Living wild engages all our senses and faculties. It provides us with a true test of our ability to recall knowledge and apply our skills. I understand that my approach to living wild and the role that curiosity and creativity play is likely a different one from what other teachers and practitioners of survival, bushcraft, and primitive skills emphasize. I don't believe that my approach is incompatible with theirs, or theirs with mine. This isn't about who's right and who's wrong. It's about what feels best for you and offers you the greatest benefit. I don't offer a strict set of guidelines to be memorized and adhered to. Instead, by fostering a creative spirit, I hope to provide you with fuel that energizes you and powers you to explore and test a multitude of possibilities. Too many rules and regulations and how-tos can stifle creativity. I'm not saying there shouldn't be any information and guidelines but rather that, instead of being guardrails to keep you on a specified path, they should be flexible and adaptable.

That's what is so amazing about our brains: they allow us to adapt to various circumstances and inputs. I'm sure we all know people who are narrow-minded, set in their ways, or whatever term we use for people who are rigid in their thinking. And those inflexible thoughts lead to inflexible series of actions. Inflexible materials break when enough pressure is applied. Flexible ones bend and go on being functional and useful. What we've come to learn about the brain—and it seems like every few years one publication or another anoints a year as the "Year of the Brain"—is that it is a remarkably adaptive organ. And that's a good quality to have in a piece of equipment we always carry with us and that weighs on average about three pounds at age twenty, and slightly less at age sixty. It's a pretty remarkable tool that helps us see, hear, taste, touch, smell, move, dream, think, and regulate our body functions.

The old way in which we frequently compared our brains was to compare them, as I did above, to computers. We learned that our brains were hardwired—that we had rigid circuits connecting various components to process thoughts. Researchers have challenged that comparison. Without going into a bunch of detail, we now know that our brains are not hardwired. The term "neuroplasticity" gives you some idea that the connections in our brains allowing us to function are "plastic"—in other words, flexible. For me, when I think of people who are creative, I think of them as flexible individuals. No, they're not yoga practitioners, but they could be. They are people who can take one set of ideas or objects and use them in novel ways. A musician works with a set of notes and produces new songs. A writer uses words and puts them together in unique sentences, and so on.

In living wild, you take a given set of objects, environmental inputs, and goals to use them in ways to solve problems that allow you to both survive and, more important, thrive.

THE THINGS THEY CARRIED

In the late spring of 2017, I was asked to teach a three-day primitive skills course at an out-of-state survival school. I designed the course to cover primitive fire making, natural navigation, stone tool technologies, glues and adhesives, primitive weapons, vessel construction, tracking, shelter making, and all sorts of primitive campcraft. In all honesty, that is a great deal to cover in three days; however, I don't stick to an eight-hour schedule. I usually go from sunup to sundown to maximize the daylight as well as the night for navigation using the stars. When teaching in the backcountry, every tree, river bend, rock structure, animal track, plant, and sound can be a lesson. For this particular course I had four students, and I knew I had plenty of time to cover all that was needed. The four students came from all walks of life: one was a police officer, one was a doctor, and two were friends who owned a small bicycle repair shop together. A solid group upon first assessment that appeared to be motivated and ready to learn. The three-day primitive skills class would require us to walk out into the bush, survive, and thrive employing only primitive skills. No tents, no stoves, no backpacks, no water filters, no weapons . . . nothing. A good time for sure with the five of us, nature, and a ton of creativity!

Before any class, I have a few routines that I like to conduct. First, we sit down as a group and discuss the tentative schedule. Everyone shares something about themselves, and I answer any questions the students may have. Generally, we try to build a sense of group cohesion by getting to know one another. Second, I hold a quasi–gear inspection or gear survey to see what people packed and what they didn't pack, and to address any questions pertaining to gear. This particular class started the same way. Keep in mind that, weeks in advance and again two days before the class start date, I send a quick email reminding all participants of the gear list, which consists only of the Four *B*s: a blade (steel or stone), a bottle (to carry and boil water), a blanket (wool or elk hide), and the "burn," a locally sourced friction fire set.

Not too complicated, really. But I also add that they can bring anything else they think they might need. Not surprisingly, that statement typically leads to some interesting experiences.

"Let's take a look at what you all packed," I said.

"So I brought a little extra," said the police officer. "I watched this YouTube video of this guy who is pretty popular in the survival community . . . He seems to know his stuff, so I packed what he recommended in his video."

"Good. Nothing wrong with that," I said. "It's a way—not *the* way . . . Now, Doc, if you don't mind me calling you that, what did you pack?"

"I packed some extras as well," said Doc. "I saw that you only required four items and thought I should play it safe with a few more."

"Same here," said the two friends in unison. "We didn't go overboard, but I think we have some baseline gear," said the older of the two friends.

"No worries, gents. Keep emptying your stuff out and let's take a look at what you have," I said with a bit of caution and curiosity. At this point I witnessed four grown men empty well over a couple thousand dollars' worth of gear onto the forest floor. I was in complete shock. I saw collectively ten knives (not joking); six, maybe seven multi-tools; saws; different camp axes; complete mess and cookware kits; sleeping pads; blankets; sleeping bags; hygiene bags; an unknown number of feet of 550 paracord; flashlights; leg holsters with mini emergency survival kits; water filters; pounds of beef jerky; MREs; slingshots; and my personal favorite, a set of throwing knives.

I know I asked for this when I said, "Bring anything you think you might need." I should expect folks to bring everything and anything, and I do. However, this is actually my first lesson.

"Outstanding gear, everyone," I say. "I can tell you all are ready for anything, and that is awesome. There is nothing wrong with being ready for, um, anything."

"That's what that guy says on YouTube: Be ready," the police officer added.

"I bet he does," I said.

"What did you bring, Donny?" Doc asked.

"Great question, Doc . . . Stand by."

THE AHA/UH-OH MOMENT

I ran to a small rock a few yards away where I had strategically cached my gear. I always stage my gear a few feet away, as this is my attention-getter for this next lesson. Behind my chosen cache rock, I grab an old mountain blanket, called a *patu*, that the men of the Hindu Kush would wear, a once steel-colored bottle now charred black from extreme use, and a small three-inch fixed steel blade. I quickly headed back to the mound of gear and my students.

"What the hell . . . ? That's it?" one of the friends said.

"In all honesty, I don't . . . ," the doctor started to say.

"Before everyone freaks out, let's discuss," I said, trying to calm them down. I explained that this is *a* way and not *the* way, but for this three-day primitive skills course, the blanket, bottle, and blade that I was securing to my belt would be the minimum gear we'd use. I routinely do this for no other reason but to drive home a point that we are creative problem-solvers and nature provides all our solutions. I have everyone stand next to their gear as I begin to call out different survival items and explain the way we will source and utilize that same item from the land. We'll take found objects and use them to suit our needs.

"That 550 paracord—grab it and put it back in your pack. Over the next three days, as a group we will make at least a hundred feet of natural cordage from different plant species that we will use for fishing and trapping," I say. "So pack it away. We don't need it." This is usually the time when the light bulbs turn on and the smiles of excitement, concern, and curiosity start to form. "All your food, all your jerky and meals in a bag, pack those away. In the surrounding hills and forests, there is a buffet of wild edibles, fish, and game that will be our sustenance for the next three days."

"This is nuts. No food? I'm not sure I can go three days without food," the police officer said. "Seriously, nothing?" he went on before being cut off by the friends.

"I'm up for it. . . . I think we got this," one friend says to the other and the group.

"If you need it, bring it," I say. "However, food—edible food—is all around us. Look down. Doc, you were wondering what I was nibbling on while waiting for you all to get your packs."

"I was. I saw you reach down and start munching," he said.

"Correct, I did." Then I reached down and grabbed an unmistakable plant and held it up for everyone to see. "This is Oxalidaceae, or oxalis, and it is one hundred percent edible."

Without fail, every one of them picked a piece and popped it in as I did the same.

"It tastes . . . ," the police officer trailed off.

"Sour," I said, "from the oxalic acid found in the plant, but it's commonly called wood sorrel and it's delicious . . . all five hundred–plus species of it," I said.

"There are five hundred–plus types of this plant?" the police officer said, still munching.

"Correct, give or take a few. We will not starve," I said with a smile. "Slingshots and throwing knives, pack them up. We will spend the next three days crafting all manner of primitive weapons to aid in our hunting efforts."

"Hell yeah, this is awesome," said one of the bike repair shop owners. "I'm pumped to learn this stuff."

"I'm just glad I kept my receipts," said the doctor. "I think I might return a few things."

Fast-forward three days and all five of us returned with no issues or mishaps. However, we did acquire quite a bit of gear during our time in the wilderness. Collectively, we had five grass mats known as back mates, five bow drill friction fire sets, three hand drill friction fire sets, around forty feet of natural fiber cordage, several rabbit sticks, one wooden walking stick per person (which also served as a thrusting spear), and several Paiute deadfall sets, premade and ready to be employed. Additionally, we caught several fish, two rabbits, one snake, and an endless number of wild edibles. In the end we walked into the backcountry with next to nothing and walked out with a whole lot more.

You might think you need boatloads of fancy gear to live wild. I hope by now you're convinced otherwise. The beauty of living wild is that you can do whatever you want and create solutions from the world around you. Whatever praxis you decide to use, just remember that the core concepts of knowing more while carrying less, leading with curiosity, and holding a loose plan will see you through. Your ability to create will reign supreme over any tool you could pack. Nature provides all.

THAT'S TRUE, BUT . . .

Let me clarify that. Nature provides all the basic resources we need. It's up to us to spot them, know how to adapt them to our needs, and decide the most beneficial means of using them to maximize their utility in helping us survive and thrive. That's where our highly adaptable brain can be most effective. In order to create, we have to employ several other types of thinking to solve problems or to produce effects that bring us pleasure. For me, thrival equates to enjoyment as well as ease. We may not be problem-free, but if our basic needs are met—remember Maslow's hierarchy—we have the time, energy, and desire to create objects and other products that bring us joy and contentment. After all, the main purpose of living wild and connecting again with nature is to enhance our well-being.

As humans, our predominant sense—the main way we gather information about our circumstances—is our vision. Our visual apparatus isn't as acute as that of many other animals. But the sensory inputs we have in our brains have allowed us to become the dominant species on the planet. There's an old joke that goes "When I was kid, we were so poor I couldn't even pay attention." That may or may not strike you as funny, but paying attention and being observant are such essential skills for success in life, and especially in survival and thrival, that they can't be overlooked (pardon the pun). We all like to think that we're keen observers and other people are oblivious, but at times we all range between those two poles. When I was in the military and working in the counterintelligence field, I had to be on top of my observation game. And the military's trainers didn't just say, as I heard so many of my schoolteachers say, "Hey, pay attention!"

They actually trained us by making us do various exercises. One in particular was memorable.

We were required to do beach runs. An instructor would be at one end of the beach and another would be positioned at the far end, say two miles away. We'd run back and forth between those two points. Running in sand isn't easy, but the point of this exercise was to test both our brains and our bodies. We'd complete one "sprint" up the beach. The instructor there would take out six photos from a folder and show them to us. He would give us a few seconds to look at them and then we had to turn around and run back to the starting point. The photos would be a pair of political officials, two well-known pop stars, and two random people. When we got back to the first instructor, we had to name or otherwise identify by some key trait four out of the six people. If we didn't, we had to run back and repeat the process until we had achieved that passing grade.

They'd do other variations of that exercise as well. We'd hump our way down the beach and be shown a photo of a woman in a bikini on the beach. And over her left shoulder there was a guy with a suicide vest on. You had to pay close attention to the big picture, because when you ran back, you were asked to provide a verbal snapshot of the terrorist and you had to keep the pretty girl out of your mind. More than that, after doing that exercise regularly for two weeks—along with a lot of other training, mind you—we were told that over the course of time we'd seen forty photos. We then, as a group, had to compose a coherent scenario that connected as many of those photos together as possible. It was always interesting to note the differences in what each individual noted and what they didn't.

How does that apply to living wild? Well, over the course of time while out in the bush, you should be alert and noticing things. In the military and in other areas of life, "noticing things" gets replaced by "having situational awareness." That encompasses a whole host of things, but for now I'm going to keep the emphasis on simple visual awareness of your surroundings. Out in the bush, being observant can make the difference between being surprised and being prepared. By using your vision to note things that are out of place—let's say scratches in the bark of a tree at a similar height in several trunks—you could have spotted a warning sign of a predator nearby. If you're not in tune with your surroundings, you're not utilizing the full capability of your best piece of equipment.

MAKING MEMORIES

Very often in my survival training courses with my students, I'll set the tone early on with an observation exercise/game. I call it the KIM game, which stands for "keep in memory." What I'll do, even before we're ready to rock and roll into the wilds, is take a ground sheet of some kind and place it over ten items that I've selected. Those items are all related to the outdoors in some way. I call the trainees over and explain what's about to happen. I'm going to lift up that piece of fabric and then they'll have one minute to observe everything that's under there. They can look but not touch. You also can't discuss what you see with anyone else. You can't write down any notes about what you observed. BAM! Sheet goes up, eyeballs dance all over the items. Sixty seconds later, I cover them up. They disperse for a few moments while I tuck all the things into my pack.

Depending on the length of the course, three, five, and sometimes ten days go by without us talking about them. Generally, on the last night, while we're sitting around that final campfire, I'll do a KIM debrief.

"Who can tell me what the ten items I showed you on day one were?"

"Oh my God!"

"I can't believe we're doing this."

After the grumbling, the collective names a few of the items. Then I dig deeper. What was the knife handle made of? What were the initials carved into it? Drilling down into the micro after the macro really drives home the need to sharpen your focus when out in nature. Sometimes I also do a preliminary KIM game, do the debrief, and then initiate another with a different set of objects. I hope, and most of the time it's true, that the second go-around is better than the first and they remember more of the ten. I sometimes even cheat a bit and tell them ten and actually put in eleven. You'd be surprised the number of people who don't even count them. During that second debrief, when they've had more success, I drill down on the objects but also on the process they used to help memorize what they've seen. I've had people tell me that they created a mental grid and divided up the objects into sectors based on their location. Others grouped items together based on commonalities. Some created a little nursery rhyme using the names of the objects.

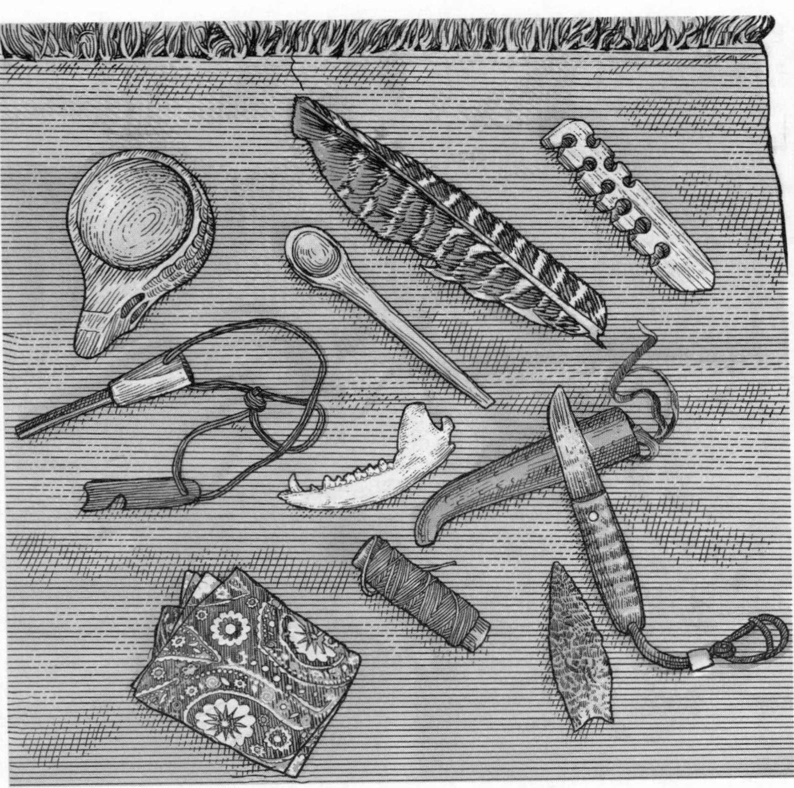

The point of that discussion is to get them to think about how they think. There is a fancy word for that, "metacognition," which is thinking about how you think. It's also about observing yourself and your thought patterns and how you tend to approach problems. Knowing your strengths and weaknesses as a thinker can play a huge part in surviving and managing risk. The same goes for understanding your level of impulse control: Do you want to come up with a solution quickly at the expense of finding the best one? Or are you such a plodding, explore-every-avenue type that you get soaked by the rain because your inner committee holds long hearings on what the best shelter option is?

FOCUSING ON WHAT'S AROUND YOU

Developing situational awareness, paying attention, and being very observant are more important today than ever before. You've probably noticed—and if you haven't, you should—that people today are highly distracted and really lacking in situational awareness. When I was growing up and learning to drive, no one ever talked about distracted driving. Today, that's a thing we all need to be cognizant of because, according to the Centers for Disease Control and Prevention, nine people a day are killed in car crashes that involved distracted driving. Their latest statistics, from 2019, reveal that 3,100 people were killed and 424,000 were injured in distracted driver crashes.*

You don't have to be driving to notice how distracted people are by smartphones. Sidewalks, grocery store aisles—even your own home—can be places to spot, and avoid, distracted walkers. Given how dangerous our non-wild lives can be, escaping to nature can seem like a great idea, but unless you develop your observational skills, your escape from the distracted could become just another aspect of our ever-increasing overwhelmed, underfocused lives.

---

* See https://www.cdc.gov/transportationsafety/Distracted_Driving/index.html.

As a kid, I didn't like going to the dentist, but there was one good thing about it: I got to sit in the waiting room and leaf through the magazines. One of my favorites when I was really young was *Highlights* magazine. And one of the features I liked best in it was the "What's Wrong?" puzzle. It was a full-page illustration and your job was to identify all the things that didn't belong in the picture. The illustrator would draw unusual objects in place of what you'd normally expect. I've seen variations on that theme with before and after photos that require you to identify differences between the first and second images. I even know someone who entertained and polished the skills of kids by rearranging items in a room after the kids got a chance to look at it briefly. In a way, survival is like solving a puzzle, a sophisticated one with a higher degree of risk than a pencil-and-paper one. But living wild offers us a chance to reconnect with the natural world and with the pleasures we took as kids in movement, discovery, finding solutions, and attuning ourselves to our surroundings. Believe me, I understand the desire to shut out noise and other sensory inputs as an adult living in a world that often feels overstimulated, and going into nature is partially about serenity. But learning how to filter out distractions from useful input is one of the challenges we all face when in nature.

Observation is a skill, and some experts in the study of cognition don't include it in the list of critical thinking skills that we all need to develop. This may be a case of picking nits, but regardless of whether observation—visual or auditory, tactile or olfactory—is a building block of successful engagement with the world around you and is foundational to more "advanced" thinking skills, it goes hand in hand with curiosity. Once we take in inputs from our senses, it's essential that we think critically and process that sensory advantage beyond the noticing stage.

BEYOND MEMORY

Critical thinking moves us beyond the realm of memorization. When living wild, it's really not possible to recall from study the hundreds of edible plants and other flora that might exist in a particular area. Again, in keeping with the notion of taking less with you into the bush, a guidebook to leaf through isn't the most desirable choice. Nor is a smartphone, even if you could acquire a signal, and unless you have an eidetic ("photographic") memory, the ability to recall an image as well as sounds and other sensations associated with it, those recalled images don't last a long time. Also, eidetic memory among adults is *extremely* rare. So the best we can do is to remember certain traits or characteristics of a typically edible plant and then compare and contrast any species we encounter with that known example. Comparing and contrasting known to unknown, or among knowns, is a crucial survival skill. Many of the decisions you will make in regard to finding and consuming water and food and making shelter and fire will involve comparing and contrasting the things you find available. Essentially, when you're out in the bush, you're going to engage higher-level thinking like comparing and contrasting to make the vast majority of your decisions.

One of the best definitions of critical thinking, and one that I've encountered multiple times in my reading on the subject, is this:

> Critical thinking is the intellectually disciplined process of actively and skillfully conceptualizing, applying, analyzing, synthesizing, and/or evaluating information gathered from, or generated by, observation, experience, reflection, reasoning, or communication, as a guide to belief and action.

This definition came from two academics, Michael Scriven and Richard Paul. The key skills are conceptualizing, applying, analyzing, synthesizing and evaluating. As important as that entire definition and those skills are, what I need to emphasize is that last bit: "a guide to belief and action." Action is what we're all about in a survival situation. So, together with those critical thinking skills, we need to carry in our brains a more pragmatic approach to solving the problems of water, food, shelter, and fire. One of those approaches is known as IDEAL, and it was developed by two guys named John D. Bransford and Barry S. Stein who crafted this systematic approach to problem-solving and wrote about it back in 1984. Here are their IDEAL steps:

- Identify the problem.
- Define the context of the problem.
- Explore possible strategies.
- Act on the best solution.
- Look back and learn.

A bunch of other problem-solving approaches work, but I like this one because it also illustrates another aspect of thinking. "IDEAL" is an acronym that serves as a mnemonic device—an aid to memory. I don't expect that most of us already follow some established pattern of problem-solving—and IDEAL may not be necessary. But when under duress and with a clock ticking, it's good to have this one in the back of your brain to pull out. Like most things, if you use the established pattern enough times, you'll find it has its limitations and you adopt and adapt to suit your needs.

I get it that a lot of this seems theoretical on the one hand, and maybe a little obvious on the other, but the point remains that I don't think you can overload your brain as easily as you can your backpack. The other thing that appeals to me about IDEAL is that the last letter, *L*, gets as much emphasis as the other steps. Looking back and evaluating what worked, what didn't, and to what degree can help save your ass the next time you encounter any problem. It can also help you save some time and energy, two very, very important resources we need when living wild or in our everyday life.

When I'm teaching and taking people out into the wild, it can sometimes feel like an artificial exercise, almost like a simulation. We chose to put ourselves out there, and unless something really unpredictable comes up, the stakes are not truly life-and-death and the potential for great harm isn't particularly high. A few years ago I was hired by an individual to teach him game-tracking skills out here in Colorado. We spent three days at altitudes around 9,000 to 9,500 feet in February. That month starts the span when Colorado receives its highest amount of snow. We were about fourteen miles outside the town of Woodland Park, up a forest service road that led into some deep backcountry. We were trapped for three days. I was aware that some weather was coming in, and we headed toward my 4x4 truck, just ahead (or so I thought) of an approaching snowstorm. We got to the truck and headed back into town. Unfortunately, as prepared as my vehicle was for those conditions and as experienced as I am in driving in winter, we slid off the side of the snow-packed dirt forest service road.

I quickly analyzed the situation and, based on my experiences and observations, I set about trying to get that truck out of the somewhat shallow ditch we had slid into. With my client's assistance, we ran through the usual tried-and-true methods. We cut down boughs from the abundant pines nearby to help the wheels gain traction and so on and so forth. None of what we tried worked. The snow fell heavier, the wind kicked up higher, and it became clear to me that we faced a real problem. This was no practice exercise.

I immediately identified the problem. We were stuck without viable transportation about fourteen miles from the nearest town. Next, I defined the context of the problem. The weather forecast had called for snow in the area. I knew enough about the various microclimates that exist in Colorado where small pockets of territory could be at great variance from what forecasters predicted. In other words, even though the snow was supposed to fall for the next twelve hours, producing five to six inches of accumulation, the snow where we were located might last for the next thirty-six hours and accumulate two to three feet. Air gets trapped between mountain peaks and settles in. We might have just been the unlucky ones over whom that meteorological effect took place. I also determined that because we'd been out setting traplines and otherwise moving for more than three days, my client was showing some signs of wear and tear. He wasn't completely beat down, but we weren't eating as regularly as he was used to and likely sleeping less than he was accustomed to. And though he had the right layers and footwear, the temperature had dropped considerably since we set out. I could see that he was cold, and even if we fired up the truck and its heater intermittently to warm up a bit, that likely wouldn't be enough to prevent his body from being further taxed.

I explored possible strategies. We could stay in the truck and hunker down, waiting out the storm. We could build a shelter and do the same. We could trek into town, following the forest service road. In evaluating each of those, I knew it was best to make a quick decision and not linger over every pro and con for each approach. In the military, as I was trained in a leadership role, and when I became a leader, one fundamental fault in leadership and problem-solving/decision-making emerged. Too often people took too much time either deliberating on their options or just hoping that circumstances would change and present a clear and obvious choice of a course of action. What I was taught, and what I practiced and later taught, was the need to make a decision as quickly as possible and act on it.

Based on my client's somewhat less-than-optimal state, and knowing from past experience that this storm was one that was going to stick around for a while—and recognizing that our food resources were limited—it was best to move out immediately rather than wait. Either way, it was likely that we'd have to walk out of the woods, so it was best to do it when we were both in the best condition possible. Better to hike through the six or so inches of snow that was on the ground (and rapidly increasing) than to make that effort after there was more snow, we

had less food to keep our internal fires blazing, and we were even more fatigued. So we acted on what I determined was the best solution. We lightened our packs down to the most basic of essentials and set out. I relied on my military training and instructed my client that I would take the lead and he was always to stay within ten feet of me. I would monitor my pace and his position, and with the tangible goal I'd given him, he was more motivated and focused.

Eventually, we did get to the nearest town and much-needed warmth and options for getting my truck unstuck.

To be completely honest, I didn't go through every one of the steps of IDEAL in sequence while using that system. I've got enough experience and training that a lot of those thoughts were instinctive and immediate. I offer IDEAL as one possibility for approaching the solving of problems whether you're in the bush or in your place of work or at home. It's good to have IDEAL in your back pocket as a guide for your thinking. I like to think of it as a routine for you to use early on as you develop your mental fitness for living wild.

Many times, people are fearful of going into nature because they are overburdened with too many what-if fears. *What if a storm comes through? What if I get injured somehow? What if we run out of water?* It's better to counteract those fears after having practiced developing your own set of what-ifs that are potential solutions to those problems. For every possible thing that might go wrong, you can think of solutions to those problems. One of the exercises we did a lot during my military training was something called a TDG—a tactical decision game. These were "classroom" exercises where we were presented with a scenario and tasked with making a decision to optimize our chances of success. For example, I'd be shown a map indicating that there was a machine-gun position here and there. These are the assets I have: twelve men, small arms, grenades, claymores. I'm leading a patrol in this direction. Then I'd be asked, "Lance Corporal Dust, what do you do?"

Again, the emphasis was on committing to a course of action after a quick assessment of the circumstances, the objective, and the resources at hand. I know that military pilots, and possibly civilian pilots, undergo similar kinds of chair exercises. They have a set list of actions to take in case of equipment failure of some kind that always begins with *I will maintain control of the aircraft*. The point of TDG games and chair flying exercises is the same: to prepare you so that your responses become second nature based on your knowledge, skills, and experiences.

Depending upon your level of each of the above, your approach and solution may differ. The word "tactical" in "TDG" conjures up images of armed conflict, but that's not the kind of survival training and teaching I do. I've come up with "SSS," or "situational survival scenario," to talk about and put in practice critical thinking skills, problem-solving, and decision-making.

Before we turn our attention to one more practical aspect of survival training—physical development—I want to end with another example of how mental fitness plays just as crucial a role in living wild as do the physical and the spiritual. When you've got all three working for you, all the what-ifs that might prevent you from enjoying time in nature give way to the pleasure that you felt as a kid in being outdoors and moving. After all, getting back to nature also means getting back to the point in your life when you were less burdened than you are as a adult.

THE SURVIVAL MENTALITY

Sometimes getting back to nature can place your life in peril. That's pretty clearly a burden. One reason why I spent the time I did in talking about problem-solving is that one of the keys to surviving a perilous situation is preparation. Being mentally prepared and having established routines to follow in your thinking—developing a series of if-then propositions—will greatly enhance your chances of surviving a situation where things go wrong. Having at the ready a set of *If this happens then I will do this, this, and this* measures—and the more of these actions you have in your toolkit, the better—can make the difference between living to tell about it and having others tell your story.

But that's only one part of the mental side of survival.

The other is the mindset or attitude you have when faced with challenging circumstances. It may seem obvious that having a positive attitude is important. That's a very trite and reductive statement. How do you develop a positive attitude? What are the composite elements that make up a positive attitude? In my mind, attitude isn't enough. You can be the biggest, brashest, loudest cheerleader, but if you don't transform that attitude into action, you may not have any better chances while out in the bush of surviving a horrific change in the weather, an injury or illness, an animal attack, or any of the dozens of other things that could go wrong and potentially cost you your life. I'm not saying that a positive attitude isn't helpful, but it has to go hand in hand with taking positive steps. Much of the rest of this book is devoted to preparation and steps, but it's also incumbent on me to share with you some of the more generic approaches that make up the attitude/action approach you need to develop or enhance.

The first of these is to set a series of immediate goals and timelines for yourself when faced with a true survival situation. For example, if you're out in the bush and find yourself lost, with darkness closing in, you set the goal of building a shelter before night falls and you have to use your headlamp. That goal is both pertinent and time-sensitive. You know that you will need to stay warm and protected from the elements, so it's a high-value proposition you've established for yourself. Rather than focusing on the *Why me?* or, worse, the *Why the f**k . . . ?* of the situation, you have a clearly established action item to complete. That will keep your mind focused and ward off negative thoughts and emotions from forming so early on in what might be a multi-hour or multiday ordeal. Having a series of these goals and accomplishing them will bolster your mind and spirit and your body.

OUR BASIC NEEDS

Earlier, I mentioned the psychologist Abraham Maslow and the hierarchy of needs that he identified as important to human development. There is another, more fundamental set of needs that we need to survive:

- shelter
- fire
- water
- food

I'll spend a lot of time in the remainder of the book discussing in much greater detail how to meet all of these needs. For now, it should be pretty evident to you why each of these are essential needs. What may not be as clear is why I have listed them here in this particular order.

THE RULE OF THREE

It has become a commonplace among survival experts to talk about the Survival Rule of Three. When things go really sideways for me, I know that I can last for three hours without shelter. I can last three days without hydration. I can live three weeks without food. As a consequence, in the example above, I used building shelter as the first goal. I may be feeling thirsty and hungry, but knowing the paradigm of shelter being the first (and shortest) of the three, my earliest goal would be shelter-related. Now, there's got to be some flexibility within this paradigm. For example, if you are so depleted by cold, thirst, or hunger that you're not able to physically perform the actions needed to establish any kind of shelter for yourself, then you must do what's necessary to meet those needs so that you can properly function. That may also mean that if you're not mentally functional, as can happen when extremely cold or hot, or in such serious caloric or hydration deficit that you're impaired, the same applies. Everyone's physical and mental threshold is different. It's important that as you undertake activities that are increasingly strenuous and the potential for risk increases, you monitor and test your endurance capabilities.

Endurance athletes talk about going into the "pain cave" during competitions, but they also place themselves there during their training. I understand that some athletes will purposely go out and train when they are underprepared so that they can experience what it's like and how to handle situations where they don't have enough fluid or food to be at their best and possibly to be at their worst. Preparation can sometimes be painful, but getting past that pain and being able to recall that experience as a success is something you can draw on later. First, you can recognize the symptoms that arise when you are pushing the boundaries of your physical envelope and know what can happen when you exceed them: complete failure of the body or a next level that you can endure. Second, by knowing what your limits are and how your mind and body respond, you can take the appropriate steps to ensure that you don't experience a complete breakdown. How many times have you heard someone say, "I'm starving," or "I'm dying of thirst." Of course, we know that they don't mean those words literally, but without ever having gotten to the point where our body has been near to those most dire states, we won't have a clear sense of what we're capable of pushing through.

Similarly, our response to the very natural reaction to fear is something that can be regulated through exposure. We've all had the experience of being afraid of a particular stimulus, then overcoming that fear either by being exposed to it gradually or immediately. Again, being able to recognize the particularities of our fear response and how we combat or accommodate our fears is another tool we all carry with us all the time.

The Rule of Three applies to all individuals and circumstances differently, but it at least provides you with a frame of reference and can help you attitudinally as well. It serves as a kind of barometer to help you gauge where you are in the survival process and as a guide to the next steps you need to take.

CREATIVITY

Just as a strict adherence to the Rule of Three isn't warranted in every case, your creativity will be tested in a survival scenario. Preparation can carry you a long way, but improvisation will most likely be what gets you back home safely.

All the tips, tricks, hacks, and equipment you bring with you are only as good as your ability to be flexible and creative. For me, that is one of the appeals of having a limited number of supplies with me. Also, it should be obvious but this bears stating: once you have more knowledge and experience, you have a larger mix of resources you can draw from to assist you in any survival situation.

An entire body of study is devoted to the psychology of survival. Many books have been written on the subject. And while the authors may use slightly different terms for the concepts and place a different level of emphasis on each, there are some commonalities. Call it adaptability or creativity, but that ability to be flexible in your thinking, actions, and use of objects can greatly enhance the likelihood of survival. When we say that an object is resilient, we mean that it can be deformed in some way but return to its original shape. That's true for people's bodies and their minds/spirits. Recognizing that nothing but death is a permanent state can help you reorder your mental state and put a positive spin on your situation. Hope and optimism have to be tempered with a realistic assessment of the situation and your circumstances. Accepting the truth and avoiding untempered optimism is essential. Being overly optimistic can lead to greater disappointment than a logical, rational, realistic perspective.

Denial, deliberation, and decisiveness are three common phases of the response to a dangerous situation. Clearly, the less time you spend in the first of those, the more time you have to think, choose, and then act. That time frame is very dependent on the circumstances you face, but the process applies widely. In most books about survival psychology, the authors acknowledge that a bit of luck influences the outcome. Accepting that that is the case, and recognizing that you have survived the initial incident, puts you in a better place than others. It can also help build the comforting fire of positivity.

One of my last points about the survival mentality was made by psychologist Viktor Frankl. He was a well-regarded psychologist and Holocaust survivor whose understanding of the survival mentality was formed under the horrible circumstances in the death camps. Simply put, he stated that those who believed that their lives had a purpose and meaning survived, while those who didn't died. Similarly, people who thought of their loved ones and friends and made it their purpose to endure so that they could be reunited with them also fared better in survival situations than those who didn't have a deep and abiding reason to go on.

Finally, one of the elements that enabled people to survive in situations where endurance was a factor was their physical condition going into the survival scenario. I'll briefly share some things that I do and that you can adapt for yourself in order to maximize your condition to maximize your chances of survival.

CHAPTER 4

BECOMING PHYSICALLY PREPARED TO SURVIVE

When I had my heart attack, luck certainly played a role in my survival. Also, I had a choice about what attitude to have going forward. I could have looked at it like it was a bad roll of the genetic dice that produced this defect in the tissues that carried my blood. I could have focused on the fact that I was young and fit and this shouldn't have happened to me. There were some moments when those thoughts darkened my outlook. But I also recognized that if I hadn't lived a healthy lifestyle, that genetic disposition toward heart and arterial disease could have been compounded by other aspects of living a more sedentary and unhealthier lifestyle. I was fortunate that I made those good choices to offset some of the bad luck I had in playing the genetic lottery. The same is true for all of you reading this book. There are very, very few genetic lottery winners who are handed the prize of excellent health and physical conditioning without having to do some work to produce a physiological state that will increase the chances that they will perform well in a survival scenario.

FUNCTIONAL FITNESS VERSUS TRADITIONAL "WORKOUTS"

I hate going to the gym. It's sweaty. It's horrible. When I want to work out, I want to work out. That means outside. I don't want to do a formal bench press; I want to roll a rock. Instead of using a squat rack machine, I want to put a log on my shoulders and carry it up a hill. If I see a creek bed, I want to jump back and forth across it instead of doing calf raises or some other leg exercise. I find those activities more rewarding because they more closely mimic what I do in my daily life. I understand the process of tearing down muscle fibers to build them up is effective for a lot of people. It makes them feel good and look good. But what I'm after is being more effective at my job and my life. Since so much of what I do involves being in the bush, tracking, hunting, and what I call Earth Roaming—being in the outdoors and exploring whatever I come across—what I do to prepare my body to endure the stresses and strains of that type of physicality needs to match what I have to do to survive and thrive in that environment. I do a lot of duck and goose hunting, and hoisting and carrying a bag of decoys along a trail to a lake or pond and then wading through chest-deep water to deploy them suits me just fine. But a treadmill and a triceps extension machine? No. Thank you but no.

I get it that cyclists need to cycle, and runners need to run, and many also cross-train by doing other forms of exercise. Whatever your specialty, the same is true. So for me the forms of exercise I do dovetail neatly with my lifestyle and profession. That's my choice, and I'm completely cool with other people's choices as well. I know some people who love going to the gym and lifting weights, doing cardio workouts on various machines, and other things. That's fine. Have at it and do the healthy things that you do and that give you satisfaction and benefits. I'm not a my-way-or-the-highway kind of guy, but I do want to let you in on my approach.

I say "my" approach, but I'm not the one responsible for creating it. The best term I can think of for what I do is something that others have called "functional fitness" or "functional training." At its simplest, it means training your muscles so that you can perform everyday activities safely and efficiently. More specifically, this type of training simulates movements you likely do every day at home, at work, or during your leisure activities. Because you are frequently using muscles and muscle groups in your lower and upper body simultaneously, these exercises and movements help you develop core stability. Instead of having workout sessions with an emphasis on arms and chest one day and abdominals and legs another, functional fitness exercises work the whole body. For more serious athletes, the fact that they target a zone of the body makes sense. But as experts in exercise physiology have determined, the whole-body approach that mimics the movements you perform in your chosen activity are likely more beneficial and efficient. They also provide an alternative, and as many of you who do exercise regularly know, varying your workout helps you stay fresh and motivated. Grinding out the same set of exercises doesn't bother some people, but I'm a more kinetic kind of guy who needs the stimulation of a varied routine. I realize that's a bit of an oxymoron, but stretching and challenging your mind is an important part of survival preparation as well.

SUIT YOUR WORKOUT TO THE WORK YOU DO

To put a finer point on functional exercise, if you're an office worker and sit at a desk all day for eight hours, consider what your body movements are and then work those muscle groups.

Here is another take on it. You sit and stand from a chair as you conduct daily activities; you walk two flights of stairs before starting work, at lunch, and when leaving work; you bend over at the waist to load copy paper in a copy machine; and you pull yourself to your desk in your roller chair constantly. Now, if we take those body movements and apply the principles of functional training, you would do box squats to reinforce your standing and sitting activities, one-legged squats to enhance your stair climbs, bent-over rows to reinforce your copy machine movements, and resistance band pulls to strengthen your roller chair desk slides. All of these simple exercise methods reflect your daily pattern of body movements and strengthen them. Most of these body movements can be done at home with simple resistance bands and a chair or even a membership to a gym. Does it make sense to do a 250-pound chest press with the above-mentioned daily pattern of body movements? Does it make sense to do 150-pound lat pull-downs? No. The aim is to create a program that reflects your daily pattern of body movement and work the muscle groups associated with it. That is why a "muscle head" will put his back out when he leans over to strap in his son in a car seat: he has not strengthened or trained the muscles used in that car seat movement. It doesn't mean you can't jog or go for a hike, but trying to bench press three hundred pounds seems a little counterproductive because you don't play offensive line for the Denver Broncos. As a matter of fact, an athlete like a football player is a great example of when pushing heavy weights away from your body makes sense . . . because that is what an offensive lineman does in his daily work. Take that office worker again and turn them into a firefighter. What are their daily body movements? That is how you build the exercises and strength training: the overall functional fitness plan is based on those daily movements. Think about yourself and your daily motions and start building on them!

In 2006, I was stationed in Okinawa, Japan. I was heading out on a deployment to Iraq about seven months after arriving and was heavy into a functional fitness routine based on what my daily happenings were going to be like when deployed. Near my house in Okinawa, I had access to a stretch of beach that I could train on. I used only what I found on the beach as my fitness tools: driftwood logs, boulders of various sizes, and pieces of thick ship rope. I cached some items in the tree line nearby to have a steady supply of fitness tools but was always curious to see what washed up. The beach was exactly one-quarter of a mile long, and it was my gym. I dragged and carried over my shoulder huge driftwood logs, simulating carrying a wounded Marine. I used those same logs and raised them onto a short seawall, simulating hauling a body into a medevac helicopter. I sprinted barefoot in the sand. I jumped over large piles of driftwood, strengthening jumping into cover. I worked on my grip strength by carrying large stones, simulating ammo cans, fuel cans, or water cans, in my hands. I did hundreds and hundreds of sprints. No matter what I did on that one-quarter-mile stretch of beach, it was tied to my upcoming deployment and the daily pattern of body movements I was going to use to stay alive in Iraq.

Today, I conduct my exercises in the mountains to reflect my daily pattern of body movements. I go to the gym outside. Just like my quarter-mile stretch of beach in Okinawa, I have locations close to my home that can give me access to the rocks, logs, hills, obstacles, and resources I need to fulfill my functional fitness ambitions. Keep in mind, my job as a survival instructor keeps me very active, so my non-workout days are teaching days, but I'm still active. It's important to add that if I'm not in the mountains teaching or focusing on my functional fitness, I still conduct numerous activities: splitting wood for winter, foraging, running, doing tasks around my home, shoveling snow when it falls, walking my dogs. The list continues. No matter what, I stay active. Those no-teaching days and no-functional-fitness days have one aim, and that is to be active. Some of my best exercises or movements to reflect my daily pattern of body movements are:

- flat timber drags and hill timber drags with various log weights and lengths to strengthen my wood-collection muscles used in shelter building
- creek jumps of various widths to simulate jumping over creeks while on a hunt or outing in the wild
- rock/boulder rolls to strengthen me for collecting rocks/boulders for shelters, smokers, deadfall traps, and fire rings when out in the bush
- overhead, between-the-legs, and lateral log/stone throws to strengthen my employment of primitive weapons like atlatls (modified spears fitted with thongs or sockets to increase throwing distance), bows, stone slings, rabbit sticks, and spears
- lots of trail runs on smooth terrain to enhance cardiovascular strength
- tree dashes—seventy-five- to one-hundred-meter sprints through wooded areas, dodging trees, stumps and logs for strengthening mobility, balance, and body control (While doing these runs, I imagine I'm chasing down an animal.)
- rock scrambling up boulder fields to strengthen core muscles and enhance body control to aid my pursuits
- one- or two-legged rock hops simulating silent game-stalking methods and enhancing core muscles and balance

I mix in a few others here and there, but these are standard. I always end with one of my favorites: silent stalks. Silent stalks are where you imagine you must approach an animal or object in the slowest way possible while remaining absolutely quiet—no noise! Your movements are slow. Every foot placement is methodical and purposeful. Breathing is steady, controlled, and quiet, so as not to indicate your position. Your eyes stay fixed on one spot: your prey, your target, or your threat. Silent stalks can start out being twenty yards and can lead to the length of an entire valley. They're done barefoot with some kind of weapon: a knife, a bow and two arrows, an atlatl, or a rabbit stick. (If you don't have one of these weapons, pick up a log and you have a club.) I like to do silent stalks last, when I'm tired, sweaty, and sore. Those may be the very conditions I'm dealing with when in a survival situation and I need food. There's the old adage that you should practice as you play, and while survival isn't a game you play, the truth of that statement still rings true.

I imagine my functional fitness exercises are all the "before" steps our early ancestors took before they finally got to their potential prey and moved in for the kill. If anything, imagine you're about to take a meal from a mountain lion. How silently would you stalk?

There are a few key elements to my functional fitness program, and these should be applied to yours as well:

- Stand or crouch when doing any exercise.
- Always ensure you can focus on the core of the body. (That is why we stand.)
- Balance and body control are extremely important.
- Ensure that your flexibility is on track.
- Your range of motion should be good.
- Use what is around you or what nature provides as your methods to push, pull, squat, lunge, run, jog, ascend, descend, twist, turn, and walk.

More specifically, I know that when I'm out in the bush, I'm likely going to need to build a shelter and a fire ring. That's why I do those rock rolls. If I'm fortunate, those rocks will all be within a short distance. If I'm not, they will be widely dispersed, and I'll have to travel some distance to gather them and bring them back to the site I've located. To be prepared for that possibility, in my training I will decide to go for a one-mile run—by far the longest practicable distance I'd travel to gather shelter-making materials. Along this training/running route, I'll be keenly observing my surroundings. If I spot a rock or a tree branch or trunk that I can use, I'll squat to pick it up. If I can carry it on my shoulders, I'll do a variation on a squat and snatch lift to hoist it onto my shoulders or rest it against my chest. I'll carry it for fifty yards or so and then drop it. I'll continue with the run and repeat that lift-and-drop sequence as many times as I come across something I can use as raw material for my shelter.

I also frequently mix in a variation on the stop, drop, and roll routine we were all taught as a part of fire safety. In this case, I don't completely come to a stop from running. I do drop to the ground and sometimes add a roll to the side. Those moments replicate what I may have to do while hunting and tracking an animal.

MOVEMENT IS ALL

I really want to stress my use of the word "movement" here. I know that when a lot of people go in for a medical exam, the doctor asks about how "active" they are. I think many people immediately go to the rigid slot in their minds where exercise and gym workouts are relegated. For me, being active or leading an active lifestyle means being in motion. That's why, to my mind, nearly everything you do that gets your body in motion, from dancing to digging fence posts, falls into that very expansive category of exercise and activity. I have a healthy, happy, and active dog named Finn. He was found eating roadkill, and I knew he was the dog for me. He poops twice a day, and I have to pick up after him, of course—but instead of looking at that as a necessary evil of dog companionship, I look at it as an opportunity. Rather than use a long-handled pooper-scooper device of some kind that keeps me from fully moving, when I'm on poop removal duty (pun intended) I do squats to gather what the dog has produced when he squats. Snow shoveling? I alternate using one hand and arm and then the other to increase the benefits of that bit of exercise activity. Nearly any movements we make during the day can be mind-shifted into a form of exercise.

Motivation is the key to establishing a higher baseline of activity. You may dread the thought of exercise for exercise's sake. I don't blame you. But when you place all kinds of movement and function at the center of your "exercise routine," they won't feel like exercise or like they are a part of a boring routine. Some people lift weights or do other forms of exercise to enhance their appearance. Nothing wrong with that: different people have different motivations. But I have to believe that everyone can be motivated to work out/engage in movement if they know it will increase their chances of surviving. I know that I find deep, deep primal satisfaction in being active in nature.

I'll take up food and nutrition in a later chapter, but you should bear in mind that it's essential that you understand your body's limits and needs prior to being in an emergency survival situation. It's beyond the scope of this book to provide you with dietary guidelines; an entire industry revolves around those recommendations and approaches. I will share with you one story about fasting that I think you might find instructive. It illustrates my point about having prior knowledge and experience that proved useful in handling situations in which I found myself calorie deprived.

FASTING AND NUTRITIONAL REQUIREMENTS

In 2008, I was in Habbaniyah, Iraq, the midpoint of the Ramadi–Fallujah corridor, working in counterintelligence. One of my local assets was a Muslim man. I knew what Ramadan was, and as the holiday period approached, I wanted to maintain the rapport I'd established with him. I also wanted to develop a better appreciation of the lives of the people we were there to assist. To do that, I engaged in fasting along with him and my interpreter. It was a bonding experience, and I learned more about him, myself, and, more important for my later life, how my body responded to these periods of consuming nothing from sunup to sundown. I spoke with this cooperating local about how he managed to do that kind of fasting every year for that month. He told me two somewhat opposing things. First, he thought of the practice as a larger part of his faith and how it would make him a better person. Second, he didn't focus on it much; instead, he just accepted that this was his reality and focused his attention on other parts of his day. If he kept his body and his mind occupied, then food receded into the background.

What I eventually figured out was that consuming food wasn't just a necessary biological function. As you may know, we can survive for three weeks without consuming food. I wasn't anywhere near doing that during that sunup-to-sundown fast. Food was, instead, a form of mental stimulation. I've never done this, but it would be interesting to record how much time I spend each day thinking about food. I know it sounds super simple to say, but in a survival scenario, don't think about food and eating. But that was my experience in Iraq. If I found other ways to occupy my mind and body, then food didn't dominate my day. In fact, I found that over time, as I did that periodic fasting, when my body had rid itself of a lot of the chemicals and preservatives that were a part of my diet, I started to burn clean. My focus was even sharper and my mental clarity better. Today, I still find that when my mind is occupied—when I'm grinding hand axes, flint knapping, or being out in the world, fully engaged in an activity—those things feed me.

I also developed a greater appreciation for rest and how to use it as a way to prevent myself from going calorie negative. The body is a marvelous machine, but it's not a perpetual motion machine. Rest doesn't mean the complete absence of activity. The two things I mentioned above—grinding and flint knapping—place less stress on the body's systems and require less energy consumption than rucking a mile with a forty-pound pack on my back. Also, rest can be—and should be, depending upon the circumstances—as complete as possible. Compare your basal metabolic rate

(BMR)—how much energy you expend while at rest as you breathe, circulate blood, process nutrients, and produce new cells (which is similar to your resting metabolic rate)—to your calorie consumption while in action. Then you'll understand how rest is a survival strategy that's crucial to success.

You can get a rough idea of your BMR using the following formula:

Women:

BMR = 655 + (9.6 × weight in kg) + (1.8 × height in cm) – (4.7 × age in years)

Men:

BMR = 66 + (13.7 × weight in kg) + (5 × height in cm) – (6.8 × age in years)

So a six-foot-tall man who weighs 190 pounds and is forty years old has a BMR of 1,810 calories. Compare that figure with this generalized table of daily calories needed:

Exercise: 15–30 minutes of elevated heart rate activity
Intense exercise: 45–120 minutes of elevated heart rate activity
Very intense exercise: 2+ hours of elevated heart rate activity

Activity Level	**Calories**
Sedentary; little or no exercise	2,172
Exercise 1–3 times/week	2,489
Exercise 4–5 times/week	2,651
Daily exercise or intense exercise 3–4 times/week	2,805
Intense exercise 6–7 times/week	3,122
Very intense exercise daily, or physical job	3,439

As you can see, in most circumstances with little to very modest amounts of exercise, your BMR accounts for most of your caloric needs. As your level of activity increases, your caloric burn does as well, but the caloric demand isn't as great as you might think. Keep in mind that these figures represent what you need in order to maintain your weight. In a survival situation, you can expect to lose body mass.

My point is that you can establish a baseline of consumption for yourself. Using the numbers above and understanding that while in an outdoor survival situation you'd likely be involved in doing 45 to 120 minutes of activity that will raise your heart rate, I'm going to use 2,500 calories as the maintenance figure. An average banana contains only 105 calories, so that gives you some sense of how much food you'd be required to scavenge or carry per day to maintain your present weight. I think of that as being in the calorie-positive zone. Anything below that will put you in the calorie-negative category.

I'll return to these concepts later when I talk more specifically about how to source nutrition. Having this bit of knowledge in advance of that will provide you with food for thought in the meantime.

PART II

ESSENTIALS OF SURVIVAL PRINCIPLES AND TECHNIQUES

CHAPTER 5

GEARING UP WITH BLADES

Earlier in the book, I made a passing reference to no-tech, low-tech, and high-tech approaches to what to take with you while outdoors. I spoke about it in terms of packing, but in my years as a student of, and now a teacher of, survival skills and primitive ways, it has become a more encompassing paradigm than that. In ways large and small, that triumvirate forms the very backbone of what I do and how I think about existing in our natural environment. So, whether it comes to ways to find and build shelter(s), build fires, locate and utilize sources of water, scavenge, gather, or otherwise secure nutrition, navigate, and reconnect with the natural world, I overlay the tips, tricks, and techniques you need to familiarize yourself (and hopefully master) with those three approaches.

As I've evolved in my knowledge, skills, and abilities, I've used the low-tech and no-tech approach as often as possible.

As the words suggest, a no-tech approach to surviving and thriving in the outdoors means taking a minimalist approach to the clothing and supplies you bring with you and how you provide for yourself. It's not just how few items you bring; for me, it's also a matter of how I source them. I prefer to travel in the outdoors carrying with me things I've made, sourced from materials that I have acquired in the outdoors, using things and techniques that I had access to and developed. As much as I might like to venture into the outdoors in no-tech mode, I do so only roughly 25 percent of the time. When I do this, I carry with me a stone blade and a clay pot. I bring with me animal hides for multiple uses. I wear a loincloth/breechcloth made of tanned animal hide, and I create a friction fire with things I source from the wild.

When using the low-tech approach, which I do approximately 20 percent of the time, I wear and carry mass-produced clothing, a steel fixed blade, a steel water bottle or billycan, and a manufactured wool blanket. I use a handcrafted flint and steel in combination with char cloth as a way to make fire. High-tech mode for me also means going out into the bush wearing massed-produced clothes. The differences are that I carry a lightweight sleeping bag or just a bag liner and bring a multi-tool, a steel water bottle, and a ferrocerium rod to light fires. I rarely employ the high-tech means. Instead, I used a combination of no- and low-tech modalities. As you can see, the amount that I take with me doesn't vary greatly from no-tech to low-tech to high-tech. It's my primal connection to those items that varies the most. The following table should help make the distinguishing differentials between the three categories clearer:

High-Tech (HT)	Low-Tech (LT)	No-Tech (NT)
Walled tent or multi-seasonal tent, fabric hammock	Canvas, plastic tarp, or netted hammock	Hides, robes, cave, leaf bed, rock overhang, shelter build
Multi-tool, lightweight camping axe, folding saw	Fixed steel blade, fixed saw tomahawk, woodsman axe	Stone blades, stone hand axe, stone saw
Ready-made meals, freeze-dried foods, MREs	Flour, salt, jerky, rendered fat, sugar, dried fruits	Hunted, gathered, scavenged foods
Cook set, water purification system, fork, knife, spoon	Single pot, steel bottle, billycan, iodine tablets	Wood bowl/shell/clay pot
Gore-Tex, nylon, fleece, microfiber (synthetic fibers)	Cotton, wool, silk, jute, hemp, alpaca, mohair (natural fibers)	Hides, skins, robes, pelts, leathers, or buckskin (sourced and personally treated fibers)
Lighter, waterproof matches, endless match, ferrocerium rod	Flint and steel, char cloth, lens magnification	Bow drill, hand drill, fire plow

What approach you take is up to you. You don't have to adhere to these categories. What I do ask, because I think it will enhance your enjoyment and provide you with the satisfaction you're looking for, is that you avoid substituting gear for knowledge, skills, and abilities. As I pointed out earlier, I was once very much a gear guy. So are most people with military service backgrounds. When you go to war or otherwise do work to defend your country, you're inclined to want to have the best and most advanced gear possible. For some people that inclination also leads you down the path toward the lightest, most advanced items available. It's easy to buy into the marketing hype, but a titanium spork won't help you meet your caloric intake needs any better than your fingers or a repurposed plastic fork from the last time you ordered takeout. It'll lighten your wallet and possibly the load you carry, but at the cost of what else?

I like this minimalist approach because it serves as a catalyst for creativity. Each of the items in the no-tech column has an original purpose or intention. It can also be used to perform other tasks. That's where your creativity comes in! It bears repeating: you can carry far more inside your head than you ever can on your back or in your pack. Along with that, the primal connection that I believe is such a large part of the appeal and the benefit of being out in nature is greatly enhanced when technology doesn't place a barrier between you and the experience.

CUTTING TO THE CHASE

I previously mentioned that one way I organize and equip myself for outings is by always having at minimum the big four with me: a blade (steel or stone), a bottle (to carry and boil water), a blanket (wool or elk hide), and the burn (fire-making tools). Over the years I've come to realize that one of the best ways to get a conversation going about outdoor enthusiasts is to mention any piece of gear. If you really want to get an animated conversation going, then bring up knives, particularly which type, manufacturer, or any other facet of knives that exists. If you want to bring a gun to a knife fight, then make a claim regarding whether it's best to bring a bushcraft knife or a survival knife as the go-to tool. There seems to be no real agreement about exactly what differentiates bushcraft from survival. Many poorly define "bushcraft" by stating that it encompasses skills pertaining to bush country. Well, technically, "bush" is an Australian term, but it has come to be used more widely than in that country specifically. However, many definitions of "bushcraft" are more precise in terms of tasks than they are in geography. I've read a number of definitions that state something very close to this list: bushcraft includes finding one's way, hunting, or finding water. That doesn't include shelter making or other aspects of survival. Survival, obviously, incorporates the concept of sustaining one's life, which means meeting all your basic physiological needs. Some people say that bushcraft relates to a means by which you live off the land.

I have no real interest in entering a linguistic jungle and hacking my way through the tangle of verbiage that gets used. What makes an activity a part of bushcraft or survival might make for an interesting discussion around the fire. For my purposes, those two terms can be used interchangeably when it comes to what activities we engage in while relying on our knowledge, experience, and a limited amount of gear to feed, clothe, shelter, and hydrate ourselves independent of structured and developed society.

MY KNIFE CATEGORIES

- **Campcraft:** This blade is ideal for cutting fire boards, skinning, shaping wood, carving notches, cutting cordage, and shaping weapons (small crafts and tool usage).
- **Chopper knife:** It can be used for work projects in campcraft but can also chop down small trees and process large pieces of wood.
- **Terrain knife:** Designed for clearing vines and large leaves, it can chop like a hatchet but it has a knife or long blade shape. It's not the best in small campcraft, but can be used to good effect with careful

hands and practice. Depending upon the location you are moving in, a terrain knife may or may not be needed. Think of a machete or kukri blade.

- **Multi-tool:** This may be the most appropriate for the weekend warrior and average hiker out on the trails. It contains a saw, a knife, pliers, screwdrivers, can openers, etc.
- **Everyday carry (EDC):** This is the knife that you have with you most of the time to do everyday tasks in and around the home.

When I was about ten or eleven years old, skinning fish with my grandfather, he told me that a good knife isn't cheap and a cheap knife isn't good. He also said that if you can't sharpen it on a flat river stone, you might as well toss it into the river.

I understand the point that my grandfather was making, but even today I'm pretty cost-conscious. My EDC is on the inexpensive side—ten to fifteen dollars—and it suits me well. I've also carried a Swiss Army knife, and its multiple tools have come in handy many times.

I've also built my own steel (and stone) knives that won't win any awards for aesthetics but perform well. I don't feel the need to have the most expensive knives at my disposal. They are tools, and that means two things: utility matters, and taking good care of them is important. That means that keeping them sharp and protected in a good-quality sheath should be high on your list of to-dos. Sometimes you may need to use a knife to chop wood, but I don't make that a common practice. Along with carrying a knife or knives with me, I also frequently bring a hatchet. Dulling and possibly breaking a knife to split wood can be a real setback with major consequences or frustrations. Knowing how to handle a knife will help you avoid accidents.

Here are the knives that I keep on hand:

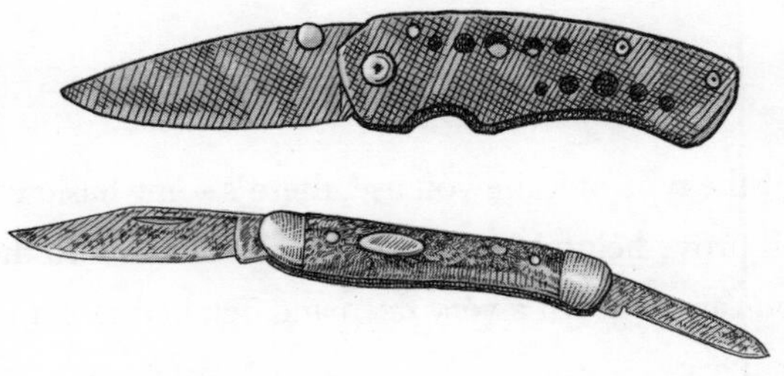

These are my EDCs. They are foldable and thus compact.

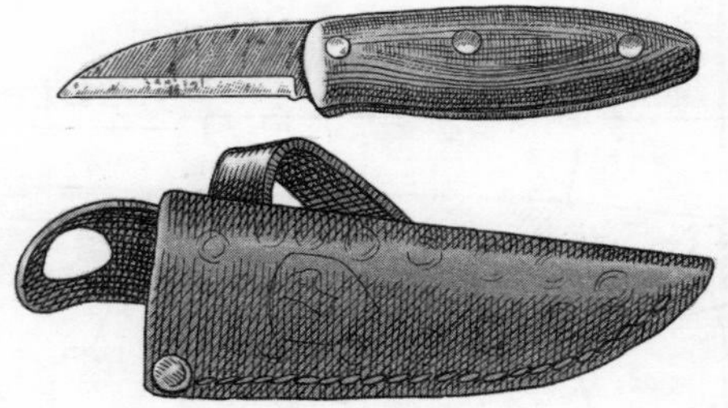

These are the knives I typically carry. They are excellent campcraft knives. Note the stout sheath that keeps me safe and the knife in good condition.

These are knives that I made myself out of old machete blades that I adapted with new handles. They are a hybrid of choppers and terrain knives and handle most tasks for me.

KNIFE BASICS

No matter the type of knife you use, there's some basic vocabulary that will prove helpful as you do more research into them. And, believe me, you can go down a very deep and detailed rabbit hole when investigating knives:

PARTS OF A KNIFE

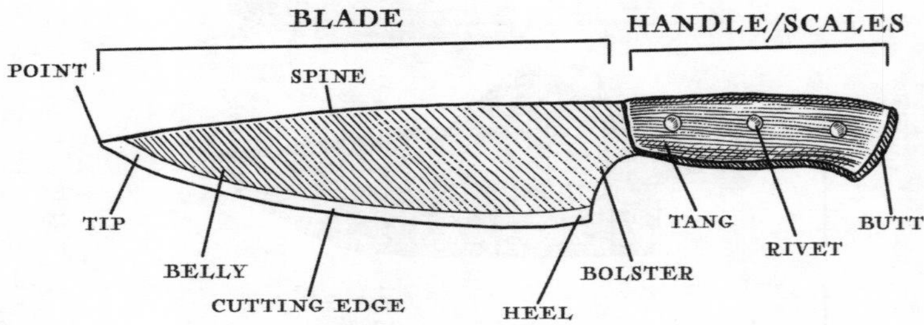

Regardless of which one you choose, I think it's important that you select one that has a full-tang blade. Full-tang blades are made from a single solid piece of material that runs from the tip to the base of the end of the butt. A half-tang or partial-tang knife has a blade that extends only partially into the handle. What you gain in weight/cost reduction is minimal in comparison to the increased durability of a full-tang blade. A third type of tang exists: a shortened tang, which has a blade that tapers once inside the handle. As before, the even more minimal weight/cost savings just isn't worth it. I also carry a fixed-blade knife. That means that it doesn't have a pivot point that allows the blade to be stored in the handle. Those pivot points are weak points because anytime you have a joint in any mechanism—even the human body—there's less structural rigidity.

The most important choice you make in a knife is the blade material itself. For centuries, steelmakers have been adding other materials to raw steel to produce better alloys. In doing so, they've made steel that is stronger, lighter, and more corrosion-resistant and durable. In many cases, the choice will come down to carbon steel or stainless steel. As its name implies, carbon steel has carbon added. Many knife manufacturers use what's called high-carbon steel. It has between 0.5 percent and 1.5 percent carbon in it. That makes it strong and durable. It also makes it less expensive than stainless. It is also generally more effective in fire starting, since it is able to produce sparks with a fire steel more easily than stainless. One downside of carbon steel is that it requires more maintenance than stainless steel. It will corrode and rust more quickly. An advantage that carbon has over stainless is that it is easier to sharpen. That's a good thing, as it is slightly less durable than stainless.

Stainless steel isn't stainless. It will corrode and it will stain, but it does so more slowly than other steels. It contains chromium, as much as 12.5 to 13.5 percent of the blade. That element helps put a surface oxide layer on the steel, which slows down the oxidation process. That layer does have a drawback; it makes these blades more difficult to sharpen—particularly in the field, when you have to rely solely on hand-sharpening methods.

Finally, in the last stage of the blade manufacturing process, a coating can be applied to enhance the quality, durability, and appearance of the knife. On some low-end knives, that coating can be paint, while more high-end knives have titanium or ceramic coatings. One type of ceramic coating, diamond-like carbon (DLC), is one of the strongest available but comes at a high price. It helps make knives with that form of titanium coating among the most durable: they can keep a sharp edge for long periods. I know that I don't just enjoy making my own blades; maintaining and sharpening them provides me with a substantial amount of satisfaction. Your mileage may vary. The same is true with a straight blade or one that has a serrated edge near the handle. Some people find the added cutting capability a serrated edge offers to be a benefit; others don't. Some find folding knives—whether manual or spring-assisted types—to be better because they eliminate the need for a sheath.

THE SHAPE OF THINGS TO CUT, CHOP, AND SLICE

Not all survival knives are created equal. That's true of the material the blade is made of as well as the shape of that blade. The blade shape determines what that particular knife is most suited to do. Again, versatility is the key. Unlike in your kitchen, where you might have a paring knife to help peel vegetables or fruits, a bread knife to cut bread, a boning knife to trim meat, and a steak knife with a serrated edge to help cut through flesh, I don't recommend carrying a series of knives with specialty functions when out in the bush. I know some people who do, but in my no-tech or low-tech, minimal-carry world I don't find that to be practical or useful. I want—no plug intended—Swiss Army functionality out of my single-blade-with-no-other-tools-attached knife. Some compromises have to be made, and my single-blade approach means that I won't have the absolute best knife for every job along with me. I'm fine with that. I don't need the best knife for every use. Adequate at most functions is better than great at one or two but lousy at many others. I've heard some car enthusiasts say that all-season tires are an abomination: they're not really good in the rain or in the snow as performance tires with maximum grip, etc. Those purists think that having winter tires, summer tires, and high-performance tires for the occasional track-day outing is the way to go. Well, if you can afford three sets and the fees to have them swapped out, then have at it. As for me, I don't want perfection to be the enemy of good enough. It's easy to fall into that perfection trap, and manufacturers and their marketing teams will do their best to make you feel like their products are must-haves.

I guess that makes me a dues-paying, card-carrying minimal essentialist who drives around with a bumper sticker that proclaims LESS IS MORE. When it comes to blade shape, that dictum still prevails. I don't need a knife with each type of blade. I want one that, based on years of experience, will suit all my needs and may not be outstanding at doing that for any one task. That means that I typically look for a knife that has a single sharpened edge.

SINGLE-EDGE SPEARPOINT

By having a single edge sharpened, the danger factor of the double-edged is greatly reduced. Also, by being able to more easily place your hand on that edge and use your body weight, the amount of force you can exert is far greater.

CLIP POINT BLADES

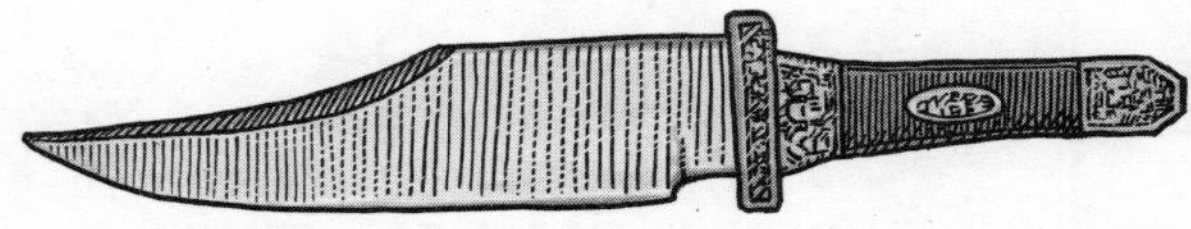

You may recognize this shape as the distinctive-looking Bowie knife. The curve of the blade makes its tip a point of vulnerability. That clip point, when too small, can easily be broken off, especially when batoning (striking) or prying. A curved blade is generally better at skinning than a straight one. That's because the contact patch is smaller. When we get to skinning techniques later on, that will become more apparent.

DROP POINT BLADES

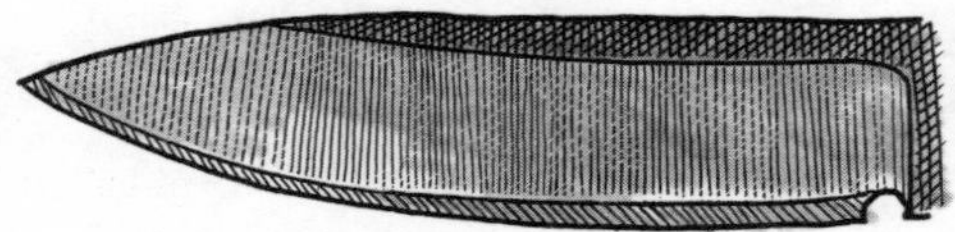

Drop point blades meet my requirements as a do-it-all-well tool. With its straight top edge, it's perfect for batoning. Its broad tip works well for stabbing, prying, carving, and notching, among other wilderness survival functions. That straight top edge is also known as a flat-ground spine. Spines can also be beveled (cut at something other than a right angle) or rounded.

STRAIGHT-BACK, STANDARD BLADE SHAPE

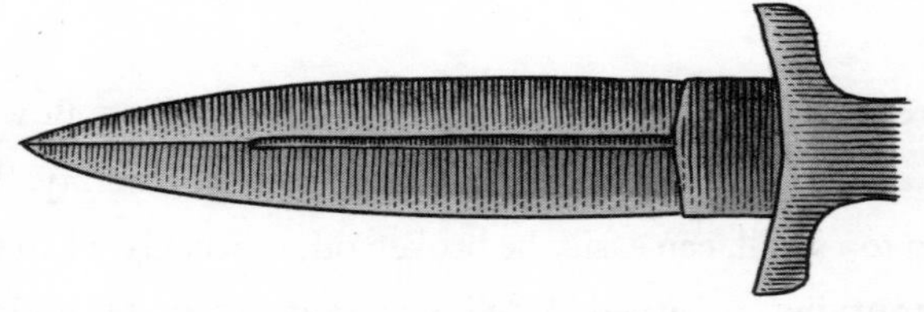

This knife features a straight spine angle combined with a traditional blade belly. This simple knife shape makes it very versatile and a good choice for chopping and cutting tasks.

SHEEPSFOOT BLADE

This one may look familiar, as it's similar in shape to many chef's knives: the blade is shorter and blunter, with a convex tip. I find that the relatively short length of these types of blades gives them good balance.

KUKRI

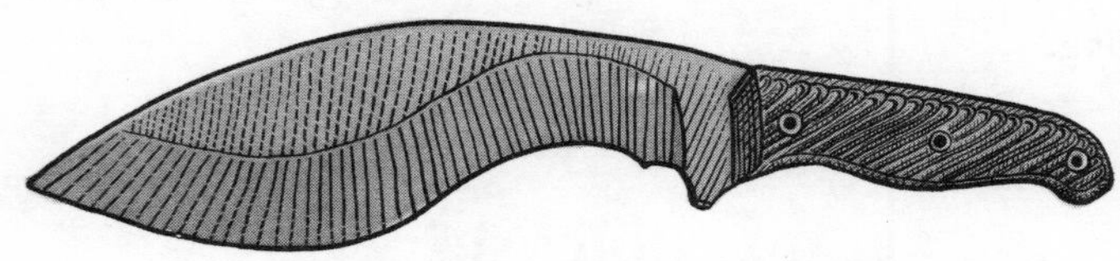

As you can see, this shape is nearly the inverse of the trailing edge. A design that originated in Asia as a military weapon, it eventually found favor with agricultural workers. They would use it to dig, harvest, and clear fields of unwanted growth. Its versatility brings to mind a machete.

TRAILING EDGE

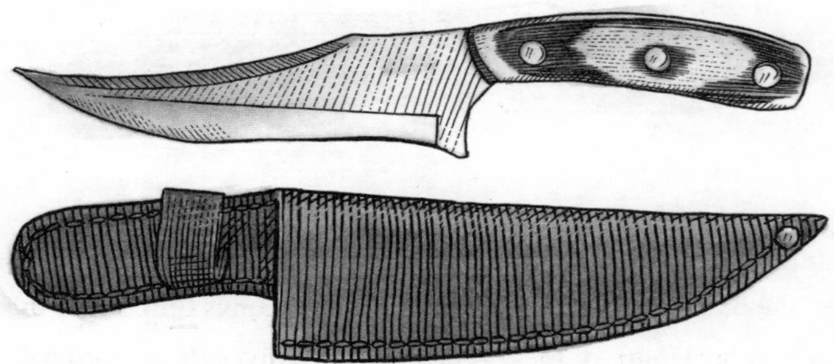

With its distinctive scimitar-like blade that has the back edge rising above the high point of the handle, these are among the most handsome shapes. They excel at slicing and skinning, while the point suits stabbing.

BLADE CHOICE SUMMARY:

- fixed blade (not folding)
- approximately ten inches (not difficult to manage but large enough to be useful)
- full tang—stronger, better weight balance
- straight edge—more versatile and easier to sharpen
- well-fitting sheath that can be attached in a variety of positions
- sharp, pointed, not overly curvy tip, like a drop point or spearpoint blade
- carbon steel (my preference only—depends on your situation)

You may have noticed that none of the knives I use have serrated edges. There's a good reason for that. Whether fully serrated or with a partial serrated blade near the handle, those blades don't provide me with the utility I need and create a greater risk of injury. Often, when handling a knife, you will need to exert leverage on the blade and shorten your grip, placing your fingers over the blade. With serrations, there's a greater risk that you will cut yourself, or you may not be able to choke down on the handle and apply enough cutting force.

CARE AND SHARPENING OF YOUR BEST FRIEND

Most outdoors people would agree that your survival knife is about the closest thing to your best friend, gear-wise. It can assist you in so many tasks and really gives you the most bang for your buck, even if it isn't a Buck knife. Because a knife has so many uses, it gets used so many times and in so many different ways. That means it endures a lot of wear and tear as it helps you skin and gut, strip, split, and undertake the myriad tasks we demand of it. As your go-to tool, it will need you to be sharp as well, and that means knowing how to restore its blade to prime condition. As I pointed out above, one of the distinguishing features of knife blades is the hardness of the steel and its shape, which contribute to the relative ease or difficulty of sharpening it, and how easy it is for it to lose its edge. After years of experience with knives and other blades, I've gotten to the point where I don't find any one knife easier or harder to sharpen. They just require a slight adjustment in my approach.

In my mind, years of technological advancement have improved our ability to produce knives in greater quantity and with higher-quality steel. Where those advances have fallen short is developing machines or processes to sharpen a knife. Old-school is still the best school, and that means using whetstones. They're also called waterstones or sharpening stones.

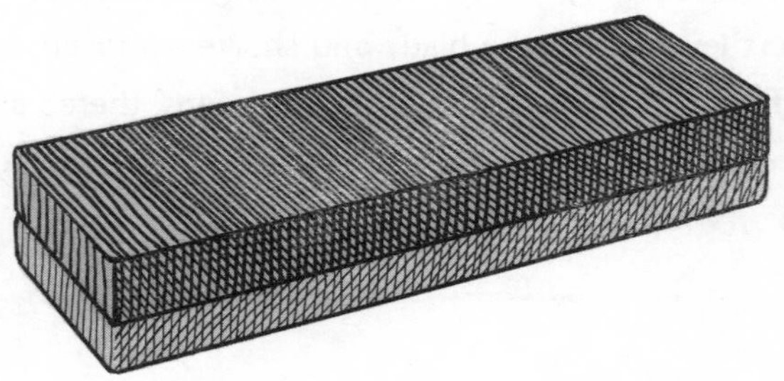

Basically, they are bits of sedimentary rock that are cut so that they have a smooth surface. When you move a blade across them, along with a bit of water or other liquid, a slurry—a mixture of particles and liquid—gets created. It's that particulate matter moving across the blade that works on the metal to remove material and thus put a new edge on it. One of the two types of liquid and stone that work in combination are oilstones. Oil has a lesser coefficient of friction than water, and that helps ease the blade across the surface of the stone. Waterstones are a bit of a misnomer. Instead of applying water while sharpening the blade, prior to beginning the sharpening, you submerge the stone in water for a few minutes.

Both oilstones and waterstones collect the swarf—the metal filings left over as you cut away the surface of the steel—and that aids in cleaning the knife post-sharpening. Diamond stones aren't really stones at all; they are pieces of metal impregnated with tiny diamond chips. Like sandpaper, these stones come in various levels of grit or coarseness and in different shapes and sizes.

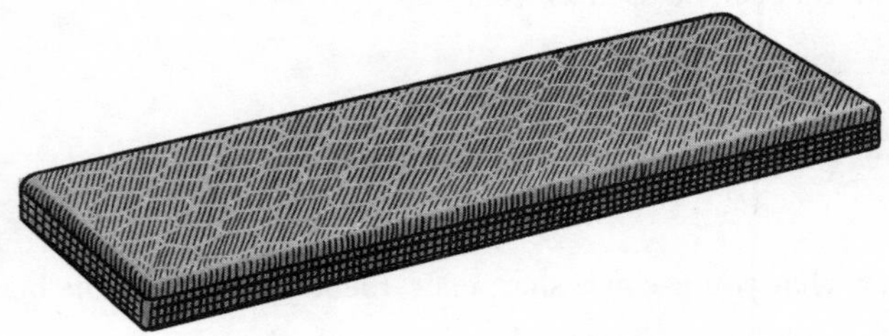

Most diamond whetstones have an irregular surface rather than a smooth one. The diamond pieces are raised from the rest of the stone, making contact with them easier.

I categorize oil- and waterstones as low-tech, while I regard the diamond stones, because of how they're produced, as high-tech. That said, all three stones are portable and can be easily carried with you out in the bush, so even diamond stones are relatively low-tech items in terms of their use. That's especially true when you compare them to at-home-use sharpeners: grinders, belt sanders, and electric knife sharpeners. I've also had some success repurposing other items as sharpening tools. First are stones that you come across while out in the bush. Smooth, flat stones work best, but most any stone can be ground against another stone to produce a fairly decent grinding stone. Again, using water to soak these or adding it while sharpening will help you produce a finer edge on a blade.

You've likely seen a movie or television show set in the days of western expansion or some earlier era when a man goes into a barbershop for a shave. The barber uses a length of leather to sharpen a straight razor before he begins the shave. This technique is known as stropping. What it does is remove some of the fine-level imperfections on the edge. Much like this, you'll see chefs using a hone, a steel rod with fine grooves in it, to do this kind of realignment of the material. I've even seen people use the rough edge at the bottom of a ceramic coffee cup as a sharpener. Essentially, anything that is hard enough to not be completely ground away when worked against the edge and provides some resistance will serve as a sharpener in a pinch. Many fingernail clippers also have a file attachment that can be used as well.

WORKING THE ANGLES

No matter what you use as a sharpener, the key to getting the best edge on a knife is understanding the baseline angle that the manufacturer or previous owner put on that blade. That's the angle you want to restore when sharpening. I have to add that you can decide that for various reasons you want to change that angle. For now, let's stick with sharpening the existing angle and not reshaping the edge. The already-established angle of the knife is known as either the rough grind angle or the bevel. That angle, like all angles, is expressed in degrees. Typically, that edge is somewhere between 30 and 15 degrees. The higher the number, the more durable the edge. For example, a meat cleaver that has to cut through meat and bone is typically made with a 30-degree bevel angle. Razor blades, scalpels, and other sharp but delicate blades are edged at around 15 degrees. Most survival knives have a blade ground to about 25 degrees, and typically manufacturers put this bevel angle in the product description.

In the drawing below, you can see the bevel clearly. The knife's edge rises up at an angle to where the shiny material meets the dull part. The difference between the flat, shiny edge at the bottom and the dull metal at the top is what gets expressed in degrees.

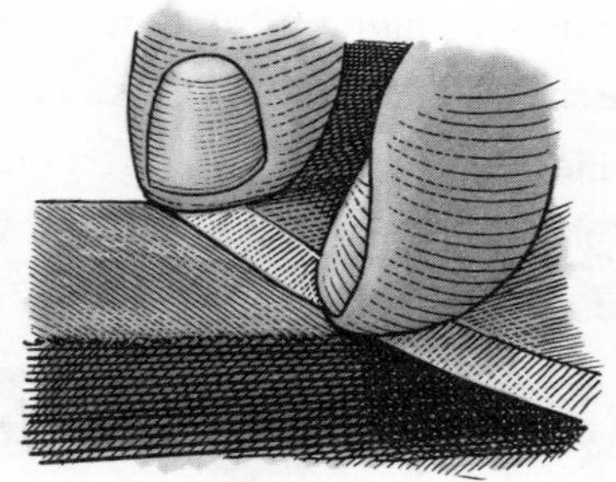

So, if you have a knife that has a 25-degree bevel on it, as you pass the blade across the stone as you sharpen it, you want to hold the knife blade at that angle to the stone. It is easier to see if the angle is correct if you hold the knife by its handle and have the blade facing up as you prepare to sharpen.

When sharpening a knife in the bush, I prefer to use water instead of oil on my stone. You can source water easily and not be bothered with carrying oil. Saliva also works well. Once you've applied water to the surface of the whetstone, you're ready to go. Hold the knife as shown above. You should be able to have a very clear look at where your knife edge is in relationship to the stone. Lay the stone against the flat edge of the knife, forming a cross. Keep the blade perpendicular to that surface. When you do that, look down at the stone. You will see a gap between the knife's edge and the stone. That's because of the blade's angle or bevel.

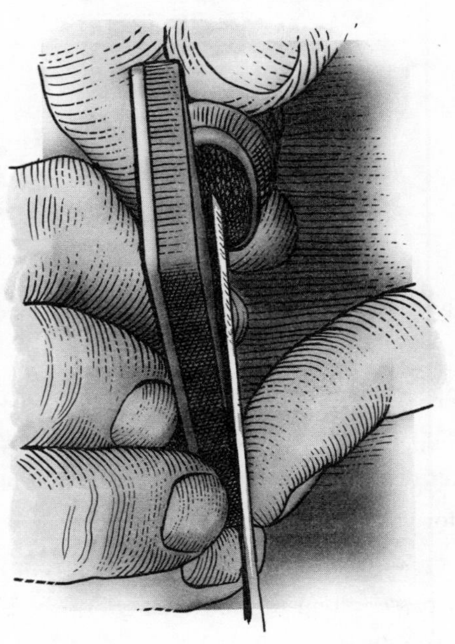

THE GAP OPEN—BAD

To properly sharpen the blade, you must close that gap. You mate the surface of the stone to the edge of the knife so that it looks like this:

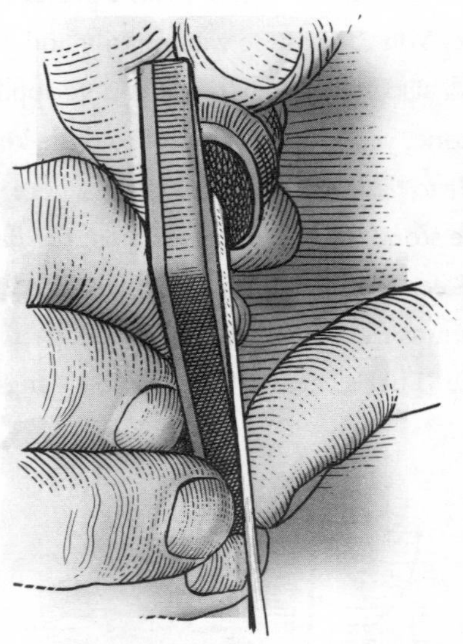

THE GAP CLOSED—GOOD

The bottom edge of the knife will be raised above the stone slightly, at an angle corresponding to its bevel.

With the edge in proper contact with the stone, you can then proceed. Work the stone up and down along that edge, applying light to medium pressure. You can also work the stone using a circular motion. Whatever is comfortable for you is okay. More important, whatever makes it easier for you to keep the orientation between edge and stone is best.

After a few passes along the entire length of the blade, it's time to sharpen the other side. The only difference here is that the tip will be pointing toward your chest as you take on that other surface. After a few passes, you may want to test the sharpness by whittling the bark off a stick. If you're satisfied that it is sharper than before and as sharp as you believe it needs to be, then you're done. If you want it even sharper, repeat the process until it meets your requirements.

AN ALTERNATE SHARPENING METHOD

The vast majority of the principles I mentioned above apply. The difference is how you orient the knife and the stone in space. The advantage of the method above is that you can work at eye level and really see if you are mating the two surfaces at the proper angle. Another option is to lay the stone down on a flat surface. Even your thigh will do when out in the bush. At home, sharpening can easily be done on a table or at a bench. The arrangement looks like this:

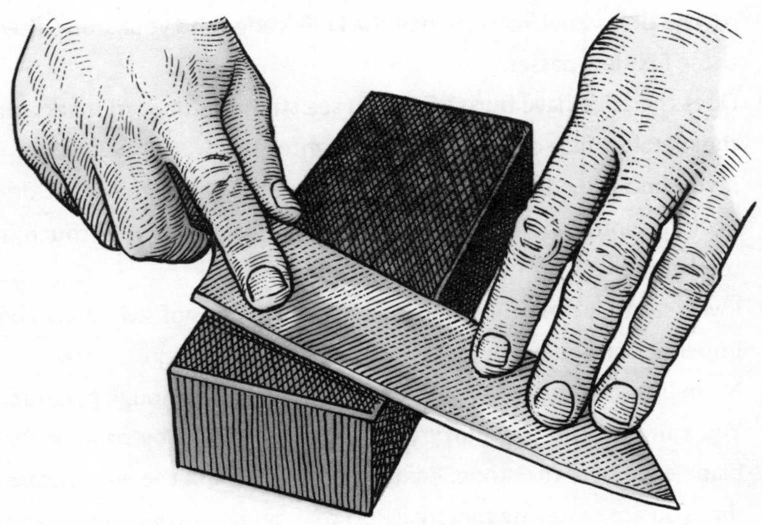

As you can see, it's much more difficult to see the edge that you are sharpening to make certain that the angle you have the edge at is the correct one. Also, your hand is in contact with the blade at several points. While this isn't highly dangerous, there is a greater degree of risk involved. That's a minor consideration in comparison to the angle issue. Keep the angle true and consistent and you'll get a sharper knife sooner.

A few tricks, tips, and troubleshots:

- Over time, you will develop a feel for how much pressure to apply on the blade. First, aim to keep an even amount of pressure throughout the stroke. Once you're able to do that consistently, then go from a lighter touch to a heavier one. The knife edge should move freely across the steel.
- You can also hear the difference between a light and a heavier touch.
- You can also hear when you may need to apply more liquid to the stone.
- If you haven't sharpened a knife before, I recommend getting ahold of an older knife, even a kitchen knife, that doesn't get much use around the house and use it as a practice blade.
- Always do a visual inspection of the knife's edge and your stone after those first few passes.
- Does the edge have burrs? Can you see striations or swirl marks on the metal surface of the blade? If so, lighten up.
- If you find the edge sliding over the stone too freely, making it difficult for you to hold the proper angle, it's likely that your touch is too light.
- If you see that the stone's surface has similar kinds of swirl marks or imperfections, then you've applying too much pressure.
- No marks at all may mean that you're not applying enough pressure.
- You can also rub the slurry that's been produced by passing the blade edge over the stone. Remember: Sharpening the edge means that you are removing material! Rub that between your thumb and forefinger gently. If it feels completely smooth or nearly so, then you're light on the pressure. If it is very gritty after those first two passes, ease back on the pressure.
- Though it's somewhat unlikely that this will happen, friction produces heat, and if after passing the blade over the stone the blade becomes hot to the touch, you need to apply less pressure.

- Going past the point where you've aligned the edge properly with the stone is the number one error I've seen committed with this technique. Doing that will dull the edge, not sharpen it.
- Match the angles and you'll have the right grind.

I'm not a big believer in the sheet-of-paper test to determine if a knife edge is sharp, particularly for a survival knife. You've likely seen someone pass a knife easily through a sheet of paper held loosely by one corner. That may look impressive, but that's a test for a highly sharp and less durable edge than what you'll want for your survival knife. Believe it or not, paper, because of its fibrous nature, can dull a pair of scissors or a knife fairly quickly. Why sharpen your knife and then subject it to a process that will damage it? Besides, out in the bush, I can pretty easily tear it with my hands, so why bother with a knife and subject it to that dulling action?

That leads me to the final matter: how to best preserve your knife's edge.

- Always return the knife to its sheath.
- If you are going to use the knife as a means of scraping food or other material off a surface, use the spine and not the sharpened edge. (I see chefs and cooks using the blade's edge all the time when transferring food from a cutting board, and I cringe.)
- When you cut up any meat, fruit, vegetable, or vegetation, clean the blade after use. Bacteria on the knife can have a corrosive effect.
- As much as possible, use the knife so that the blade is perpendicular to what you are cutting, slicing, or chopping.
- Apply oil to the blade to keep moisture out. Moisture can also have a corrosive/oxidizing effect on the blade and contribute to dulling.
- Sharpen the blade frequently. It is much easier to fine-tune an edge than it is to do a more substantial sharpening.
- The care and feeding of your knife to keep it from dulling is nearly as important as, if not more important than, mastering blade sharpening. The old ounce-of-prevention cliché does apply here.

As I've spent more and more time in the bush, I've come to recognize the value of having one go-to knife. My generally minimalist approach to gear was a hard-won battle. I appreciate the true craftsmanship that goes into the commercial and artisanal production of a knife. That's why I've also invested the time and energy into making my own stone blades. That's a subject for later exploration, but it's also another way that creativity and a no-tech/low-tech ethos guides all that I do.

OTHER BLADES

As much as it's important to have that one go-to knife with you, there are times when you need other tools that cut and chop. If I'm not doing a super-fast, super-light, maximally minimalist outing, I will take additional tools with me. Among these are:

AXES, HATCHETS, AND HAND AXES

What's the difference? They all chop, right? That's true, but they aren't interchangeable in purpose and in name. A hand axe is a stone tool, while the others are made of steel. Hatchets and axes are similar handheld tools, but they're not the same. Each has its strengths and weaknesses, and deciding which is best depends on what you need it for. In this guide, we'll compare the hatchet and the axe so you can determine which is the right tool for you. Hatchets are short, one-handed axes that are commonly used for chopping, hammering, and backyard work. A regular axe has a longer handle and requires two hands to swing; it's more powerful than a hatchet, and is capable of felling large trees and chopping logs.

- Both tools often have a wooden handle and a steel head.
- They're both primarily used for chopping wood.
- Hatchets are best for light jobs, while axes can handle bigger chopping tasks.

Full-sized felling axes are between thirty-two and thirty-six inches long, while a boy's axe is a little shorter, at twenty-eight inches. Hatchets measure roughly eighteen inches in length.

AXE

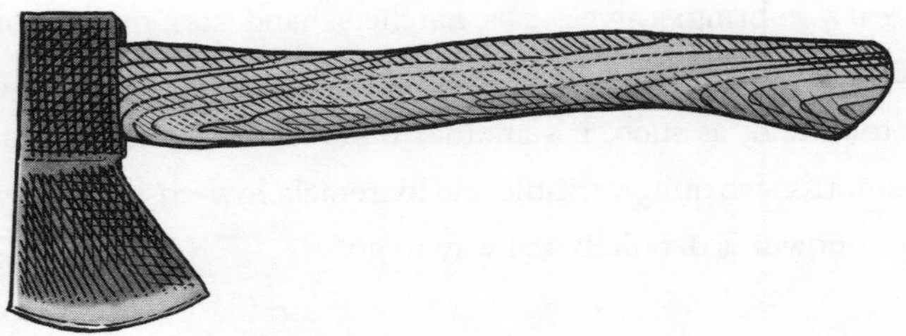

HATCHET

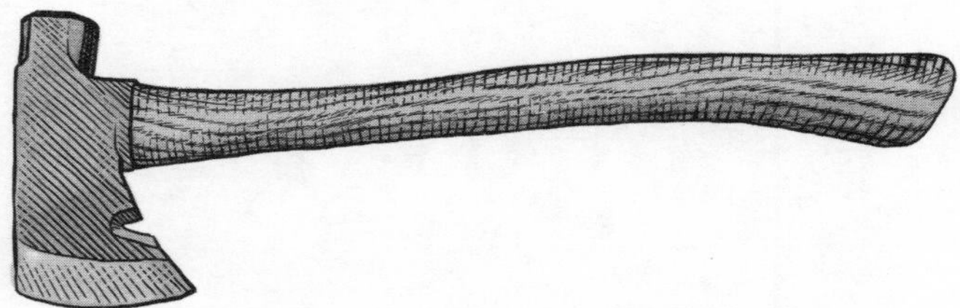

HAND AXE

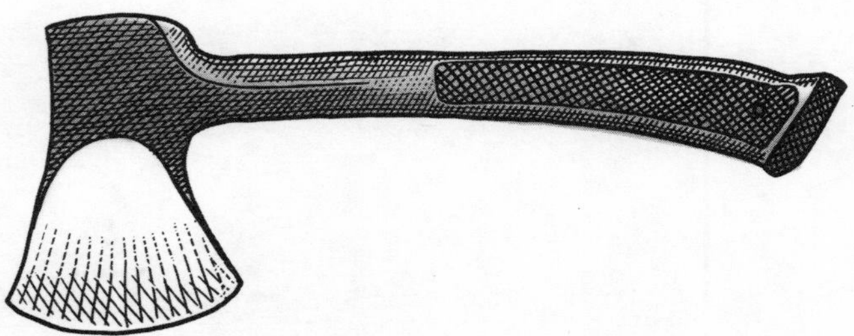

Manufacturers also produce multi-tools based on the axe/hatchet as well as various folding saws. I've found that the right axe or hatchet may not be able to loosen bolts, but for the vast majority of my needs out in the wild, they are the best option.

In the next chapter, on shelters, you'll see how these tools can be employed. You'll also learn about a paradigm that I use to determine the types of shelters I'll build. It can also be useful as a way to think about all the gear you bring: knives, axes, hatchets, hand axes, multi-tools, etc. The TOWERS concept, which you're about to learn about, is an analytical tool, and, as such, it's another one that only takes up space in your brain. It's also quite versatile and extremely low-cost. Less gear and more brainpower is definitely the way to go.

 CHAPTER 6 

SHELTERING

Finding or making shelter is most essential to your survival. It requires you to use your problem-solving skills and your physical capabilities. The brain and body need to work together to preserve each other. When you're out in the wild, I can't say if it's better to have an abundance of brain or brawn working for you. The two must work in concert. In teaching my survival/bushcraft classes, I frequently use the acronym "KSA." Those three letters stand for "knowledge, skills, and abilities." I have been growing, refining, and mastering my knowledge, skills, and abilities for years. Another way of expressing my evolution is to think of it this way: in a sense, by having a no-tech ethos that guides me, I've devolved. My aim is to master as many primitive skills as I possibly can. I want to have the knowledge, skills, and abilities that ancient people possessed and refined to survive. They had no other option but to use as much creativity as they could while using any materials they could find from whatever environment they existed in.

There are no written records to show that early man developed a system like ours with a division of labor where people work in highly specialized fields. Until human beings began to cultivate rather than solely hunt and gather, the only real "specialty" that early humans mastered was survival—by staying warm, by staying safe, by feeding and drinking, and by procreating. They also survived by paying attention, developing a highly refined situational awareness, and being creative and learning through experimentation and observation. Calling how they existed "primitive" is not quite accurate: that term applies only retrospectively. When the first humans made stone cutting tools, they were on the "cutting edge" of their technological advances. What I aspire to, then, is to go back to that point in human history and be a master of their most advanced knowledge, skills, and abilities.

So I aim to help you utilize all your survival, bushcraft, primitive living, and wilderness self-reliance knowledge, skills, and abilities to live. As I always say, I have my way of doing things and teach it to others, but it is not "the" way. I have established the no-tech/low-tech/high-tech paradigm and employ it in my outings, but it's up to you if you want to take bits and pieces from each of those categories. Again, as much as these KSAs help us survive in the outdoors and under potentially lethal circumstances, the vast majority of us won't face those dire situations. We could, and we need to be prepared for them, but for the most part we get out there because we are looking for the satisfaction of a good time. I'll freely admit that sometimes, when we go through a bad time, that's way more fun than when things go well. But, no matter what, KSAs—whether that knowledge is of twenty-first-century tech or primitive tech; high-tech carbon fiber, Polartec High Loft fleece, and solar-charged electronics or stone tools, vegetation cordage, or scavenged food—the end point is the same.

I think it's important to understand the difference between knowledge, skills, and abilities. Many people group knowledge, skills, and abilities together and use them interchangeably. There are crucial distinctions among them. Knowledge, skills, and abilities are essential for any person who embarks on an outdoor experience.

- **Knowledge** is what you know: facts, concepts, or theories. Take, for example, the fire tetrahedron: fires start when a flammable or combustible material, in combination with enough oxygen gas or another oxygen-rich compound, is introduced to a source of heat or ambient temperature above the flash point for the fuel and is able to sustain a rate of rapid oxidation that produces a chain reaction. Knowledge is typically the information you find in manuals and textbooks. Knowledge is something you can cognitively recall, like knowing the fire tetrahedron or even the "Happy Birthday" song.

- **Skills** are things you do, like singing, rebuilding a car engine, or throwing an atlatl. Skill requires technique to execute. When you put a skill into action, you employ knowledge to execute the skill, like singing "Happy Birthday" on key and on time. To have mastery of a skill, knowledge and abilities must be mastered as well.

- **Abilities** are natural or built-in. Abilities allow us to do something. Between skills and abilities, a fine line exists to determine if something is learned or innate. Abilities are innate traits or aptitudes that a person adds to a task or situation, like singing "Happy Birthday" with a naturally harmonized voice or throwing an atlatl with athletic precision. To put it in very simple terms, abilities are natural or innate, whereas skills are behaviors that have been either learned or acquired.

For the most part, knowledge, skills, and abilities do not function independently. For instance, if you're a bowhunter or archer, you may have the innate ability to keep your hands and arms in a steady position while acquiring your target, but a skill for shooting and hitting the target is what you learn from hours and hours of archery practice and study, which results in knowledge. Like skills, abilities can also be sharpened and improved to a certain extent. For instance, you may have the skills to swim, but your ability to swim fast comes from possessing strong arm, back, and leg muscles. You can develop those with regular training, proper diet, and exercise. This shows you can combine ability and knowledge to create skills you can use. Even though knowledge, skills, and abilities are different in many ways, I group them together into the acronym "KSA" for a good reason. As you read ahead, know that, for example, something like small-game trapping could have several KSAs associated with it. Small-game trapping is made up of several sets of KSAs. The same is true for nearly any task you undertake: they are a collection of KSAs.

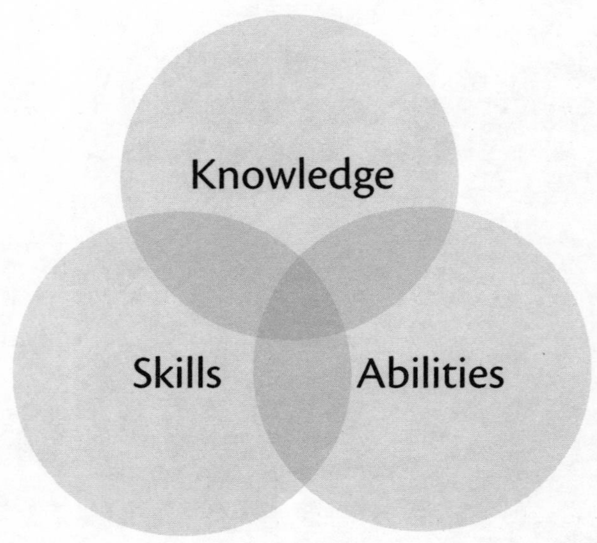

Shelter is one KSA that everyone who heads out in the bush must be well versed in. Picking the correct location, utilizing the appropriate resources, and building a shelter based off the weather are all vital requirements. However, I don't break shelter building into types of shelters you should know. Instead, I break shelter building into a group of factors that will influence the type of shelter constructed. Shelter building can be one of the most creative aspects of survival and thrival. People discover building creativity and abilities when they break the rules of shelter-building conformity. Let's not restrict our creativity by going with only the tried-and-true, established types of shelters. Certainly, you can use them as a starting point, something you can (pardon the pun) "build" off of, but don't limit yourself to copying what you know. Use that knowledge in conjunction with your skills and abilities.

Nature can provide many options and resources that can take the standard debris hut and turn it into something amazing and long-term. Anytime I teach shelter making, I do not stress the type of shelter made but factors like *time*, *occupants*, *weather*, *energy*, *resources*, and length of *stay*. I call this the TOWERS concept of shelter building. As I discuss this concept, you will find that many individual factors influence the others.

Time. Time is of the essence when you're out in the wild. When I say "time," I mean two aspects of time: how much time it will require to build and whether I have enough time to build it. I have attempted to build shelters in the dark, and I can tell you that it did more harm than good. Without the correct allocation of time to build the shelter and time left before the sun sets, tragedy can strike. When we don't consider time, it can and will be extremely difficult to build an elaborate shelter for multiday living—or even something simple to get you through the night. I believe time to be a very easy equation to solve. By my usual assessment, I need two hours to build my shelter. But if I have only thirty minutes of daylight to accomplish it, then I need to rethink my shelter-building options.

Project ahead and allocate enough time to build based on future actions during your journey. This does not mean you cannot build once the sun has set. A low-tech or high-tech approach can mean bringing along lanterns or using the latest in LED technology headlamps. For the purposes of this explanation of TOWERS, I'm going to use no-tech methods and approaches. Consequently, without artificial light, you need to consider the time and light available to safely construct the shelter. Additionally, you can be pressed for time based on incoming weather. If I plan on building a huge, extravagant shelter, but severe lightning and rain is thirty minutes away, I clearly do not have enough time. That means I must take a different approach to finding or creating a shelter that will meet my time, safety, and comfort needs. I look ahead and consider what is the best thing I can do now to help me get through (i.e., survive) and also thrive (keep myself in the best shape possible, mentally and physically) so that I can continue on my way the next hours, days, and even weeks of my journey. Time is a resource related to how you allocate all your other resources.

Deciding not to build a shelter is also a valid choice. Like all choices, it has immediate and long-term consequences. That's why I spent time talking about problem-solving and decision-making earlier. I knew that TOWERS was in your future and wanted to lay the groundwork for it before building on these concepts.

Occupants. The number of occupants is going to greatly influence the shelter constructed in a couple of ways. For example, if you are out with four people, your shelter must be big enough to house and safeguard four people from the weather and any unwanted visitors that go bump in the night. This also means you have four people to help build the shelter and collect resources. Going back to time, the number of people can greatly increase productivity if time runs out. Unfortunately, group decision-making frequently takes more time than solo decision-making does. It all depends on the individuals who make up that group.

Weather. Weather can be complex and multifaceted. Weather encompasses current and future conditions based on the duration of where you stay. Weather is also seasonal. Suppose I'm out in winter and I see snow clouds in the distance. In that case, I will want to construct a shelter with excellent insulation, even though currently there is no snow. Living in Colorado, I'm very aware of the state's monsoonal patterns. That's right: Colorado, like regions of the Southeast, has a summer weather pattern with clear mornings, a chance of midday rain, a period of clearing, and then another chance of evening precipitation. Those rains, more frequent at higher elevations, are often accompanied by lightning. People who want to bag a "fourteener," one of the many peaks that top out above fourteen thousand feet, are advised to ascend early, bag the peak by noon, and then descend. The Rocky Mountains are rocky, but they also comprise minerals that are lightning attractants. Situational awareness is key.

Weather elements influence and determine shelter locations and design based on wind force, wind direction, sunshine, visibility, precipitation, temperature, humidity, and cloud cover. Simply put, the elements of weather are and always will be necessary for you to battle against, overcome, or mitigate. We build shelters to reflect wind, block out intense sunshine, shield us from precipitation, help control our body core temperatures, and protect us from elements of weather. The saying "Location, location, location" is important, but here we mean weather, weather, weather.

Energy. This is best understood as the energy required to build the shelter and the energy required to live in it. We all understand that in order to construct a shelter, we will burn through caloric stores in our bodies. Without proper energy, a shelter could cause more harm than good. I am sure many people have seen what I call the "human deadfall shelter." It is a poorly constructed type of shelter with a main ridgepole that is weighed down to the point of failure while a hopeless survivalist or bushcrafter sits underneath, taking photos for social media. Complete shelter failure is near in this case, with a rebuild around the corner requiring more energy. If I were to create a poorly designed shelter and fail to consider falling temperatures at night, I could spend the entire night shivering, attempting to heat my own body from my rapid movement. My body's automatic response to cold would deplete my energy stores. Then I would have to wake the next morning to gather more resources to improve my insulating layers on the shelter, thus burning more energy. If you properly construct a shelter the first time, you will avoid the over-expenditure of energy doing rebuilds and lots of maintenance.

The same could also be said for shelters to block the sun and make shade or lower temperatures. If constructed poorly, the cooling effect will not take hold and cause the person underneath to lose more water, thus creating the need for expelling more energy to find more water. There is no perfect energy output solution. This is just a consideration point to think about.

Resources. In an ideal situation, you would have all and every type of resource available to build your shelter. Hopefully, they would all come from one immediate location; if not, maybe another area would serve you better. Having numerous construction resources—wood, branches, logs, grass, mud, clay, leaves, etc.—to build the physical shelter are key when selecting the shelter location. If I pick a perfect location to build a shelter but have no resources around, I might want to rethink my location. Resources like firewood, fresh water, food options, natural sunlight, and safety—from animals, weather, and the natural environment—can impact the shelter construction and placement as well.

You could bring some resources with you. This would depend on the trip you are conducting. Items you might bring include axes, saws, and blades. You could also bring tarps and hides and even hammocks, large plastic leaf bags, and other materials to be used for constructing the shelter.

Stay. The duration of your stay will greatly dictate the shelter you build. Why build something elaborate when you are passing through an area and will need shelter for only one night? Duration of stay does not mean a shelter must be bigger; it just means it must last longer and provide you with the requirements you will need over a period of time. I have slept behind more giant rocks in piles of leaves than I have in actual shelters. I keep it simple.

SITE SELECTION

Terrain and other environmental conditions are highly variable, so it's difficult to come up with a single set of guidelines for selecting the best location for your survival shelter. There are a few principles that apply. Many of them are covered in the *R* for "resources" in the TOWERS paradigm. However, I want to cover some of this ground in a bit more detail. This will give you some things to consider in the next section when I present you with some shelters and ask you to evaluate them.

Being in wooded terrain can be a real benefit in a survival situation. Wood is a source of fuel for fires to keep you warm. (Most people who die when stranded outdoors expire from exposure/hypothermia.) Having a fuel source nearby is enormously helpful. Fallen branches and trees are great materials to use to build shelters. In the pages to come, I'll use the term "deadfall" to name these things that nature provides. If you walk into any heavily wooded area, you'll likely see dead trees that have fallen to the ground. You'll also see many that have gotten hung up in the canopy.

Stages of hypothermia:

- shivering
- slurred speech or mumbling
- slow, shallow breathing
- weak pulse
- clumsiness or lack of coordination
- drowsiness or very low energy
- confusion or memory loss
- loss of consciousness

When selecting a site for a shelter, finding a place away from hung-up trees is a good idea. When the wind blows, they can be shaken loose and fall. Not being near them, and particularly under them, is a basic safety precaution to take. So is avoiding anything poisonous or venomous or even just frustratingly pesky that flies, crawls, stings, or bites. Besides the obvious insects, that includes plants like poison ivy and others that cause an inflammatory response when you come in contact with them.

Level ground is ideal. As you no doubt know, very little terrain is perfectly flat. But building a shelter at a low point where rain will run down and form a pool isn't advisable. A quick scouting mission will reveal places where moisture collects. Leaving yourself high and dry in this sense isn't a bad thing.

Orienting the direction in which your shelter will face is also important. In the wind, building anything broadside to it creates a large surface for it to act against. Knowing from which cardinal direction the prevailing winds come is a good practice. Facing the shelter's entrance in the opposite direction of that wind, reinforcing more strongly the sections that face into the wind, contribute to your shelter standing strong. The exception regarding where to locate the opening is if you need the wind to act as a cooling agent in hot weather.

In the photos that follow, you'll see various shelters that I've seen others build. I'm going to discuss in detail only low-tech and no-tech shelters. You can go down a very deep rabbit hole in your own investigation of all the types of commercially produced shelters, from bivy sacs to the most elaborate tents; that information is out there. I don't use those high-tech shelters, so, in light of my emphatic reliance on TOWERS for more than just wilderness experience, I believe that our collective resources are better used in the low- and no-tech domain.

In my time in the wild, I frequently come across shelters that others have constructed, used, and then abandoned. When I come across them, using TOWERS as my guide, I may use them or not. Even if I don't, I frequently do a TOWERS assessment as a kind of forensic analysis—a guessing game, if you will—to determine the circumstances under which they were constructed. I use my KSAs to assess what their KSAs were as well as how TOWERS might have, or should have, played a role in their decision-making/problem-solving.

I wish you and I could be out in the bush encountering these shelters. We could do this analysis together, but that's not possible. To solve that problem, I'm including illustrations and descriptions so that we can imaginatively go on this trek and examine various shelters.

You should examine these illustrations and consider how each aspect of TOWERS played into the choices these parties made. I will offer my assessment for the first of them to give you some idea of what goes through my mind when out in the bush. I also do this when assessing what my students have decided to do.

Keep in mind that I'm less interested in your knowing the names of these things and what distinguishes a tepee from a wickiup from a lean-to. In my experience and my teaching, I let TOWERS be my guide instead of language and naming.

Time. Because the tree trunks resting against the rock ledge don't have any branches on them, I guess whoever set them there was collecting deadfall in this heavily wooded area. They didn't want (nor did they need) to take the time to chop down and delimb fresh trees. Using those rocks was also a time-saver. They didn't have to collect as much deadfall to provide 360 degrees of coverage. Also, the number of trunks they used to form the wall was relatively few and they did nothing to fill in the gaps between the trunks.

Occupants. Having seen this shelter in person, I better understand the size that this illustration may not fully convey. It was approximately forty-five feet in length. From the base of the rock to the base of the deadfall, leaning trunks varied with the shape of the rock at approximately seven feet. In a pinch, a relatively large group of five to ten people could have fit in there, depending upon whether they were willing to sit up or lie prone. For a solo spot or a smaller group, this could range from spacious to comfortable, with enough room for gear storage and a place for a fire.

Weather. This illustration depicts a snow scene, but I don't think that it was built as a winter shelter. There's just simply not enough protection from precipitation, frozen or otherwise. Also, as the drawing is oriented, the side closest to you is facing southwest, and as result the farthest point is facing northeast. Given that the prevailing winds are from the west, this selection and orientation of the deadfall used as a wall/roof material isn't optimal. The other possibility is that rain, snow, or wind weren't present or imminent when it was quickly built. Also, they used bare trunks only, with nothing filling the gaps between them. The lack of limbs with pine needles on them indicates that there was no need for the insulation and protection value that pine boughs can provide. Fair-weather and fair-season construction seems like a likely build scenario. That said, in high winds and falling precipitation, if it's a small number of occupants, you can press yourself against that rock. First, it isn't going anywhere: the wind isn't going to knock it over. Second, utilizing a rock as a wall and an overhang reduces the amount of resources you need to gather and the amount of energy you expend getting materials and putting them in place.

Energy. This was a low-energy build. As I pointed out, gathering nearby deadfall was likely the source of the one wall. Given how heavily wooded the area is, it's likely that the builder(s) had to travel no more than fifty yards at the most to get those few limbs. In terms of energy, chopping and delimbing are on par with finding and carrying. However, when you have to do both those things, which they would have, the caloric consumption doubles. Why exert that much energy when the environment and conditions don't dictate that need?

Resources. Essentially, the same as above. It's clear that what was needed to build this was all close at hand. In the winter, with that much snow, water was not an issue. Whether there were food sources at hand is difficult to say. If this was winter, animal tracks would be clearly evident. Materials to make traps would also be readily available. This one doesn't offer much protection from the elements as others might, and the same is true for protection from wildlife.

Stay. Depending upon the season, you could use this shelter for quite some time. The lean-to elements aren't great, but they'd be adequate in fair weather and in a fair season. Again, the rock isn't going anywhere. Whenever I can, I like to use rock ledges/overhangs, either on their own or in combination like this one. So, as I indicated, even without the added allocation of resources for finding and propping up that deadfall, this site could work on its own. That's especially true if you have additional materials you brought with you to help increase insulation value and/or protective covering.

Similar to the first shelter, the one depicted in this illustration was constructed primarily from deadfall. Rather than trunks being placed leaning against a rock ledge, they are propped against a living tree in the center of the rough circle. (That tree functions as a ridgepole.) A few boughs are visible, but no effort was made at the time of construction to fill in gaps with more of them. In prehistoric and historic times out here in the West and Mountain West, this construction style was one of the most common. In less heavily wooded areas—deserts and plains—other choices would have to be made.

THE HOW-TO

To begin, the first pieces are leaned against the standing tree's trunk. Ideally, the ridgepole/standing tree will have branches or notches in which those uprights can rest. Subsequent ones either rest on the deadfall or the live trunk. Trial and error are the best teachers when it comes to how to get each of the uprights to remain in position. I sometimes think of these as pole-vault shelters because the method I use is to heft the root end of the deadfall up to my shoulder for dragging it into place. I then drop that root end in place where I approximate that, when I lift it, it will reach the live trunk in the desired location. I then plant that root base in the ground like a pole-vaulter does with his pole, walk a few steps back while still holding the piece aloft, and then when I feel I have the correct leverage, I walk it up hand over hand until it's perpendicular to the ground. With it fully balanced and under control, I put a choke hold on it, widen my stance, and then lower it as gently as possible until it's securely in place.

I don't advocate for the "T-I-M-B-E-R!" method of dropping them from that fully upright position. I think it's especially unwise to plant that root end and thrust the deadfall trunk at an angle other than 90 degrees. Letting them fall into place like that may bring back childhood memories of leveling an enemy with a dropped or felled tree. The sound of crashing timber may also bring some childish delight. But in constructing a shelter of this type, it's important to place those first few leaning pieces carefully and make certain that they are secure. Think of home construction. A solid foundation is essential for the framing to rest on.

If you try to let the first few trunks drop into place instead of carefully leaning them, you're going to be making more work for yourself. In the end, you'll wind up doing more deadfall repetitions, and that will soon sap your Energy and suck up your Time. Yes, it will take more Energy to lower those trunks into place instead of allowing gravity to do its thing, but, in the long run, dropping them is penny-wise and pound-foolish. If you're out in the wild, practicing these skills and moves or using shelter building as functional exercise, the drop-in-place method might be fine. But in a true survival situation, your TOWERS assessment will likely tell you otherwise.

Here's a better look at the early stages of a shelter build and the crux of the early pieces resting in notches or against other uprights:

And here is a longer view of that relatively spare framework:

Whether you opt for a shelter that is low to the ground and at a shallower angle, or one with greater height and a steeper angle, it depends on your needs and what materials are at hand. You may only find or be able to carry certain lengths of deadfall or cut timber, and as a result your choice will be made for you.

The circumference of the circle, the height, the number of supports, and whether you rely on deadfall only depend on your TOWERS analysis. This is where your problem-solving and creativity merge.

A quick note on panic, adrenaline, and the desire to get it done *now*. Those three things are normal and natural but could be counterproductive if you don't have correctives for them. For example, you may have visions of erecting a structure similar to the one above, but conditions may dictate that you don't have the time or resources to make that survival fantasy come to life. Don't panic. Don't get your adrenals pumping overtime. Get comfortable with all in due time. How? By having a backup plan that allows you to address your most immediate needs as efficiently as possible. Live to play another day and then reassess and see if you really, really need an elaborate structure or really, really want one. Balancing need and desire is crucial in life, especially when your life is on the line. (Later I'll get into making teas, some of which can have a calming effect on you.)

One of the ways to keep from entering a panicked state is by making a choice and taking immediate action. That doesn't mean mindlessly doing anything that comes to mind is advisable. At each step, assess your progress and remain situationally aware. That will allow you to adapt to changes and stay in the moment. Focusing on the past or the future—bemoaning bad choices made earlier or engaging in negative self-talk and berating yourself—is not a good use of your time or your mental, physical, and emotional resources. All that gets more complicated when out in a group, and you may feel that you're in jeopardy due to someone else's missteps. Try to stay positive and realize that any divisiveness reduces your chances of coming out of a bad situation in good shape. Yes, it is possible to think selfishly and think of the collective's welfare, too.

This is a variation on what you saw in the illustration depicting the use of a standing tree as a center pole. Notice that it is an even more elaborate setup of deadfall resting against a live tree. Based on the size of some of the trunks in the left foreground, I'd have to guess that more than one person was involved in the construction of this, or that lone individual had Yeti-like strength. Of particular note here is the inclusion of a doorway with an annex or vestibule-type space. The footprint of this shelter was quite large and had both low-angle and high-angle walls/ceilings. This was no quick, get-me-to-the-next-day endeavor. Using TOWERS, it was easy for me to make those assessments.

One of the main reasons shelter building is so important to us is that it allows us to rest. And the most important form of rest we need in a wilderness survival scenario is sleep.

As Americans, we have a complicated relationship with sleep. We all know that our bodies need it. The body is a remarkable machine that can restore energy to itself. It requires us to slow down, sleep, and reduce our energy output so that we can go back out refreshed and rejuvenated.

Too often we restrict ourselves to a specific time of day to get that rest: at night. Yes, I'm aware of our energetic cycle and the reality of contemporary life that reserves and reveres sleep patterns after the sun goes down. But by not sleeping or napping during the day, people are seriously creating major physical health problems.

Much of the entire rest of the world takes naps during the day. Why are we afraid to do it? On the flip side, the Marine Corps taught me how not to sleep. This is pretty simple, such as when you're on a mission and when your fellow Marine to your left or right needs sleep more than you. Mission is always the priority and troop welfare is always second. I scavenged that concept of "mission priority and troop welfare second" in regards to sleep during my heart attack recovery. My mission was to recover from my heart attack and sleep was my key to it. My body needed to heal and recover. I did not want to rush it. However, I eliminated much of the insomnia contributors, thereby enhancing my personal welfare (troop welfare): no alcohol, no nicotine, no caffeine after a certain time, no food after 8:00 p.m., no TV in the bedroom—I will never get one, as I would rather be doing other things—no technology, go to bed void of emotion, eliminate hot temperatures, eliminate light, install soothing ambient noise, and if one of us is having trouble sleeping, we don't rustle around and wake the other. This is my general model for sleeping at home today and it still produces six to eight hours of sleep at night. When I'm in the backcountry teaching, hunting, gathering, scavenging, or Earthroaming, my sleep is amazing. My naps during the day are even better. I love sleeping in caves, improvised shelters, large piles of leaves and grass, in animal hides, in the open, on sunny hillsides full of flowers and berries, in a rainstorm protected from above, in falling snow, and, most important of all, next to a fire—man's first TV! Sleeping wild is awesome, as many of the "insomnia" factors don't exist at all. Your priorities change and your mental focus is trained on ensuring your safety and warmth during the night. You're not thinking about what someone you will never meet and holds no personal value to you said about you online. Let's be honest: credit card debt worries don't survive in the wild, especially when you're sleeping under the stars next to a fire in a bed of leaves and grass.

More crucially, in a survival scenario, sleep helps us restore our energy so that we can be clearheaded, make good choices, and have the physical capacity to do what needs to get done.

As with most of the others so far, this structure combines a live trunk as a center ridgepole with deadfall uprights. Once that was completed, for added protection, the creators placed horizontal branches stacked on roots. Here in Colorado, aspen trees are abundant. They compete for resources—light and water—with the pines and frequently lose. Aspens are like a vine, one continuous organism connected by a thin underground root. As a result, when they die and fall while young, it is easy to stomp out those curved pieces where they emerge from the soil and use them as they were used here in the foreground. Placing those thicker, shorter lengths around the base of the structure created a kind of foundation on which the horizontal branches were positioned.

I have seen other variations of this framework and sheathing technique. Trimming live limbs and using grasses, leaves, and other forms of vegetation as "siding" will provide insulation and weather resistance value. All of that requires an additional expenditure of resources, and making a wise, TOWERS-based calculation guided the thinking here.

This close-up illustration gives you a better look at the root/trunk foundation and various materials used for the horizontal layer. Frequently, deadfall will have small projections from the union where branch meets trunk. They are ideally suited for us as hangers for horizontal pieces—or, as they are technically known, battens. Fallen trees that are in a state of decay will often give up their bark layer very easily and can be stripped by hand without the use of tools. In a way, they resemble shingles that you can place on the roof or the side of your shelter to fortify it.

Below is another view of this technique of applying additional material to the framework.

Obviously, that outer gap layer doesn't have to be applied horizontally. An additional layer of deadfall of a smaller diameter can rest between any gaps. Vegetation that grows in long stalks can also be arranged vertically. I've sometimes used either cordage I've brought with me or fashioned from materials at hand to secure it to the frame. If you are out doing a combination of low-tech and no-tech and have tarps with you, you can easily wrap or hang them from the frame. Depending on wind direction or a desire to have more shade, if you don't have enough fabric to cover the entire circumference, choose the best spots to suit your needs and place them there.

AN ALTERNATIVE SOLUTION

What I love—and I think most people who go out in the natural world to replicate primitive shelters do as well—is the creative aspects of these efforts. If I'm not in a great rush to move along and am "camping" rather than in a real survival situation, I take great pleasure in adding onto and refining structures like these. Somewhere on the cellular level, we transmit an energetic impulse to not rely on someone else's labor to provide us with shelter. And this isn't just an American rugged-individualism thing. I've been around the world a bit, and I've seen similar impulses and innovations in approaches satisfying this need to create and be secure.

The Marine Corps taught me how and where to sleep. When there was an opportunity to get a forty-five-minute power nap in, you took it because you never knew when the next opportunity to sleep was. You didn't sit around jaw jacking. You closed your eyes and slept! Marines have this amazing ability to sleep anywhere: in airport lounges before heading out on a deployment; inside a Port-O-Shitter on a machine-gun range (that was me, Private First Class Dust, pants around my ankles, mouth open and out cold); on helicopter rides (guaranteed slumber ops); in long-as-hell resupply convoys during training; in classes; while cleaning weapons; while conducting preventive maintenance on vehicles (me again, Private First Class Dust, checking for undercarriage leaks, mouth open and snoring) on field days; after patrols; during lunch breaks, smoke breaks, and piss breaks. Hell, if your ass can grab a few and nobody is going to get killed, have at it.

As a consequence of my military experience, my comfort needs for sleep are likely fewer than what others may have. That said, I do believe that, under the right circumstances, the most minimal of "shelters" will do. Conventionally referred to as "bough beds," these structures are simple and quick to construct. If you've ever assembled flat-pack furniture, you'll marvel at how little time can lapse between work time and shut-eye.

Essentially, the bough bed consists of two perpendicular rails laid a few feet apart. Whether you chop down a tree or use deadfall, these log rails should be approximately as long as you are tall. You can also stack branches for a "headboard."

Once those are laid in, it's all about gathering whatever you can find that will fill the void between the two rails that will make for the most comfortable "mattress" you need or want: leaves, grass, pine boughs, or other plant material. Depending upon your TOWERS assessment and your softness preference, lay in that vegetation to provide you with the necessary support and insulation value. Generally speaking, in winter, getting about six inches above the snow or cold ground will provide you with enough of an air gap to keep you warm.

For me, the best bough beds are ones where I have a layer of small pine branches that compress rather than stab me when I lie on them. Boughs generally have a curve to the smaller offshoot branches: Lay them so that they are convex rather than concave. Large branches with few fresh needles don't do much to aid the comfort factor. Once that initial layer is in place, I like to use dry leaves and grasses as a top layer. If I need more warmth, I can burrow down underneath that top layer and then gather the leaves or grasses I've scattered back over me as a vegetation blanket. I can also use a tarp or other piece of fabric as a layer that I keep close to my body and stack vegetation on top of that.

Given that I almost always bring an animal hide with me, I can either use that to lie down on or place on top of me for a cushion or insulation.

Obviously, you can make a bough bed inside a shelter as well. Keep in mind, though, that if you also create a firepit inside the shelter, the addition of those dry leaves in the bough bed means a greater risk of a spark or an ember from the fire igniting that bed.

As I frequently remind my students, nature provides all. It's our job to take advantage of that fact. In the illustration above, a windblown tree that has fallen is an ideal starting point for a shelter. Rather than using an upright trunk as a ridgepole on which to rest upright logs and branches, that angled trunk provides a shallower angle for building the shelter's side walls.

There's one possible drawback of the fallen tree strategy: the trunk may not be stable and could collapse. I do a quick recon on that potential problem and climb on top of it and even jump up and down a bit to test its sturdiness. Those few seconds of testing can save you time, effort, and possible injury. Also, a tree that has recently fallen is better than one that appears to have been grounded for a while. A fresh tree will still have some green leaves or, if it's an evergreen, needles. The branches that are holding up will still be firm and therefore less likely to snap and have the trunk collapse.

Another advantage of a more recently fallen tree is that it is less likely to have been invaded by bugs. Bees and other stinging insects sometimes build nests near fallen trees and can present you with an unwelcome housewarming present. Other wildlife may do the same and surprise you with their presence when you're trying to sleep.

ADDITIONAL NOTES ON KEEPING WARM

There are many ways to take advantage of what nature offers you. Winter survival's most difficult challenge is staying warm. Depending on the type of clothes you're wearing, you can get wet if snow is on the ground or falling from the sky. If you sweat a lot and you're wearing clothes with too much insulation value, the cooling effect of evaporation can lower your skin temperature and your core temperature. In very cold temperatures, you can reach a hypothermic state in a matter of hours. Finding and/or building a shelter in cold temperatures requires you to think and act fast.

Snow takes, but it also gives. Snow is a very good insulator. Because of that, for any of the shelters above where deadfall has been used to form walls, packing snow in the voids will make those shelters more weather tight and increase the insulation value of those walls. Similarly, in deep snow, a snow cave can be a viable option. A word of caution: because snow can seal so well, it's important that, in making any snow shelter, you have some ventilation so that enough oxygen is available.

If you have enough snow, you can quickly build a variation on the bough bed:

- Use your feet to stomp down the snow to near or at ground level, forming a shallow "grave" eighteen inches wider and longer than yourself. The idea is to have a stable platform on which you will lie. You can also use a short length of a tree trunk as a digging or tamping tool. Essentially, what you've formed is a kind of shoebox without a lid. You can add snow from around the cutout you created to increase the height of the four sides.

- Gather pine boughs and cover the ground that you exposed. The goal here is to be at least a couple of inches off the cold ground.
- Find sticks that can span the width of the box. Lay them out approximately one foot from one another. These should be sturdy enough to support the weight of boughs.
- Lay pine boughs across the horizontal "rafters" to form a roof.
- If you have a tarp or tarps, you can use them to supplement the bough floor and ceiling.

It's been my experience that snow caves can be somewhat time intensive to build and the potential for collapse great, especially for first-timers. This bough box can be done relatively quickly and, with a roof, offers good protection from falling snow. The more boughs you add to the floor and roof, the greater the insulating value. When finished it should resemble this:

You could also do something similar in other seasons. Instead of building snow walls, use deadfall to form the box and then lay in boughs, add tarps, etc.

Nature Provides All

You've probably noticed that after a snowfall, when melting begins, rings clear of snow form fairly quickly. Those areas are known as thaw circles. The reason they form is because when the sun shines in the woods, the dark trunks absorb more light than the white snow, which reflects those rays. The trunks then become like radiators: they emit that heat and it melts the snow nearest to them. Trunks are round, so thaw circles are naturally produced.

You can use this heat absorption phenomenon to your advantage. If you're cold and need a rest, entering one of those thaw circles can help. Also, one advantage of using a live tree as a ridgepole is that the additional thermal value can possibly make a difference in maintaining your body temperature above the point of hypothermia (95°F). Another advantage is the base of the tree. Less snow reaches the ground because of the overhanging branches.

Here's an example of how to take advantage of snow's positive sheltering benefits:

ROCK SHELTERS

Natural shelters and structures are amazingly efficient and effective, and I always seek them out. Many natural shelters and structures start with a small rock wall, a rock overhang, a single boulder, a tree stump, a mound of earth, a downed tree or trees, or even a strange piece of terrain. Many primitive peoples used rock shelters to take advantage of what nature provides. Like snow, rock gives and rock takes. When exposed to the sun, rock absorbs the sun's rays, producing a warming effect. Rock acts as a windbreak. A rock ledge can provide an overhead canopy to keep the sun from baking you or precipitation from freezing you. Rocks heated in a fire can be brought inside a shelter to provide a source of heat.

Caves are one form of rock shelter. Caution should be taken when using some natural shelters, like caves. Many snakes, scorpions, centipedes, rodents, bats, bears, big cats, and just about anything that can get inside will make a home of a cave. Check the area for bones, poo, dead animal remains, tracks, and anything that doesn't look right or smells extremely bad. Caves are also subject to cave-ins and rockfalls, especially if you light a fire in a cave. The heat from a fire can crack, split, and explode pieces of a cave, causing a cave-in. Check the floor of a cave for loose rock that has fallen as an indication of possible cave-ins or rock breakages. The cave floor is the best indication of what can fall from the cave walls and ceilings.

I view natural shelters and structures as work enablers. Imagine coming across a large boulder that creates a perfect windbreak. I would use it as it is: a wall that I don't have to build. I build a leaf-and-grass bed next to it, knowing the wind is blocked and no rain is coming, and then I crawl in for the night. Shelter done!

Depending upon your TOWERS assessment, any of the three rock formations shown here could prove to be an effective shelter solution. As before, the addition of tarps, fabric, clothing, etc., can enhance the protective value of these locations.

When it comes to shelters, being creative is the most important rule. Remember, nature provides all and can greatly assist by providing a roof or wall for a night. Shelters should be built for the needs and wants of you and your group. I could have listed fifty types of shelters I have built and lived in, and, yes, you could probably replicate them with ease. Build your shelters following the TOWERS concept, and you can never go wrong.

TOOLS, GEAR, AND EQUIPMENT

Tools, gear, and equipment can be brought to assist in the construction of a shelter. Tarps, trash bags, and plastic sheets all afford quick shelter builds and can most definitely save time and energy when used. Axes, saws, and hatchets clearly will aid in chopping and cutting of wood for shelter construction. Rope, string, and cordage can be assets.

However, all the tools, gear, and equipment I just highlighted can be sourced from the natural environment.

Here are a few ways you can use minimal gear and tools to provide yourself with shelter.

WEDGE TARP

You can quickly be set with minimal coverage by using a tree branch, a trekking pole, or some other sticklike object as a means to support this simple shelter. Cordage can help secure the open end, while tent stakes or found sticks can help secure the perimeter. This shape is ideal to use in windy conditions. It's low-profile, but it's still also crucial to put the lower end facing in the direction of the prevailing winds to prevent the tarp from filling up and acting like a sail.

BURRITO TARP

Another minimalist shelter can be made in short order and requires nothing but the tarp material itself. Begin by spreading the tarp out flat. Then fold as you would a large tortilla: one long side about one-third of the way toward the center and then again. Keeping the bottom side on the ground, lift the flap you formed by folding and lay down inside. Draw the flap over you. You can also do a fold-and-flap at the bottom for and additional seal. With plastic tarps, you run into the problem of breathability and moisture/condensation forming. Depending on your TOWERS assessment, that may not be a factor mitigating against its use, especially when considering how little time it takes and what little gear is needed. If you're not good at folding, then rolling yourself into the tarp will also do.

A-FRAME TARP

Using either cordage you've made or brought with you, string a guyline around two trees with as much tension as needed to prevent slack/sagging. Drape a tarp over the guyline and secure the bottom with stakes if you have them, or use rocks, branches/trunks, or other heavy items to secure the bottom.

DESERT TARP

Hot weather can also be seriously problematic, of course, and a desert survival shelter is a variation on what desert peoples have used for centuries. It is also known as the double roof tarp. That doesn't mean you need two separate tarps. One large one will do, but having two tarps makes the shelter's construction easier. When you exploit the nature-provides-all reality, you're using the principles of thermodynamics to keep you from suffering hyperthermia—a dangerous rise in body temperature.

- Dig a slightly larger than body-size hole in the ground, about one to two feet deep.
- Drive sticks at each of the four corners of the hole. Be sure that at least two feet of the sticks projects above the top of the hole.
- Tie off each corner of a tarp near the very tops of the stakes.
- Tie off each corner of the second tarp twelve inches below the top of the stakes. For the one-tarp method, simply fold the tarp and keep the twelve inches between the two layers.
- Use guylines to support the stakes and either drive the stakes as you would with a commercial tent, or use rocks or other materials to secure them.

In hot weather, I frequently see my dogs pawing at the ground to remove the top layer of warm dirt before lying down in the cool dirt they've just exposed. We can learn from them.

Being below ground level is one element of cooling that the desert tarp setup provides. The other is the double roof. Each one provides a layer of protection from the sun. The top one takes the most brutal solar beating. The plastic material will heat up and can radiate down onto you. That's where the second layer comes in, providing an additional heat barrier. The air sandwiched between the two will be heated, but the air will be cooler beneath that second tarp layer. Add that to the cooling belowground effect, and you can lower the temperature without causing hyperthermia, which produces the following health problems:

- Whole body: dehydration, fatigue, flushing, thirst, excess sweating, fainting, inability to sweat normally, lightheadedness, low blood pressure, nervous system dysfunction

- Muscular: cramping, stiff muscles, muscle spasms
- Gastrointestinal: nausea, vomiting
- Respiratory: fast breathing or shallow breathing
- Also common: elevated core body temperature, fast heart rate, delirium, dry skin, headache, mental confusion

TARP HAMMOCK

This is an ideal way to get you off wet ground or away from crawling pests.

- Spread out the tarp.
- Roll one of the long sides to the midpoint.
- Roll the second long side to the midpoint.
- Tie a sheet bend knot around each of the two ends of the tarp.
- Securely tie the ends of the rope to a tree after wrapping it around twice and making sure that it has dug into the bark securely.
- Allow for sagging and settling of the knots when determining height of the rope wrapping.

The rolled sides of the hammock can help secure you, but they can also be unrolled and cover you so that you have a burrito-hammock combination. If you're not careful about wrapping yourself up in the tarp and it rains, water will pool in it. It may not be the best in wet weather, but it will keep you above the fray.

As a low-tech tool, tarps are extremely versatile, lightweight, and compact. As the illustration below demonstrates, you can quickly and easily get yourself under some form of cover by having a tarp, a length of paracord (a lightweight nylon rope), and a little creative thinking.

TREE SHELTERS

Many evergreen trees have branches that are low to the ground. They also spread widely from the trunk. As a result, they offer a very quick solution to your shelter needs. With a few strokes of an axe, you can, if necessary, clear a few boughs that you can use as a cushion and insulation and to spread over you for additional cover. With the addition of a tarp draped over some of the limbs, you can increase the protection and warmth of this canopy, all in a few minutes. This won't be an ideal solution for a longer stay, but when the weather or darkness is closing in on you, sheltering beneath an evergreen will do a lot to help you conserve your energy so that you can push on after getting some much-needed rest.

NATURE ISN'T OUR ONLY PROVIDER

Sometimes human nature provides. As I pointed out earlier, I frequently come across shelters that others have constructed. When truly out in the bush and not in designated camping sites where you always disassemble your shelter and pack out everything you brought in, leaving a shelter in place is fine. Sometimes in your exploring you'll come across things besides shelters made from natural resources. On a recent venture into the woods, I came across a little-used logging or mining road. Someone had cleared it years ago, but new tree growth was evident. Rather than meandering my way in and among older growth, I took the easier route along this "avenue."

To my surprise, I came across an abandoned truck. Of course, I spent some time contemplating how it got there and other details of its history. I was miles from any paved roads or residences. It was in fairly decent shape for its age—but a quick examination showed that its motor was gone. More questions followed, but that speculation was good mental exercise. What did that have to do with survival? I knew that I'd stumbled across another energy-saving resource that could aid some other traveler at some point.

Though the windows were out of the cab of this abandoned truck, its roof was intact. You could easily place tarps or other materials to fill those voids. This long-bed truck had ample room to spread out in, getting you off the ground and on a fairly level surface. The bed also had various attachment points so that you could improvise a tarp roof. You could also find a ridgepole or run guylines from various points to set up one of a variety of tarp shelters. Then you could settle in for a good night's rest and wonder how a truck had wound up so far in the woods.

PACKING OUT THE IMPORTANT POINTS

Don't forget two of my core concepts: Know more and carry less, and nature provides all. Tools, gear, and equipment are nice to have, but can create a nasty dependency. The saying "All the gear and no 'idea-r'" applies here, as people become so dependent on a tool or equipment that many can't do without it. I am amazed when I hear students and instructors say, "If only I had a [fill in the blank], I could [fill in the blank] all the time." Learn how to source and make your own gear and you will truly be able to execute the construction of any form of shelter.

 CHAPTER 7 

FIRE

The ability to make fire is essential—even lifesaving. Fire will cook your food, boil your water, keep you warm, ward off unwanted visitors, aid in signaling for help, keep you entertained, and help you connect to the past. The knowledge, skills, and abilities (KSA) of fire making are endless and should be mastered. Far too many times I have witnessed survival students and survival instructors with impressive knowledge of friction fire methods and amazing skills and accuracy in building friction fire sets fail miserably. The reason? Because they lacked the physical ability (they tire out) to create a small coal that would eventually become fire.

You should always carry a fire kit of some type. I know I said that I often source them from the land, but I want you to focus on the mastery of the KSA of your chosen fire kit. Your fire kit can fall within any of the tech-level categories. If you are in the no-tech category, maybe a hand-drill friction fire set native to the area you are in is your fire kit of choice. If you are in the low-tech category, employ a flint-and-steel set that throws sparks into a local type of tinder to start a fire. If you are in the high-tech category, utilize a ferrocerium rod as your fire starter.

No matter which of the three categories you're in, master the fire-making KSA specific to your fire needs. I recommend that every one of my students strive to achieve mastery for every level. Once you can make fire in all three praxes consistently and without failure, you must then create failure. What I mean by this is purposefully breaking, losing, or reducing the number of fire-making tools and materials you have prepacked, or otherwise creating an issue that you must overcome. Purposely varying the difficulty of the conditions under which you make fire will help you succeed later on when unforeseen circumstances arise. For example, let's say you have chosen the no-tech fire-making method of the hand-drill friction fire set. Using that set, you want to be able to rou-

tinely generate enough downward pressure, speed, and clean rotation to create a coal, place it in a properly constructed tinder bundle, and blow it into a flame in various conditions every single time. This shows a level of mastery and routine execution of a skill reinforced through knowledge and abilities.

Practice fire making at home under optimal conditions (dry weather, dry wood). Once you have become proficient at that, practice doing it under suboptimal conditions (wet weather and wet wood). You don't want to be out on an expedition and face worst-case-scenario conditions for the first time. Having prior experience to fall back on will reduce the pressure on you to produce and conserve much-needed energy.

Here are the fire-tech methods that correspond to each of the three tech categories:

HIGH-TECH

- stormproof matches
- ferrocerium rod
- chemicals
- butane lighter

LOW-TECH

- flint, steel, and char cloth
- solar refraction
- fire piston
- standard matches

NO-TECH

- bow drill friction fire
- hand drill friction fire
- fire plow
- fire saw

THE FIRE TRIANGLE

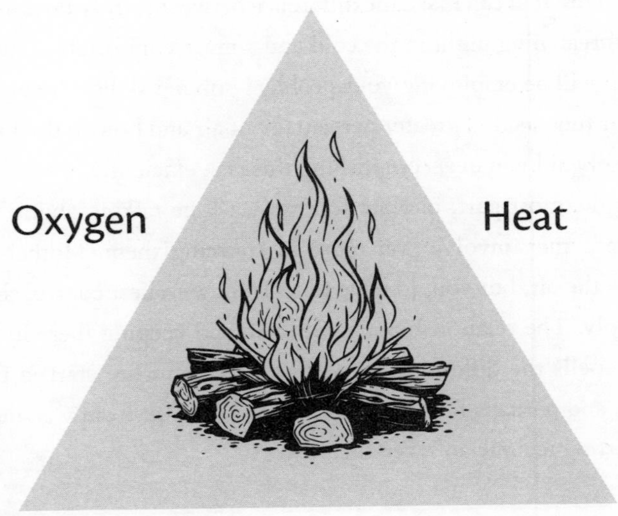

At its simplest, there are three component elements of a fire. Fire is a chemical reaction to the combination of these three elements. Think of your vehicle's internal combustion engine. In order for it to run, it has to have the right balance of heat, fuel, and oxygen in the combustion chamber in the right proportion and at the right time. Just as your vehicle's engine won't run properly, or maybe at all, without the proper air-fuel mixture, you need the proper balance of these two members of the trio to start a fire and keep it going. Your car has an engine control management system that controls all three elements.

In starting and maintaining a fire in the wild (or elsewhere), your brain is your fire management system. You've likely used it as such somewhat mindlessly many times before. Somewhere buried in our genetic code is a reminder that fire is good and has made our lives not just possible but better. Consequently, it's hard for many humans to resist the temptation to poke and prod at a blazing fire or one that's dying out.

When you do that, you're likely not considering how you're altering the air-fuel mixture. You just watch and see how the flames intensify or decrease as you move the fuel, turn the log, etc. Out in the wild, when starting a fire that can make the difference between a truly uncomfortable or life-threatening night in the cold and a more comfortable/survivable one, you will be employing your problem-solving skills. Understanding that your fuel needs a greater percentage of air and how to do that safely will greatly aid you in accomplishing this task efficiently.

For the most part, in what follows we'll be talking about fuel and heat, since they involve you more in sourcing them. Mother Nature provides the air, but you do have to learn how to best control that oxygen supply. The relationship among them and keeping them in balance is what spells the difference between a successful fire start, a frustrating one, and perhaps failure. It also helps keep you from wishing that a "fire-starting technician" were nearby.

The Seven *Ps*: Proper Planning and Preparation Prevents Piss-Poor Performance

This statement was drilled into my head during my military training. It applies widely but perhaps no more so than here in creating fire. It's essential to gather all the materials needed and think about all the variables that can affect your ability to produce a potentially lifesaving fire ahead of time. Time spent in advance will prevent you from wasting time with troubleshooting and do-overs later.

WHEN HAVE YOU REALLY GOT A FIRE GOING?

The process of producing a thriving fire consists of four stages. Only when you get to stage four and maintain a blaze have you, in my mind, really achieved fire. I also like to think of it this way: there are four phases of wood you go through in creating a fire . . .

1. Tinder
2. Kindling
3. Wood
4. Fuel wood

Based on this, then, you only truly have a fire going when you're burning fuel wood. During any of the other phases, the material you have ignited can be easily blown out by wind, extinguished by moisture, or otherwise snuffed out.

Utilizing any high-, low-, or no-tech approach requires that you know how to source and prepare tinder bundles, kindling, wood, and fuel wood. Each should be prepared prior to attempting to ignite them. Best-case scenario: all the materials you use in each of the four stages are as dry as possible. There's the old expression that you need to keep your (gun) powder dry, and that's the case with fire-making materials. As much as water is your friend in a survival situation, when it comes to making fire, it is your enemy. The more moisture involved in the process, the more difficult starting and extending the life of your fire will be. Moisture isn't an enemy you can't overcome, but expending resources unnecessarily in a conflict with it can have other consequences for you down the line.

LET'S TALK TINDER

Getting tinder ignited is the first stage of making a suitable fire for heat, cooking, and all the other ways we use it in the bush. So, whether you're using any of the high-, low-, or no-tech methods listed above, you will need a tinder bundle at the outset of your fire-making endeavors.

Tinder is any material that can easily ignite and stay lit long enough so that you can transfer that ignited bundle to your kindling. Among the many materials you can source in the wild to make a tinder bundle are:

- dry leaves
- dry bark
- dry wild grasses
- dry stems and stalks of various vegetation
- dry fur
- dry fungi
- dry cattail heads
- pine needles
- pine cones
- fatwood

The last of these, fatwood, needs some explanation. It is an excellent fire-starting material because it contains a chemical, terpene, in its resin that is the main component of turpentine, a highly flammable liquid. Fatwood, then, is a dried wood that is impregnated with resin.

Pine trees produce resin as a way to protect themselves from insects and diseases. It is notable for being tacky to the touch, thick, and yellowish in color. Resin and sap are not the same thing. Tree sap is less viscous (i.e., it's thinner) and clear. You can source resin from pine trees that have been severely scarred (the bark has come off sections of the trunk) or from dying or fallen pines. When one of those things happens to a tree, the resin runs down the trunk toward the ground.

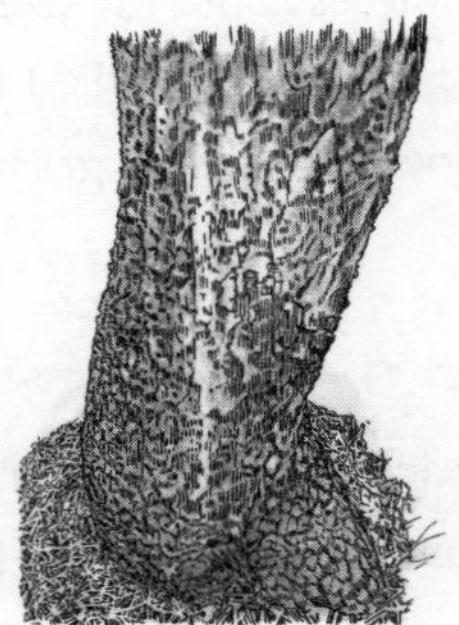

Impregnated with resin, pine wood looks different. When you strip away a piece of this fatwood, you'll notice striations of darker, amber-colored material within the lighter grain of the pine:

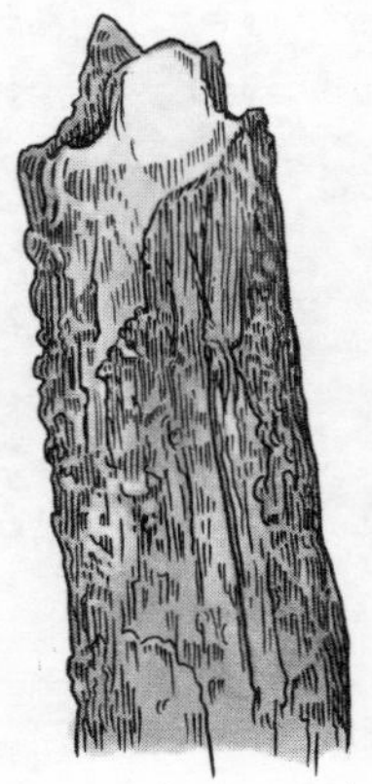

Think of it this way: fatwood is like a charcoal briquette with a fire-starting flammable material already in it. Because it has that additional flammable material, when a spark strikes it and that resin is ignited, it burns longer because it has an additional fuel source. Eventually, the wood itself will catch fire, but at the outset the resin is in flame.

Fatwood fire-starter sticks are commercially available. I pack fatwood I've sourced and processed with me because of the abundance of pine trees available here in Colorado. I find a piece of fatwood and then, using my knife, I process it by shaving off pieces about the size of cornflakes. I put them in a bag along with my fire-starting tools. I use those in combination with a small pile of the fatwood flakes to get my tinder bundle going.

Nature provides all. You may have noticed in your time in the woods that beneath some pine trees, piles of bark shavings have accumulated. When dry, these are already partially processed materials you can use in your tinder bundle.

You can also bring from home:

- dryer lint
- pocket lint
- shredded paper
- cardboard
- cotton balls

I prefer to source tinder from my location out in the bush, but I sometimes also carry along tinder bundles that I prepared at home in the case of an emergency. No matter what raw material you use for the tinder bundle, you must process it to make it as effective of a fire starter as possible. Using a knife, a stone, or your bare hands, you manipulate the material to break it down into a fibrous state by moving along the full length of the material. Similar to sharpening a blade, which results in scarf forming, bits of the material as fine as dust will be a by-product of processing. Whether I use my pant leg, a rock, or other surface on which to hold the tinder while working it, I collect that by-product along with the larger fibrous pieces. All of these materials are combustible when they come in contact with a spark or a flame.

The next step is to form that processed tinder into a bundle. Typically, that bundle will look something like a bird's nest. Process enough material that the bundle is larger than your hands and requires two hands to hold it. Here's a typical tinder bundle I might process:

KINDLING

Smaller is better at this stage. I've seen many ignited tinder bundles get consumed and die out without igniting the kindling because that second phase of wood was too wet or too large. Think of matchstick- or toothpick-diameter pieces. Six to eight inches in length is ideal. Better to build in multiple stages and maximize the material's flammability—of which size is a factor—than rush and use large pieces of wood too soon.

Nature can be cruel and kind simultaneously. Many pine trees are diseased. One of those diseases produces an effect in which limbs dry out and twist. These brittle, dry branches can produce an abundance of kindling that you can harvest in just a few moments with little effort. These diseased limbs are easily identifiable. They look like skeletal fingers.

Before attempting to light the tinder bundle and kindling, you must have a fire lay ready for action. As with the various types of shelters you can build, I'm far less concerned with you being able to name all the fire lays you can make. It is far better that you know the advantages and disadvantages of each and how to select the right one for the environment you are in.

One of the most commonly used fire lay shapes is a cone. Being wider at the base makes it easy to erect either stick by stick (time-consuming) or by forming them into that shape as you gather them. It's not always the most stable shape and prone to collapse in windy conditions, but only if you haven't chosen a fire site away from the wind.

Similar to the above, you can build a fire lay that uses a center pole to stabilize the sticks arranged around it. That center pole, like the others, should be dry. Drive a pointed end into the ground a few inches, leaving a foot or so exposed. The one drawback is that the center pole takes up some space from where you want to put the tinder bundle; of minor concern is that the center pole also interferes with air circulation. But this offers a good alternative if you're having trouble getting your sticks and twigs to stand up.

I hope by now you've recognized how shelter-like these builds are. Here's a variation using horizontal pieces to keep the vertical ones in place. This takes a bit more time and resources to build, but if you've been using TOWERS, you assessed the situation fully and made a good choice based on that.

Much like building a shelter using a rock ledge or a fallen tree as an initial supporting structure, you can do the same things when creating a fire lay. As you can see, there's an open end where you can slide your tinder bundle beneath the wood fuel with some ease.

My go-to option for a fire lay is the X lay. It plays the wind well.

SAFETY MATTERS

Most often, because I've done this thousands of times, I don't experience much difficulty getting a tinder bundle started and transferred to my fire lay to get my kindling aflame. However, through trial and error and assisting many students with these steps, I've figured out what to do when it's a struggle getting from the initial stages to a full-on fire. It may be obvious, but you need to be careful when attempting to make fire. Remember, your time and energy are finite resources, and spending it treating any injury, particularly a burn, is an inefficient use of them, as well as negatively affecting your chances of survival.

Using your hands, gloved (fire-resistant) or not, could get you hurt. To avoid getting burned by flames or embers, I do as our ancient ancestors did to thrive: I use a tool. Again, Mother Nature can provide all, and this tool is available in nature for use. Utilizing rocks and sticks in the fire-making process can help make this a more "hands-off" exercise.

To avoid direct contact with flames, use a stick rather than your hands to transfer your tinder bundle to the fire lay. If you've ever seen a pizza chef using a long-handled tool (a peel) to get an uncooked pizza into the oven, then you've got the picture. Lay that single large stick on the ground. Place a few more smaller sticks across it to form a small platform. Once you've got your tinder bundle lit, place it on the platform and then lift and carry the tinder bundle to the fire lay and place it in position. Moving the tinder bundle in this manner also helps feed the fire oxygen, one of the three elements of the chemical reaction.

As I said, I normally don't employ this method of air control. I simply blow on it to keep it alight. On a windy day, this carry-stick method gives you another option when your initial ignition stage produces so much smoke that it's difficult to keep your eyes open as you move your face close to the lighted tinder bundle.

I could go on, but as you know by now, I want you to have knowledge and apply your skills and creative problem-solving ability to fashioning tinder bundles and fire lays. Go out and experiment with different methods and materials of different shapes and sizes.

IGNITION

There are a number of variables to keep in mind, depending on what method you use to produce spark or flame to ignite the tinder bundle. But once the tinder bundle is burning, there are a few common tips and tricks to transforming that initial bit of combustion into something more easily sustainable.

I often fold the tinder bundle over itself to get as much combustible material in contact with the flame as possible. Second, I bring it up head high and blow gently as many times as needed to keep the red embers glowing. Once more of the bundle catches, I continue to blow to keep the fuel-to-oxygen ratio optimal. Once I'm confident that the tinder bundle is in good shape and the chances of it going out are slight, it's time to get it to the fire lay.

CARRY ON

I probably don't have to say much more about transferring a tinder bundle that has caught flame. For the most part, the flames will initially be in a confined space within that material. A couple of suggestions will help:

- Ignite the tinder bundle as close to the fire lay as possible to avoid carrying it farther than you have to.
- Don't move in so much haste that air currents extinguish what may be a fairly small flame.

FEED THE FIRE

Once the fire lay is ignited, it's time to keep feeding it, keeping in mind the same principles as before: dry fuel, appropriate-size pieces, a stack that ensures good airflow, etc. Having as much of that additional wood/fuel on hand at the outset makes the whole process go smoother. Essentially, the higher and hotter the flame gets, the larger the pieces of wood that you add. If at some point the fire seems to be dying, adding additional tinder materials is in order, as is increasing the amount of oxygen through blowing on the embers. You'd be surprised how much time it takes to get embers reignited and a fire going again after an active flame has been extinguished.

COOL YOUR HEELS

I can't stress enough the importance of preparation, patience, and persistence in getting a fire started, regardless of the method you employ. I know you want to be warm, but in order to do that, you have to stay cool. Or, put another way, having a hot head won't get your fire started any quicker or help it last any longer. For most of these methods, physical strength and endurance don't play a prominent role. In some they do, but even in those cases being calm and calculating and maintaining your situational awareness will do more for you than solely trying to muscle your way through the process. Of all the essential skills you need for wilderness survival, fire making is the one in which your problem-solving skills will most come into play.

You can't solve the problem if you *are* the problem.

THE HIGH-TECH WAY(S)

Now that you know the basics of getting through the initial stages of making a fire, let's quickly take a look at the high-tech methods and materials you can use to get that tinder bundle going.

Stormproof matches. With a thick coating of phosphorous applied to an approximately three-inch-long stick and a striker affixed to the box, these matches will light in wind and rain and either stay lit or be easily reignited. Although they are about as foolproof an option as there is out there, you do still need to take some care with them. Primarily that means keeping them dry before use. If the box is degraded by moisture, the striker becomes less stable and matches are more difficult to light (though some brands provide you with extra strikers). The added length means that some manufacturers' models will stay lit for as long as fifteen seconds. Clearly, keeping that tinder bundle and fire lay as dry as possible is the key, even with these bad boys.

Ferro rod. Like many, I generally refer to these rods using this shorthand name for the synthetic alloy they are made of. The substance ferrocerium is highly flammable. Ferro rods require a hard surface such as a knife blade or a rock to initiate sparking. When struck against a hard surface, it produces intensely hot sparks that can top out at around 6,000°F. Friction heat produced by rubbing them against a hard surface instead of a sharp strike also ignites them at the relatively low temperature of 338°F. They are commercially available, come in different dimensions, and are available with or without handles.

One of the easiest ways to use a ferro rod as a fire starter is to take the tip of your knife and place it in the center of your tinder bundle. Be sure that the tinder bundle is on a flat, dry, and secure surface and that you are near the fire lay. Position the knife so that the handle is at about a 60-degree angle to the supporting surface, with the spine of the knife facing upward. Use the other hand to scrape the ferro rod along that surface in a horizontal sawing motion. (Now you may see one of the disadvantages of a dual-edged knife: rubbing a ferro rod along it will contribute to dulling.) As you experiment with the ferro rod, you will get a sense of how much pressure to apply. You'll receive immediate feedback: no sparks flying means more pressure is needed. Ferro rods are durable, and a pack of them can be used to start a hundred or more fires.

FERRO ROD WITH STRIKER

Not much to add here, except that instead of having to source and use a hard object, these rods come with a durable striker for that purpose. Often the strikers are relatively small in comparison to a knife blade or a rock, so your hand could come in contact with the rod or be closer to the sparks and flame. Depending upon your hand size and sensitivity, the rod/striker may or may not be best for you.

MAGNESIUM FIRE STARTER

Most ferro rods are impregnated with some percentage of magnesium because this element is very chemically reactive. It is an earth metal and its easy ignition and flammability make it very suitable for igniting a flame in a tinder bundle. Magnesium fire starters like the one above are sold in different shapes and sizes but are generally small rectangles. Sandwiched between two pieces of magnesium rests a piece of flint. These fire starters are sometimes packaged with a small metal tool, often with a serrated edge, that works as a striker. They are very portable and generally very inexpensive, often less than four dollars.

Unlike with a ferro rod, where rubbing it across a hard surface or striking it against one produces a spark, magnesium fire starting is a two-step process. First, take the striker and position it above the tinder bundle. Scrape it along the piece of magnesium. Shards or flakes of it will come off and land on the tinder. (Pro tip: When using this tool, it's often best to grind some of the tinder until the pieces are very small and some of it is ground to dust. Place those smaller bits in the center of the tinder bundle and place the magnesium bar over that powdery material.) By trial and error, you'll learn how much magnesium needs to be flaked off. Given how inexpensive these bars are, it's better to use more than you think you might need rather than less. If you use less and you get no ignition, you can always scrape off more.

Next, again using the striker, with a vigorous downward motion, drag that serrated edge along the flint to produce sparks. The sparks will ignite the magnesium, which will ignite the tinder, which you will use to light the fire lay that will eventually ignite the larger pieces of firewood. Through patience and by practicing the techniques of bush/survival craft, you will learn how much pressure you need to apply to get a spark.

ELECTRICAL FIRE STARTER

Electrical fire starters come in various shapes and sizes, and some look very much like butane lighters except that they require no sparking mechanism to ignite the liquid fuel because they produce an electrical arc fire. Just press a button to produce an arc of electrical fire across two poles, hold the tinder to it, and proceed from there to the fire lay. These fire starters are very useful in wind and rain, since there's no exposed flame. Many are rechargeable USB devices.

PLASMA FIRE LIGHTER

A relatively recent development, plasma lighters bear many similarities to electric ones. In this case, a high-voltage electric current moves between two nodes, creating an arc of plasma. (It's beyond the scope of this book to get into the various states of matter that exist. I say that knowing that research scientists say that 99.9 percent of all matter in the visible universe is in a state of plasma. But I can't state what plasma is, so trust me.) This arc can light your tinder bundle and spark a late-night discussion around the campfire about the origins of the universe. Use sparingly! Those discussions can get "heated."

POTASSIUM PERMANGANATE

Potassium permanganate (PP), an inorganic substance, is an oxidizing agent that is used in industry and medicine and as a disinfectant. It can also be used in combination with glycerin to produce a flame. Handle PP carefully and wear a pair of gloves when using it. You can find it in some hardware stores, but because it is used in water treatment, pet stores that have aquarium supplies may have it.

Pour a teaspoon or so of PP onto your tinder pile. Next, using the eyedropper that frequently comes with vials of glycerin (readily available in pharmacies), squeeze a few drops on top of the PP. Be patient. It takes a while for the exothermic (heat-producing) chemical reaction to take place. A few minutes later the tinder bundle will begin to smoke and then flame. Proceed as usual.

LOW-TECH FIRE TECHNIQUES AND TIPS

As I indicated earlier, I believe that everyone who goes out into the wilderness needs to master at least one form of fire making from each of the three main categories I laid out. While high-tech means are reliable, that doesn't guarantee that things can't go wrong and you won't need backup options. Also, as you advance in knowledge and skills, going down the tech scale will likely bring you deeper satisfaction, and that is what thriving in the outdoors is all about.

FLINT, STEEL, AND CHAR CLOTH

In the winter especially, when the TOWERS analysis lets me know that quickly getting warm is of the essence, I carry a fire-starting kit made up of a steel striker, a piece of flint, and char cloth. That's the ideal composition of that kit, but I also vary from that, particularly when it comes to including flint.

Flint is a sedimentary form of quartz. It's also categorized as a variety of chert, but its origins are less important than its properties and uses. Flint was often used by early humans to make tools and start fires. You can still do both of those things today. When struck by a hard material like steel, it will produce sparks that can ignite your tinder bundle. It has been used so widely by many groups of people that its name is often used generically to describe any fire starter.

When out in the bush without my premade kit, I will find other species of rock that are hard enough to produce a spark when struck by a hard object. In the past, marcasite (a mineral also known as "white iron pyrite") was frequently used, and I use it sometimes as well. But in my estimation, carrying a piece of flint is a very efficient use of resources. Mind you, it does take some preparation at home, but that time is well spent in comparison to sourcing it in the field.

Here is a piece of raw flint:

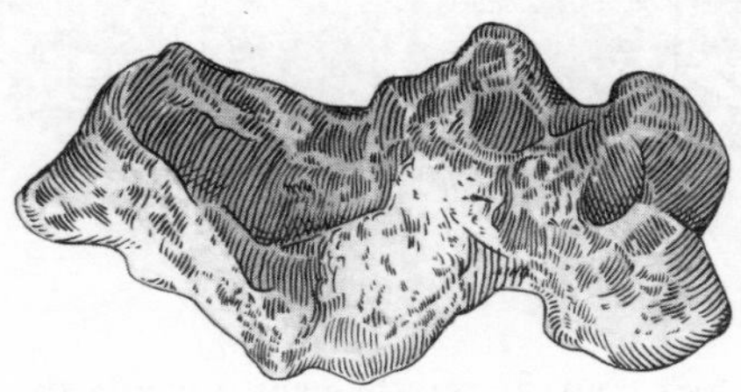

This is what it looks like after it has been knapped:

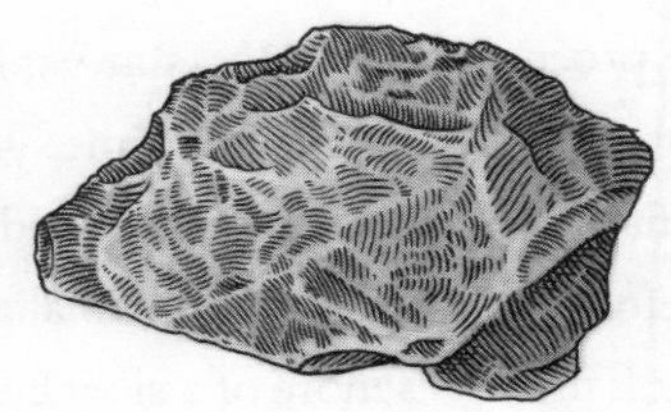

Knapping is the process by which flint is shaped through the process of lithic reduction: taking it from its natural state by removing some parts in order to create a tool or other object. Flint knapping is one of my favorite activities, and we'll return to this topic later in the book.

In my prepared kit, I carry a fire striker made of carbon steel. For centuries, blacksmiths and others produced these in large numbers, since they were in such demand. You can purchase them today, and many are reproductions of the shapes and styles that go all the way back to Roman times and the medieval period. Here's a typical one:

As you can see, your fingers fit neatly inside the nearly complete ring, and the straight edge is what you bring in contact with the flint.

The third item in my kit (I carry all three of them in a corded pouch) is char cloth. While it's possible to create a spark using just the flint, chert, quartz, or other stone that produces sparks when struck by steel, char cloth makes the process easier. Sparks are ephemeral. When you are working with flint and steel for the first time, you will see just how quickly those sparks flare and are then extinguished. It may take generating many sparks before your tinder bundle is alight. Char cloth gets ignited by a spark, but it produces more of a slow burn. Think of the orange glowing embers on a charcoal briquette. It will never flare up into a flame; instead, it will glow. That glow has enough heat in it that when it's placed in the tinder bundle, it can ignite those more flammable materials.

Char cloth, as its name suggests, is a bit of cloth or other material that has been charred. In other words, it has been partially burned. Char cloth is frequently made from fabrics such as cotton or canvas. It is commercially available, but you can also make char cloth yourself from old cotton T-shirts and such. I generally carry pieces precut in about two-inch squares.

ACHIEVING IGNITION

I look at my flint and identify the straight edge it has. I then take my square of char cloth and align one edge with the edge of the flint. I make sure to place that material on the top edge of the flint and not the underside. Using my nondominant hand, I hold the char cloth in place. I then use my dominant hand to hold the fire striker. I hold the flint away from my body a bit. I sometimes do this seated and tuck my elbow into my gut to support that arm. Then, with the striker in the other hand, I come down in a descending blow, similar to one you'd deliver if you were using a hammer. In other words, keep your upper arm still while moving your elbow, forearm, and hand in a downward strike. It doesn't have to be a violent or energetic motion. I bring the very edge of the striker gently into contact with the very edge of the flint in order to produce sparks. Move with precision. Edge meeting edge will produce sparks, whereas blunt blows with large surface areas contacting each other won't. When produced, most sparks will rise and then fall onto the char cloth.

Because the fabric is charred, it will ignite easy and produce a glowing ember. It will not flare up into flame and will most likely not spread across the entire surface of the fabric. It will sit there like a tiny glowing coal. Because it is in such a state, be very careful when blowing on it after seeing that glow dim. You want to keep it as bright orange as possible. Gentle breaths and care when moving and transferring it to the tinder bundle are the order of the day.

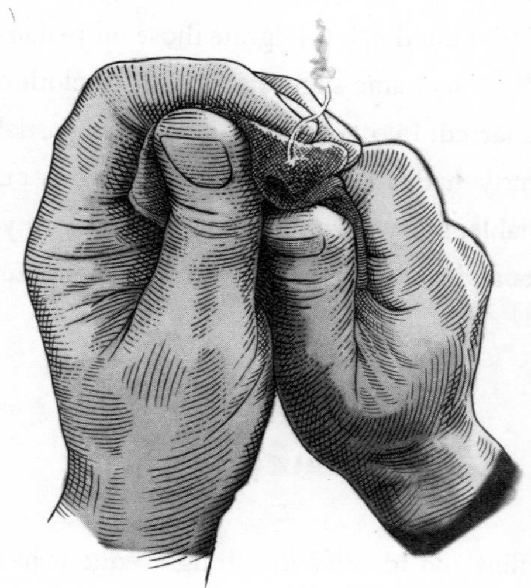

Once the char cloth has glowing orange spots on it, nurse it with soft breaths as necessary, being mindful of how fragile that ember is. You also need to be careful not to inadvertently expel any saliva. Carry the ignited char cloth to the tinder bundle and proceed as usual with the fire lay. I frequently try to increase the size of the ember/coal by folding the char cloth so that a few more fibers of it catch fire. Be careful not to smother that original ember. That may sound obvious, but relatively refined motions aren't always easy to make when it's cold and your manual dexterity is compromised.

Also, I sometimes tear off a piece of the char cloth that I've been working with and add that to the tinder bundle before placing the lit section on it. Having more char cloth in the mix inside the tinder bundle increases the chances that it will go up in flames.

Char cloth is especially useful when your tinder is not completely dry and brittle. It's also effective when environmental conditions—rain, high humidity, etc.—make sparking the tinder bundle directly problematic.

There are many online tutorials to learn how to make your own char cloth. Among them, this one from wikiHow is nicely illustrated and concise: www.wikihow.com/Make-Char-Cloth.

SOLAR REFRACTION

This one may bring back memories of childhood when a magnifying glass producing a few curls of smoke was about the best thing in the world. Rather than using friction to spark a flame in your tinder bundle, the sun's rays are an effective way to get it burning. One obvious drawback to the method that follows is that the sun doesn't shine all the time. But, as a fallback to others and a bit more added to your KSAs, I'll briefly shed some light on another method.

Whether you use a pair of eyeglasses, a parabolic mirror (one that is curved and has a bowl-like surface), a magnifying glass, a filled, clear plastic water bottle, or a soda can, directing that refracted beam of light into a precise point is essential. A focused beam is what you're after. That most often means holding the refractor perpendicular to the sun's rays, and you'll have to make some distance and angle adjustments to get that tight bright dot where you want it.

I bet you're wondering about the soda can. Well, the bottom of the can is concave but dull. If you can get some kind of abrasive material to polish it to a higher sheen, it can act much like a parabolic mirror. Of all the implements listed above, the magnifying glass, because it intensifies the light beam, is the best choice. Manufacturers produce magnifying glasses that are made for the express purpose of fire starting. Solar light can be harnessed to produce temperatures of up to 1,800°F. So, along with friction and chemical reactions, it is a viable low-tech option.

FIRE PISTON

Originally used in ancient Southeast Asia, fire pistons exploit heat and compression of a gas, in this case air, to combust materials placed inside it. Most automobiles sold in the United States have internal combustion engines in which the fuel is ignited by a spark plug. Diesel engines, which power some cars but many trucks and other heavy equipment, don't utilize spark plugs to ignite the fuel inside the cylinder. Instead, they use compression. Fire pistons apply many of the same principles as a diesel engine. A piston rises and falls inside an airtight cylinder powered when you press down forcefully. Inside the cylinder is a small bit of tinder or char cloth. When the piston descends, it compresses the air, raising the temperature to the point that the tinder or char cloth catches. It will produce an ember similar to what the flint and steel did on the char cloth. That ember is then used to ignite the tinder bundle.

The illustration above depicts a handmade fire piston from the Philippines. Most mass-produced fire pistons today are made of metal. I've also seen some hand-made ones. Any fire piston will produce embers very quickly and easily. However, it's your skills in transferring and nursing that ember and how well you selected materials for and prepared your tinder bundle that make the difference between an easy initial step and a successful fire.

STANDARD MATCHES AND BUTANE LIGHTERS

The old reliable for millions of campers for generation after generation, matches and butane lighters are low-cost and easy to use, but singed fingertips and abraded thumbs are downsides. About as portable as anything you might bring, they are a legitimate, no-frills, low-tech option.

NO-TECH METHODS

I believe that, more than anything else, beginner and wannabe outdoor enthusiasts are most fascinated by, and aspire to start a fire using, no-tech methods. I'll dispense with any other introductory remarks other than to say that you can either make bow-drill or hand-drill friction fire tools at home ahead of time and carry them with you, use found materials out in the bush, or employ some combination of the two practices. I enjoy making them out in the field but also bring with me one bit of material for the bow drill to eliminate fashioning it there.

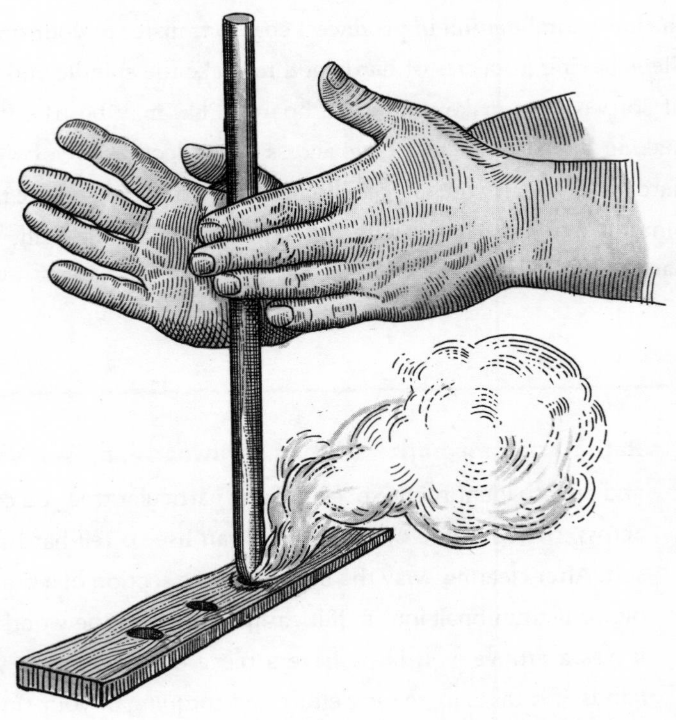

Let's get started with the less complicated of the two: the hand drill.

The advantage of the hand drill for making friction fires is its simplicity. Because it's made up of just two pieces, if you make one at home and carry it with you, you'll find that it is light and doesn't take up too much space.

There are two key components of making a hand drill that, unless done properly, can make them problematic. Getting the equipment right is the first priority. If your equipment isn't in good order, no matter how much strength and endurance you have and how fast you can spin the drill, your chances of successfully producing a coal or ember decrease. The two parts are the spindle and the hearth board. (These are also known as the drill and the fire board.)

The hearth board is a relatively short length of wood that you fashion from a tree branch. Some survival experts will tell you that the ideal combination to produce a coal to transfer to your tinder bundle is having a species of hardwood to make the spindle and a species of softwood to make the hearth board. That may be true if you are making one at home and have access to a selection of softwoods and hardwoods. So, if you opt for a home build, go ahead and use that combination and experiment with different species. In the field, you may have to use wood of the same species.

Rather than memorize a list of hardwoods and softwoods and how to identify the species of any particular tree you come across, there's a rule of thumb you can use to tell hard from soft. After clearing away the bark layer of a section of a branch, dig your thumbnail into it. If it easily penetrates the wood and leaves a groove, you likely have a piece of softwood in your hands. If it takes increasing effort and torquing of your thumb to get through the surface layer, you're handling a piece of hardwood.

When making one out in the field, you likely have a smaller selection of tree species and other materials. Shrub trees can often be used to make the drill as well. Your first task is to cut or chop a softwood branch to length. About one foot in length is sufficient. As with all aspects of fire making, the drier the wood, the better.

Next, using your blade, whittle along the two opposing surfaces of the round branch to produce two flat sides. Ideally, the hearth board's thickness will be slightly less than one inch from flat top to flat bottom. I'll explain why that's important in a bit. The width of the hearth board can also vary, but generally three to six inches is sufficient. Anything much less will make it less stable to press down on.

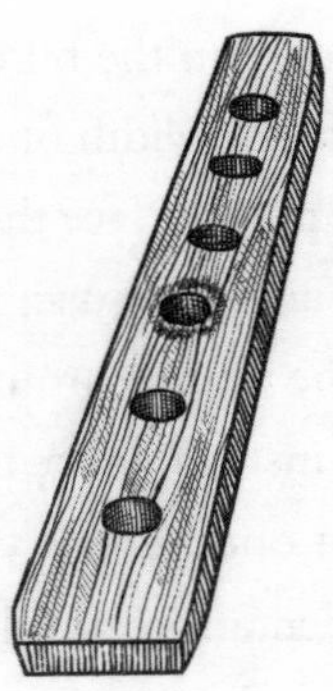

Once you have your hearth board flattened, turn your attention to making the spindle. Here, thickness matters, too. Because you will be putting pressure on the drill as you force it into the hearth board to create friction, it needs to stand up to downward forces. You don't want the drill to bend and produce a wobble as you spin it. The diameter can vary, but something slightly less than the width of your thumbnail is optimal. The drill's length should be about the distance from the tip of your fingers to the crook of your elbow. I've found that taller drills can be a bit unwieldy because the center of gravity is a greater distance from the stable platform of the hearth board. The length I've described allows you to maximize your leverage as you both spin the drill and press its tip into the hearth board.

As with much of what I teach, the dimensions I use here fall under the heading of "my way but not the only way." If you have really large hands and a thinner spindle doesn't work for you, modify what I suggest and use one of larger dimensions. If you don't want to take the time or have the tool needed to cut the hearth board to an exact length, use a piece of found material that will work for you. Part of being creative is being flexible and adaptable.

After you've whittled the spindle of your hand drill, with the handle end slightly larger in diameter than the bit end, use the bit end as a guide. It should be approximately the width of a pencil. Use your knife to sharpen it to a slightly smaller point. Place the drill tip approximately in the center of the hearth board and then, using the point of your knife or the sharp edge of a stone, scribe a circle around the tip. Don't trace it to the exact dimension of the tip; instead, make it about one-eighth of an inch wider. Once you've got that outline, use your blade's tip to carve out a shallow pilot hole–like indentation. While you're at it, you may want to make several others in case the first one isn't the right size. Test to see if the spindle's tip spins freely in that hole. The hole shouldn't be so deep that the edges of the bit catch on its sides. You want a point of contact solely on the bottom of the pilot hole.

After you've prepared the two pieces, perhaps the most critical step comes next. You need to cut a V-shaped notch in the hearth board from its perimeter to the edge of the indentation. This notch serves as a kind of chute, allowing the passage of material to flow out of that shallow hole and onto your coal catch—an item such as a flat piece of bark, a knife edge, or a flat rock that allows you to safely carry the coal to the site of your tinder bundle. Avoid using dry leaves, since they're flimsy and your coal can easily burn through them and fall to the ground.

Next, either while seated or standing, with the drill and the hearth board firmly in place and the capture material in position, take the handle end of the spindle and place it between the fingers of your hands, held as if in prayer. Then vigorously rub your hands together as if trying to warm them. Place enough inward pressure that the drill remains between them and spins as your hands move down the length of the drill. Use enough downward pressure that your hands spiral toward the hearth board. Repeat this several times. If the drill keeps hopping out of the pilot hole, then you may have one of the following problems:

- The indentation may be too shallow.
- The pointed end of the notch may be too large.
- The hearth board is not staying firmly in place.
- Your drill is really imbalanced.
- Operator error is occurring and you're struggling to coordinate the rubbing movement with the downward movement and your hands are moving on different planes.

Correct as needed and reengage.

You should see some powder being produced. Some will cling to the sides of the pilot hole, but it should not build up to the point that it flows over the edge and onto the top surface of the hearth board. It should, instead, fall through the notch onto a surface that can capture it and eventually an ember. Alternatively, you can place the tinder bundle beneath it. I don't like this method because, given the size of the hearth board, you won't have room for much tinder.

If you don't see any char powder, you need to stop and assess. Are the dimensions of the pilot hole and the point of the drill correct? There has to be a point of contact sufficient to produce friction. Does the drill seem to be spinning freely throughout its rotations or is it getting hung up? That may indicate it's hitting the edges of the pilot hole or that you aren't keeping the drill perpendicular to the hearth board. Again, assess whether or not you are placing enough downward pressure. Do you see a darkening of the wood on the tip of the drill and/or the bottom of the indentation? If not, you may need to increase the pressure and speed with which you're moving your hands.

Make adjustments as necessary and repeat. If all goes reasonably well, you should begin to see smoke after some time. Take heart at that: you're getting there. The question is: How close are you getting to being there? Patience and persistence once again come into play. A sprinter's mentality isn't the best one to have here. Start out at a steady, sustainable pace. When you start to see smoke, then increase rotational speed. Keep an eye on what's happening in the pilot hole. That first bit of smoke results from the contact between the two pieces of wood. If you start to see a second wisp of smoke, then you really know you've made progress. That second wisp is coming from the ember produced by that powder igniting. It is sometimes difficult to see if there is an ember, so while you continue to turn the spindle, blow lightly on the accumulated material in the notch. Adding oxygen will get any ember to glow more brightly.

If all goes well, the tinder bundle will catch and you can proceed with its careful handling and transfer, then nurture it into a full-on flame.

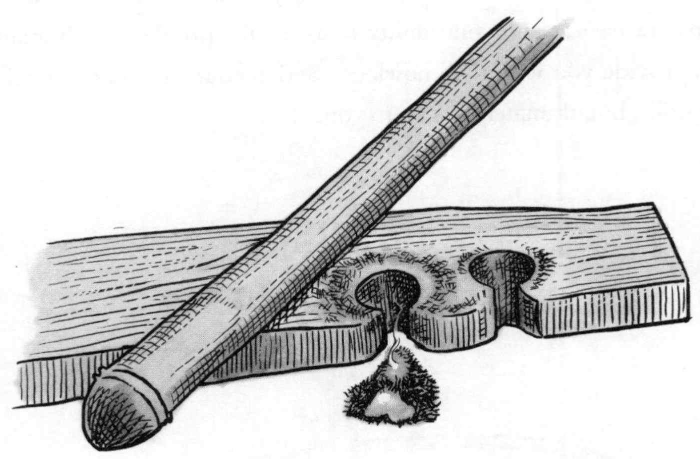

TROUBLESHOOTING

Why can't you get a suitable ember?

- The pilot hole you carved may be too close to the edge of the hearth board. This can cause the spindle to slip out and/or destabilize the hearth board, making it hard to get the spindle up to a proper number of revolutions per minute.
- Bad placement of the pilot hole can also cause that imbalance at the worst time, so that the char powder that has been produced gets spilled out.

The size of the pilot hole has to be the proper depth, as I pointed out above. If it is too deep and close to the contact point where the friction, and thus heat, is the highest, additional char powder will build up on top of it and smother those would-be embers. This can also happen if you use the same pilot hole from the same hearth board to light several fires. Each time you do, that drill point digs a bit deeper.

As with so much of what's necessary to acquire these skills, situational awareness and your ability to assess the problem really matter. I can provide you with the knowledge and encourage you to practice all the skills, but ultimately it's up to you.

BOW DRILL FRICTION FIRE

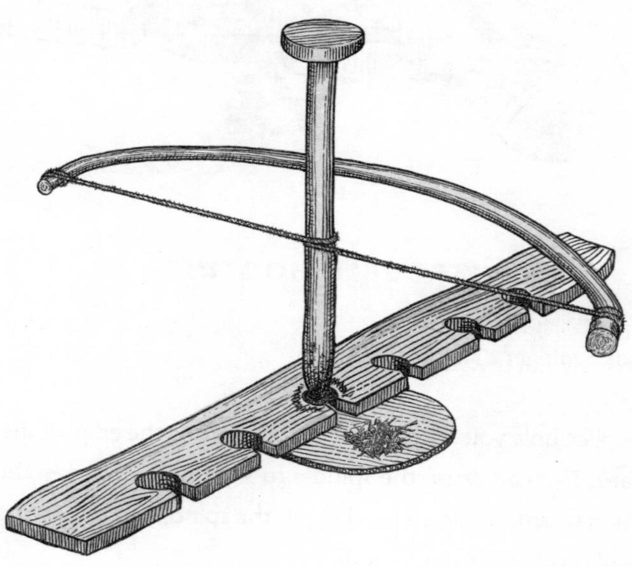

All of what I said about the spindle and hearth board applies here. Those two parts of this fire-making tool are the same. What's different is that instead of spinning the spindle between your hands, you fashion a bow, much like one used on stringed instruments, to rotate the spindle. Because of this, I'll move ahead to the most pertinent part of the preparatory stage, making a bow.

- Find or cut to size a stick that has a Y-shaped notch at one end. Choose a stick (or cut one to size) two to three feet long. Somewhat green wood about the thickness of your thumb is best. Overly dry wood, and especially deadfall branches, will likely break. The bow wood should have some flex to it. The length does matter, because as you perform the sawing motion to get the spindle to turn, you want to have the best range of motion possible.

- At the opposite end from that Y, cut a channel or groove that will receive the other end of the material you will use to string the bow.

You don't want a second Y. You need to be able to adjust the length and tension of the bowstring easily.

You can slide that material along that gouge, effectively increasing or decreasing the amount of material between the two ends of the bow. That also reduces or increases the tension. Hold the material in that gouge with your thumb.

Use a length of pre-stretched buckskin for the bowstring. I also like to bring a bearing block that I made in advance from an antler: this bony material generates far less friction than wood does. While you want some friction at the contact point between the spindle point and the pilot hole, less friction overall allows the spindle to turn faster. That produces greater speeds, which in turn translates into hotter temperatures to ignite the char material into an ember.

The same is true of the antler-bearing block. It's roughly rectangular and fits easily into the palm of my hand. I round off all the edges so that when I bear down on it with some pressure, it won't cause me any discomfort. It also has a pilot hole centered in it to receive the spindle. Again, with less friction at this point where producing heat doesn't matter, it spins quite freely.

You can take all these premade parts with you and leave your bow at home if you make a new one in the field. The next step is to use this device to make a fire.

When you're out in the bush and ready to make a fire with the bow drill, do the following:

- Find a flat rock or place the blade of a wide knife on a flat spot on the ground. Rest your hearth board on that. The blade or rock will serve as a coal/ember catcher.
- Get down on one knee. With the foot of your raised leg, hold the hearth board in place.
- Insert one pointed end of your spindle into the pilot hole of the hearth board. The spindle should be about the length of your fully spread hand from pinkie to thumb. This shorter spindle than the one used with a hand drill has a lower center of gravity and provides greater control.
- With the bit end inserted into the hearth board, ready your bow and buckskin bowstring.
- Use a reverse wrap tie on one end of the bowstring. Loop that knot around the Y end of the bow.
- Place the bow on the hearth board with the bowstring facing the spindle. Do one quick wrap of the buckskin around the spindle.
- Secure the loose end into the groove that you cut into the bow at the non-Y end.
- Place the bearing block on top of the spindle. Make sure that the spindle is perpendicular to the hearth board.
- Grab one end of the bow and draw it back and forth in a sawing motion. Instead of using short strokes, it's important to use long ones in which you fully utilize the entire length of the bowstring. Stay attuned to the pressure you're applying downward through the bearing block. Monitor the spindle angle to keep as close to 90 degrees as possible. Observe when smoke begins to come from the contact point. Once it does, you've arrived at the sweet spot. Continue to saw while slowly increasing downward pressure as the volume of smoke increases.

When you push down on the bearing block, you want to maintain a single point of contact between the spindle tip and the pilot hole. Any wobble, or a too-tight fit (closed off) where the spindle tip contacts all edges of the pilot hole, will increase friction at those points. That undesirable contact at the pilot hole's edges will reduce the spindle's rotational momentum.

You don't want too much friction at the top. Speed is your friend, and as you know, friction reduces speed. Too little friction at the bottom as a result of slow spinning makes it less likely that you will produce enough heat to get char material to make a coal. Put another way, you don't want any part of the spindle tip to come in contact with the pilot hole in the bearing block. If you ever see smoke coming from the bearing block, you know that the pilot hole is closed off. Make adjustments either to the hole or the point of the spindle.

FIRE PLOW

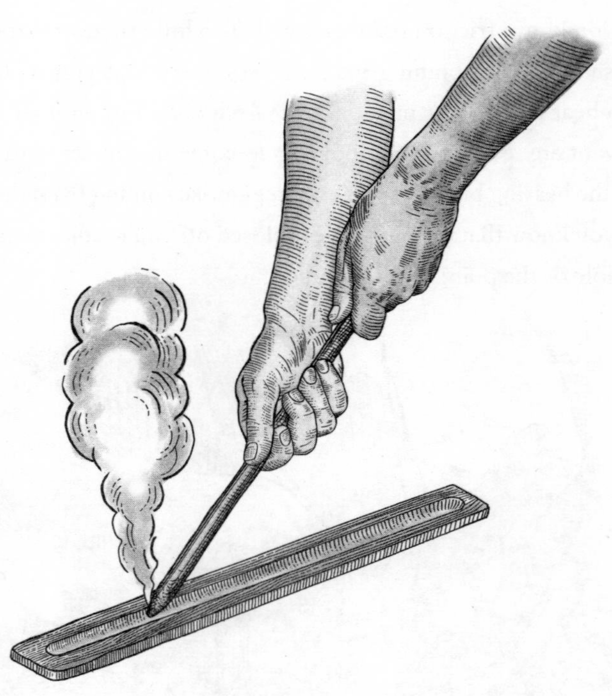

This is friction fire making at its most basic. As with the hand drill, it's just two pieces of wood. One needs to lie flat and have a groove carved along in the middle of its width. To aid in oxygen flow along that groove, you should carve a second, shallower groove into it. The second piece of wood has a dull point formed on its end. That pointed end should fit fairly tightly within the center groove of the first piece. Pressing forward and pulling back on the upright piece will produce friction like the first two no-tech methods I described above. The same principles apply to handling the production of coals as with the others.

FIRE SAW

This fire-starting method works effectively with easily split softwoods, such as bamboo. As the drawing above shows, you slide a split piece of wood through notches cut into a full length of that soft material to produce friction heat. By loading tinder inside that intact piece, the vigorous sawing produces heat that will set the tinder alight.

Whatever method you use to get a fire going, I'm sure you will enjoy the satisfaction of having provided yourself and others with a means to meet many of your survival and other basic needs. While it would be possible to survive for a time without fire, the sense of security a fire provides can't be dismissed. Also, as you'll see in the next chapter, having a fire to cook with and to purify water can help keep you healthy, perform many survival tasks, and generally better enjoy your time out in the wild.

CHAPTER 8

WATER AND HYDRATION FOR SURVIVAL

Sourcing water is the third of our four survival priorities. More specifically, though, you need to source it and purify it. It's never enough to just find water; you have to ensure that it is safe to drink before consuming it. Unfortunately, much of the water we source from nature is home to a variety of pathogens that can do us great harm and possibly kill us. That is why I want to stress the important distinction between purifying water and filtering water. Purifying water means eliminating as many pathogenic (disease-causing) organisms as possible. Filtering water means eliminating particulate matter like dirt, sand, vegetal debris, and such. Filtered water from a natural source will look better but it won't necessarily be safer for you.

At home, we rely on a massive infrastructure to bring safe water into our homes. Out in the wild, we don't have the luxury of going to a tap to get water that we presume to be safe (i.e., won't make us sick or kill us). Therefore, we have to rely on a variety of measures to eliminate microorganisms, bacteria, and parasites. Potential illnesses from these pathogens include giardia, dysentery, hepatitis, and hookworm.

I have had dysentery more times than I would like to admit due to consuming untreated/impure water. While I was fortunate to have had access to drinking water on these occasions to make up for what I was losing due to severe diarrhea, I was miserable. I was also unable to think clearly. In any survival situation, your ability to effectively problem solve will dictate your outcome to a great degree. As I keep stating, your bodily resources are just as important as the tools, equipment, and other survival resources you create or find in the wild.

Water is essential to life in so many ways. If you don't have enough of it in your system, your ability to move is compromised because water helps lubricate our joints. That means building shelters and fires can take longer due to your body's stiffness and pain. Water helps regulate our body temperature, digest our food, deliver oxygen throughout the body, and flush out waste. A lot of recent research has centered on proper hydration and maintaining good brain function. Current findings suggest that some cognitive abilities and mood states are positively influenced by water consumption. Obviously, being able to think as clearly as possible is crucial to your survival in the wild.

HOW MUCH WATER DO WE NEED TO SURVIVE?

I wish I could provide you with a simple chart that lists your body weight, your sex, and how much water you need to consume each day to sustain your life. This is a critical question with a complicated answer that will vary from person to person.

Worst-case scenario, to maintain the functional level you had going into a water-deprivation scenario, you need to replace the amount of water that you lose each day through urination, perspiration, and respiration. Keep in mind this is inexact, but one way to determine this take-in-to-replace-what-goes-out worst-case scenario is to take your body weight and divide it by 20 percent. For example, for a two-hundred-pound person, you'd do this math:

$$200 \times 0.20 = 40$$

That means this individual would need to take in forty ounces of water just to maintain that water equilibrium. If they did anything to increase their respiration and perspiration rates—being active, for example—they'd need to consume more. If they were in a hot, humid environment, they'd perspire more and thus need to replenish a greater amount. Same for those who suffer from dysentery or diarrhea.

Because of physiological differences related to body composition, a two-hundred-pound woman would need to consume less than that: roughly thirty-two ounces, approximately 22 percent less than a man.

If you get less than that amount, your body can compensate. A third of the water you hold in your body is outside your cells. When in a dehydrated state, that water gets absorbed by the cells so that they can maintain their functional state. Also, when in a dehydrated state, the body goes into water conservation mode. Both of these responses contribute to us being able to survive without any water for roughly seventy-two hours. If you have some water, however intermittently and sparingly, you could possibly extend your life beyond that three-day window.

Because so much of this is dependent upon the individual's health, age, height, weight, gender, activity level, and environmental variables, these are very much ballpark figures. Also, though I've been using "water" so far, you can take in other fluids and count those toward your total consumption.

Dehydration is a condition in which the body isn't able to function properly because of insufficient fluids in the system. If you're moderately dehydrated you'll experience some of these symptoms:

- thirst
- dry mouth
- decreased frequency of urination
- dark yellow urine production
- dry, cool skin
- decreased or no perspiration
- headache
- muscle cramps

If you don't rehydrate, you may advance to severe dehydration, during which you may suffer from:

- cessation of urination
- very dry skin
- vertigo

- rapid heart rate
- rapid respiration rate
- fainting
- confusion
- irritability
- lack of energy

Less commonly, you can also enter a state in which the consumption of too much water can be problematic. This is known as hyponatremia. By consuming too much water, you reduce the amount of sodium in your blood. Hyponatremia is the most common type of imbalance in our electrolyte levels. Its signs and symptoms are:

- vomiting
- nausea
- headache
- memory loss
- confusion
- fatigue
- loss of appetite
- irritability
- muscle weakness
- cramps
- seizures
- decreased consciousness/coma

Clearly, some of the signs and symptoms of underconsumption and overconsumption are similar. One of the easiest ways to monitor your hydration balance is to monitor what volume of fluids you are taking in and, more significantly, what you are expelling. Regular urine color ranges from clear to pale yellow. Dark yellow to orange urine is an indication that you aren't getting enough fluids. Consistently clear urine, plus some of the symptoms listed above for hyponatremia, may indicate you are in a hyponatremic state. Hyponatremia is the name of the condition when you have a low concentration of sodium in your blood. To ward off hyponatremia, athletes and others have come to rely on manufactured sports drinks, salt tablets, and even pickle brine to make sure they keep their sodium levels in the correct range. Of course, you can also add salty solid foods to your intake to cause the same result in blood/sodium levels.

ENSURING THE PROPER WATER SUPPLY

When going out on an expedition, it's best to carry pure drinking water. That's not always possible, since multiday trips will require that you carry gallons of water. One gallon of water weighs a little more than eight pounds. Spread that out over a week, and you're carrying, initially, fifty-six pounds of just H_2O, and that's just to keep your in-and-out water balance at an equilibrium. To fully satisfy your thirst and keep you operating at your best, you'd need much more than that.

Many times when I go out into the bush, I'll do a preliminary scouting mission and cache water at various spots when I know that the location I've selected doesn't have abundant natural water supplies. My other option, especially when I believe I can source water, is to bring a filtration system or a means to boil water. The vast majority of the time, I use the second of those approaches. Even boiling water before drinking it doesn't guarantee that some pathogens won't still be present. Experts differ on the length of time you need to boil water to kill all waterborne pathogens. They do, however, all agree it's the safest method to make water as safe to consume as possible. The Centers for Disease Control state on their website that for altitudes below 6,500 feet, boiling water for one minute will do the trick. Above 6,500 feet, they call for a three-minute boiling period. (The time differential is a result of the fact that water boils at a lower temperature at higher altitudes.) Even if not every pathogen gets killed in the boiling process, you're considerably reducing the level of risk. I've always taken my chances on boiled water being safe, and thus far, this approach has kept me from getting sick.

I try to keep it simple:

- Water boils at 212°F.
- Waterborne pathogens, viruses, bacteria and parasites die when exposed to temperatures between 165° and 185°F.
- In the process of reaching 212°F, your water will pass through that 165°-to-185°F range for some minutes.

Good to go.

Purifying water through boiling is another reason why your ability to make fire is so critical.

SOURCING WATER

Every season brings new challenges and opportunities with regard to sourcing and consuming water.

I like to think of sourcing in two ways. The first is direct consumption. By that I mean finding a source of water that you can consume safely without processing it first. For example, you slurp morning dew off vegetation and swallow it. You could also use that same source later by sweeping it into a container for future consumption. In either case, you do so without additional processing or purification.

The second classification of water sources I make is delayed consumption. You find a source, but before you can consume it, you have to process it to make it safe to drink. If you are out in the world, it's likely that you will not be very near a water source—a lake, pond, creek, stream, puddle, or sip well. But looked at from another perspective, you're never *not* near a water source.

SUBCATEGORIES OF WATER SOURCES

We can break sources down into three additional categories beneath the direct consumption/delayed consumption umbrella:

- surface water: oceans, lakes, streams, rivers, creeks, etc.
- groundwater: seeps, springs, and aquifers
- atmospheric water: rain, snow, hail, dew, mist

Among these, atmospheric water fits into the direct consumption category, especially if you are out in the wild and away from atmospheric pollution produced by industrial plants, etc. Groundwater may be safe for direct consumption, but care should be taken if animals use the water and/or if insects or their eggs or larvae are present. Surface water and atmospheric water are the most obvious ones for us to spot, but all three categories reveal themselves if you're paying close attention and can read the signals that nature provides. Groundwater is the hardest to access, since it rises from beneath the earth's surface. If one of these sources is not readily visible, here are a few tips on how to read the signs that will lead you to water.

IT'S ALL DOWNHILL FROM HERE

Water flows downhill. It will always seek the naturally lowest-occurring point. By knowing that incontrovertible fact when sourcing water, you should head downhill. Sometimes "downhill" doesn't mean a large, obvious change in the gradient. In the mountains, it generally is, but all downhill sections of terrain don't always lead you to water. Look for two pinch points: a ravine where converging slopes come together.

Ravines can be broad or narrow, steep or shallow, but they have all been formed by erosion. That means that water has produced them. Ravines are like gutters on your home that collect rainwater and channel it. In some of the more level areas on pitched terrain, frequent rain may pool before reaching a flowing stream. If not, then follow the ravine farther down. It will lead you to either another ravine or a valley. Once at the lowest point, there may be a stream or other source of a quantity of water that you can then filter and purify.

LOOK FOR THRIVING VEGETATION

Trees, bushes, grasses, wildflowers, and other vegetation all need water to survive. Where they grow and show their lushest colors and quantity, you're likely to find a nearby water source. Sometimes that source will be groundwater. Desert environments will sometimes contain lines of trees or thickets of brush. Those are most likely following a creek bed. It may be dry, but when it rains, some water will follow that bed and can be collected. A dry creek bed or a dry area of grasses or even a cracked mud surface are worth investigating. They're evidence that at some point in the past, water was present. Dig a few feet below the surface and you may find it has collected water. It will need to be filtered and then purified for safety.

LET CREATURES BE YOUR GUIDE

You're not the only one out there. Animals are present, and they, too, need water. Larger animals will leave tracks. Frequently you will be able to spot game trails that they've created in moving habitually to a water source.

Many insects, particularly bees and mosquitoes, serve as indicators that water is nearby because both of these species must stay close to a water source in order to survive. Their fellow airborne creatures, birds, can also serve as a guide. When you spot them, follow their direction of flight. They could lead you to surface water or groundwater.

SNOW AND ICE

At the height of winter, these two can be abundant sources of hydration. Even as spring turns into summer, at some elevations and in some shaded areas snow may linger. I've heard some experts say that you shouldn't ever consume snow and ice unless it has been melted first. The logic is that the energy needed to metabolize it is more of a detriment than your hydration need. That's too broad of a statement to be truly beneficial. Depending upon the length of time you've gone without water, you may need water to survive to think clearly and/or to take other survival measures.

RAIN, FOG, AND MIST

All atmospheric water can be consumed directly or stored for later consumption. Wherever rainwater collects—on your skin, on your clothes, on your pack or tarp, or on vegetation—it is worth drinking at that moment or storing for later. Water wrung from a T-shirt may not be as palatable as your favorite spring-fed, vitamin-enhanced mini-mart purchase, but it will keep you hydrated.

VEGETATION

Consuming water from plants and fruits is a great way to get nutrition and hydration efficiently. In some jungle environments, large vines carry a large quantity of water. When cut, a near stream of water flows from them.

YOU CAN SOURCE WATER BUT CAN YOU CARRY IT?

I mentioned in chapter three the four *B*s of my minimal approach to supplies. One of those was "bottle." I always carry a single-walled steel or aluminum bottle with me. That's because it allows me to collect, carry, process, and store (CCPS, pronounced like "sips") water. If your hydration system doesn't allow you to do all four of these things, then I wouldn't carry it. Too often I see people out in the wild with double-walled metal bottles that keep water chilled. Double-walled bottles are heavier than single-walled bottles, and saving weight is always a consideration. I also don't recommend plastic bladders or bottles. They have multiple points of failure: bite valves, hoses, and caps, for example. These are susceptible to leaks. Plastic can also be more easily punctured. That makes them more of a liability than they're worth. Any steel water bottle also has the added advantage of serving as a signaling device. If you ever get separated from a group or otherwise lost, it makes a loud ringing sound when struck with another object.

A buddy of mine was once out on a thirty-mile training run for an ultra-marathon—not a typical survival scenario, but it became one. This was in a desert environment with no water sources along the little-traveled route he'd chosen. He had a running vest with various plastic flasks and a three-liter plastic reservoir. The fitting that connected the hose to the reservoir developed a leak, and mile after mile he lost precious ounces. By the time he got within six miles of his car, he was completely out of water. He became hyponatremic and dehydrated. Fortunately, his symptoms weren't so severe as to cause permanent damage, but he got disoriented and took a wrong turn on the trail, and those six miles ended up being ten before he safely returned. Endurance runners want to pack light, and steel may not be the best option. But given all the circumstances he had to factor in, packing light should have been lower on his priority list. Again, problem-solving and anticipating worst-case scenarios is an essential part of your wild wisdom mindset.

DIGGING A SOLAR STILL

This tried-and-true method of using what nature provides is particularly useful in the desert but can be applied in other areas as well. It's particularly effective in desert environments because this is a solar-powered water producer. Even in the most arid areas, you can source water.

All you need is a sheet of clear plastic and a container to capture the drops of water that will condense on the plastic when, through the greenhouse effect, moisture from the soil evaporates, rises, and condenses. As above, locating a sandy wash or a depression where rainwater might have once collected is important.

Here are the steps to take to construct this potential lifesaver. I'm basing this on you having a six-foot-by-six-foot sheet of plastic.

- Dig a hole that is approximately four feet across and approximately three feet deep.
- Dig a second hole in the center of the first hole that is large enough to fit your capture vessel inside it.
- Place your capture vessel inside that smaller-diameter hole.
- If available, place any green vegetation along the walls of the outer hole. This will assist in creating more moisture.
- Spread the plastic over the larger hole, securing the four corners with rocks. The plastic will sag but shouldn't make contact with the soil at the bottom of the pit.
- Place a small, round rock centered over your capture vessel. Gently push this rock down, making sure it stays centered over your container.
- Once the sides of the plastic are at about 45 degrees, stop pressing down.
- Use rocks and other surface materials and seal the entire edge of the tarp.

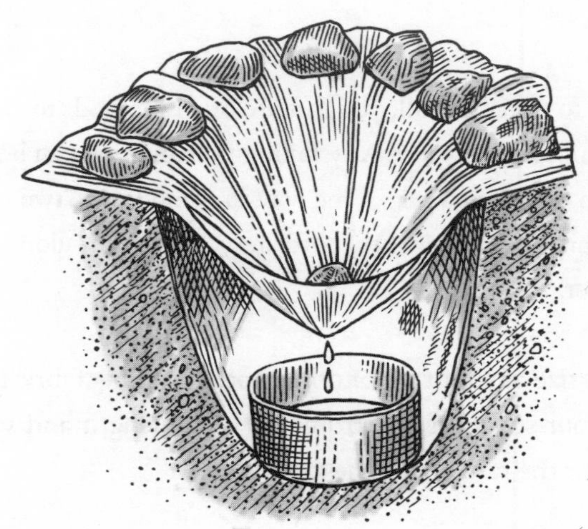

It may take as long as an hour to build a solar still. Once construction is completed, it's time to wait. The sun will heat the air inside your sealed hole. That heated air will draw moisture from the soil inside the hole. That moisture will then condense on the surface of the plastic. Because the plastic sheet is angled, the moisture will run down the sides and then fall into the capture vessel.

The water that is captured has been heated and may be suitable to drink. Purifying it by boiling is an added insurance measure. You can expect to collect as much as a quart of water per day using this method.

A slightly more sophisticated process involves using a plastic tube. While constructing the still, place one end of the tube in the bottom of the container and run the other end outside the perimeter of the plastic. The tube can then be used as a drinking straw. The advantage is, of course, that you don't have to unseal and reseal the hole in order to gain access to the container. I typically wouldn't take a length of tubing with me, but in a desert environment this might be a good idea. A hollow vegetal reed may work as well.

With such a relatively low amount of water production, this may not be the most efficient use of your energy stores, but in an arid environment it may be your only option.

ATMOSPHERIC WATER COLLECTION

In addition to the solar still, you can use other methods to capture and reserve atmospheric water. Any falling precipitation can be collected on a tarp or in open containers. One way to combine the two is to set up an elevated tarp using branches, cordage you brought along or made, and a container.

- Using the size of your tarp or other water-catching fabric as a guide, prepare four stakes of approximately equal length and sufficiently tall to keep the tarp above the ground.

- Drive those four corner posts into the ground, again using the size of your tarp or other water-catching fabric as your guide. (The greater the surface area of the catch, the more rainwater you will collect.)
- Tie off two corners of the water-catching fabric as close as possible to the tops of the posts.
- Tie off two corners of the water-catching fabric approximately one foot above the height of your water container.
- Place the water container midway between the lower tie-off posts.
- Either by using the gromets in the tarp or through a hole in the water-catching fabric, tie a rock to your cordage.
- Place that rock in your water container.
- Make sure that the funnel end of the tarp remains in place by tightening or loosening the cordage as needed.

The next step is to wait for precipitation to fall. If you have brought only one container with you, it will be beneficial to improvise. If there is a large stump of a tree nearby, you can take your knife and carve a bowl into it. Not only will it fill up with rainwater that is coming down, you can transfer water from your collection container to it. You can also take one or more lengths of tree trunk and carve a small bowl or bowls into them to be left out to collect falling precipitation.

Your situational awareness and ability to read the weather come into play here. By scanning the sky or knowing the weather patterns in an area, you should become aware in advance when it's a good time to set up a collection device. Also, by practicing this at home, you'll have a sense of just how much time you'll need to set one up.

TRASH BAG TRANSPIRATION

Think of this as collecting vegetation sweat. Plants don't perspire, but they do transpire. Plants use only a small fraction of the water they absorb through their roots to sustain themselves. They use much of

> **Leakproofing Your Wooden Containers**
>
> Whether it's the base of a stump or holes carved into lengths of branches or trunks, you can prevent too much water from seeping into the wood by charring it. Take a few hot coals from your fire and place them in the center of the bowl you've carved out. By blowing downward on the coals, you'll transfer the heat into the wood. Allow that portion of the wood to char and smolder. That charring process will provide a kind of seal or coating to the insides of those bowls. You can scrape away the heavier portions of that char or just filter out any flakes that get into your drinking supply. Or you can just suck it up when drinking them.

it to keep themselves cool. So when the weather is hot, water moves from the roots and rises through the stems and into the leaves. From there it evaporates, much like our sweating does, producing a cooling effect.

You can trap that evaporate by:

- placing a rock or other weighty object inside a clear plastic bag
- placing the open end of the bag over a leafy tree branch or a shrub
- tying the open end of the bag to make a good seal
- releasing the bag and allowing the weighted end to sink (Ideally it will rest on the ground, but if you secure it sufficiently, the bag can dangle.)

During the course of the day, the leaves will transpire and the evaporation will condense inside the bag. Either poke a hole in the bag after water has collected and drink or allow the water to flow into a container.

Tie up the hole so that you can repeat the process. Alternatively, untie the bag and retie it after drinking or storing the collected water.

Warning: Be sure that you don't bag a poisonous plant.

Be aware: The water may take on the taste of whatever leaf you've bagged. You won't be able to filter out that taste, but unpleasant-tasting water is far better than no water at all.

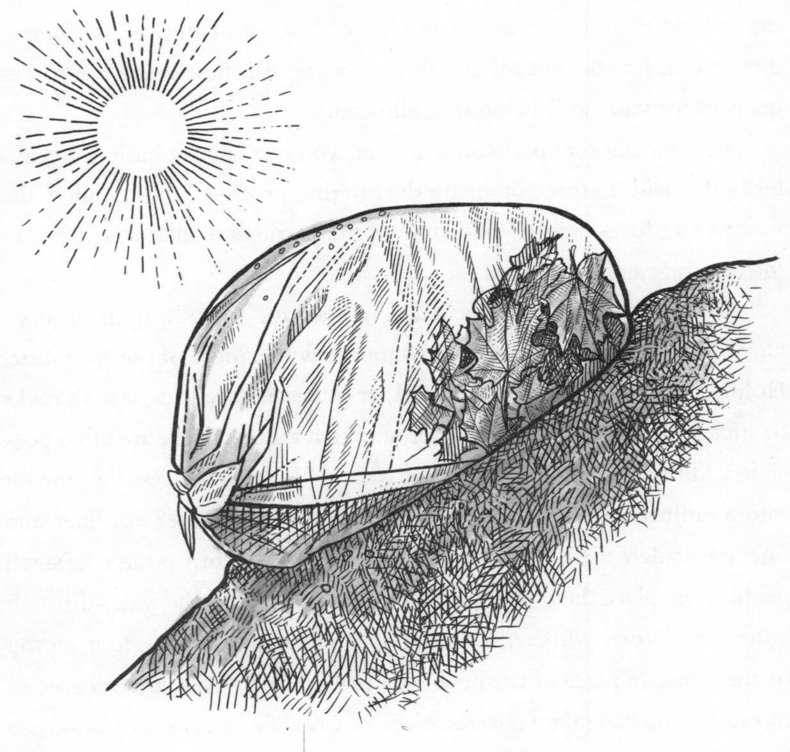

GO FOR A HIKE

In the early morning following a heavy dew, walking through vegetation dripping with moisture can help your water supply. If you're wearing long pants or if you have socks on, you can squeeze out the moisture that soaks into those fabrics. If it collects on your skin, you can squeegee it off and into a collector. Every little bit of water helps.

FILTERING WATER

In some ways, this is more about cosmetics than it is about safety. When I'm out in the bush with my dogs, they have no qualms about lapping up brownish-appearing water from a mud puddle or "chunky" water from a ground source filled with sticks and leaves. For most of us, that's hard to stomach, and, truth be told, some of the soil, sediment, dirt, sticks, leaves, and other debris in water can have negative consequences for your well-being if swallowed.

To filter out that particulate matter, you can make a basic water filter in the field. Before you begin the filtering process, you can allow the water to sit for a time so that some of the particulate matter will rise to the top and can be skimmed off.

Ideally, you'll have a second container for this filtration process. Cover the opening of the second container with a piece of porous fabric. Holding that in place with one hand, or otherwise securing it with rocks or sticks, pour your collected water onto that fabric. There are other possible additions to this pour-through-fabric filtration process that turn it into a multistage operation. At each stage, you will filter out finer and finer particulate matter. After you've done the first fabric pour, take small pebbles and place them on top of the fabric and repour the water through your filter. Next, you can take sand if it's available and place it on top of the fabric in place of the pebbles. Finally, for an even finer degree of filtration, you can take a charred piece of wood from your firepit and use it as a filter. Many commercial water filters use charcoal in their systems.

PURIFYING WATER

The order of possible water contamination ranges from least safe to safest:

Least safe	Surface water
Possibly safe	Groundwater
Safest	Atmospheric water

Why is this so? Mostly because the most common way water becomes unsafe to drink is through us—by what passes through us, more precisely. When we eliminate solid waste, with other animals doing the same, harmful bacteria and parasites are deposited in surface water and groundwater. The good news is that those contaminants can be removed. The other main cause of water being made unsafe is runoff from agricultural chemicals, heavy metals, and radiation. The good news is that those generally aren't present out in the wilderness. The bad news is that most purification techniques we use in the wild won't get rid of them.

COMMERCIAL WATER FILTERS

Even though these are described as filters, they do help purify the water to a great degree. They have fine-mesh filters and activated charcoal through which untreated water passes. The main difference among them is how you get the water to move through that filtering system. As a high-tech, low-risk option, these really can't be beat.

ULTRAVIOLET FILTERS

Intense UV light can kill most microbes. UV lights have to be powered somehow, and that means you need batteries or an external energy source. That makes them less than ideal in a low-tech/no-tech scenario and adds an extra weight and space consideration. An additional drawback is that the water must be fairly clear at the outset.

CHEMICAL TREATMENT

Whether its iodine, chlorine, or other compounds you can add to water to kill the baddies, the biggest downside to these additives is that they add a nasty taste to the water to make it safely potable. They also take some time to work—between half an hour and a full hour. You don't need quarts and quarts of these liquids, so space and weight aren't much of a factor.

HERBAL FIXES

Some plants naturally have antibiotic properties. Some have an alkaloid that can be used to purify water. They contain a substance that neutralizes harmful microbes. Chewing the roots of these plants before and after drinking potentially contaminated water could lower the risk that you'll get sick from drinking it.

That's a lot of "coulds," because Western scientists and researchers have only begun to really tap into the benefits of the five hundred thousand varieties of plants on our planet. I'll explain the connection between what plant and planet sink is in a bit.

In the next chapter, on food, I'll go into the benefits of plants in greater detail. For now, know that, for example, Oregon grape, a shrub found with some regularity in the Pacific Northwest, is one of those edible roots you might ingest when drinking untreated water.

BOILING IS BEST (FOR ME)

I return to this point because, as a low-tech/no-tech practitioner, this is my go-to method most of the time. I bring a metal container that I can place over a fire to boil water before consuming it.

One alternative to placing water over a fire to get it to boil—if you don't have the means to suspend your metal container safely—is to heat rocks in a fire and then place them directly in the water container. Repeat as necessary with other heated rocks to get a good steam and boil going.

Preparing yourself for the right season, the right region, and the right terrain will dictate what you bring, but, as always, the most important things you can carry with you are your knowledge and your experience. Understanding how to source, filter, and purify water when not near readily available lakes, rivers, and streams will give you confidence to go the distance.

 **CHAPTER 9** 

FOOD

Without a doubt, all four of the essential needs—shelter, fire, water, and food—have a physical component. They also have a psychological and emotional aspect. For some people, being warm and dry is more of a mood elevator than having a full belly or a good night's rest. In recent years, we've used the word "hangry" to describe what happens to someone whose blood sugar dips and they undergo a transformation from friendly to fearsome. If we don't eat, just as when we don't drink enough, our ability to function mentally and physically can be affected. Add that emotional component and you get the triad of decreased mental, physical, and emotional depletion. It can produce some very negative consequences for us when in a true survival situation. We can survive for many days without eating. But, in my experience, the satisfaction that comes from procuring a meal through our own devices delivers many different kinds of fulfillment beyond just our physical requirements for energy: the mental and emotional benefits are huge.

THE HIGH-TECH WAY

As with all things survival related, we can take a high-tech approach to meeting our food requirements. As you should know by now, that's not my preferred option, but what works best for you is what really matters. Maybe some of my "distaste" for high-tech foods has to do with my own personal history. Back in the day, when the military's meals ready to eat were an innovation and not an irritation to our bowels, the options were fairly limited. Today, as you likely know, dehydrated meals are abundantly available and offer a lot of variety. The main limitation they possess is that if a foodstuff has been dehydrated, then it needs to be rehydrated in order to be consumed. However, they can be very tasty

and fulfill our nutritional requirements, so I recommend having a couple along in case of emergency. The same is true for the various goos, gels, energy chews, and bars that endurance athletes consume. They can give you a quick shot of needed energy and don't take up much room, but, again, most of them require or come with the recommendation that you take water with them in order to maximize their benefits. If water's abundant, then no problem. When water is limited in availability, then use them advisedly when you feel a case of the "hangries" coming on.

THE NO- AND LOW-TECH WAYS

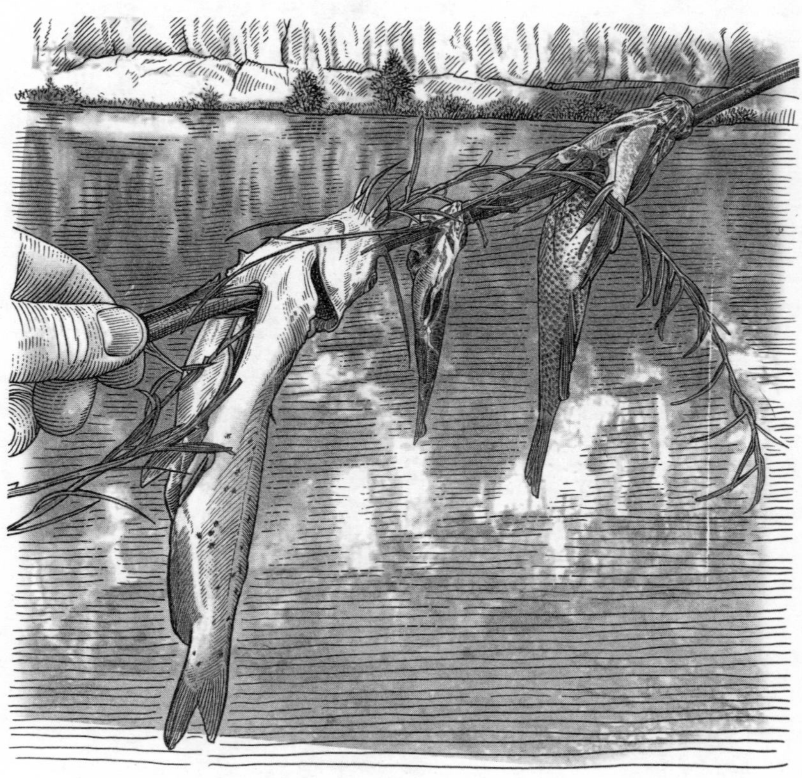

Throughout this book, I've advocated for taking a more no-tech-to-low-tech approach to being out in the wild. I prefer to use those two levels myself when thinking about food. In fact, I sometimes go very old-school in my preparation. I often bring these "staples" along with me: flour, salt, jerky, rendered fat, sugar, dried fruits. With this fairly limited set of carry-along foods, I've been able to meet my nutritional requirements. That means I'm looking at food as nothing more than fuel instead of a highly flavored delicacy to tantalize my palate. When you look at that list above, its reminiscent of pioneer or cowboy days out on the range or the frontier. Those staples feed my imagination as well as my cells.

In this chapter, my goal is to focus on the low-tech end of the scale. The following story will suggest why I enjoy going out and dining primal-style whenever possible.

Two years ago, I was teaching two active-duty Army Special Forces personnel (Green Berets) some important survival skills they wanted to brush up on. We were up at sunrise to check some traps we'd set the afternoon before. An aroma was carried to us on the wind we all recognized: blood and meat. We soon came upon a freshly killed mule deer. Steam rose from the body, emanating from fresh wounds to the neck. I knew instantly that this was a very fresh kill. The mountain lion that took the deer down had to be right nearby. All my senses were suddenly heightened as my adrenal glands pumped out their product. It was like my vision had turned to high-definition TV. I scanned the area, paying particular attention to the tree line less than a hundred yards away. We'd interrupted that big cat's morning meal. It was likely going to do what predators often do when they sense that their cache is threatened: attack. We left quickly.

After we retreated a few hundred yards, I couldn't resist: I told the other two students to go back to our camp and that I would join them in a few minutes. I stealthily made my way back to the kill site. I knew I wasn't acting in the smartest of ways, but the thought of a venison backstrap for lunch was too great a temptation to resist. I belly crawled to a vantage point and sniffed the air again. This time the kill smell came from a different direction. Sure enough, the mountain lion had come back and tugged the mule deer toward the tree line. It had only gone maybe fifteen yards. I scanned again and understood that the feline had gotten a whiff of me and retreated. Before, when it was the three of us, we'd outnumbered that lion and asserted our dominance. Now the killing field was leveled.

I continued to scan and assess and decided to take my chances. I walked slowly down the opposite side of the hill with a slight bend in my knee, eyes alert, ears open, with a small four-inch knife in hand, ready for whatever might emerge from that rocky tree line. My senses, my awareness, and my primal instincts were in full force. I felt alive and energized that the source of our next meal—my tribe's meal—was just a few seconds away.

Once I got to the mule deer, I quickly thrust my knife blade between the shoulders and ran it along the spine toward its tail. I pulled hard and fast on the meat flap, still watching the tree line a few yards away. I implanted my blade a few inches out from my original cut mark and made one parallel cut along the same line of direction toward the tail. I pulled a two-foot piece of meat from the mule deer's back and slowly started to walk backward to the crest of the hill. I never took my eyes off the tree line as I knew I was under observation.

Never in my life have I felt more connected with my primal past. Never in my life have I felt with such certainty that I could be a meal to some other predator. Never in my life have I eaten so wild! I walked back to the camp where my two Green Beret students were waiting patiently. On catching sight of me, they said almost in unison, "Now I've seen it all!" I explained to them that food comes in many forms and their ability to scavenge food from the wilds might be something they would have to rely on one day. In the meantime, we set about getting our fire going again to roast the backstrap. Eating wild is a survival skill that everyone must experience.

HUNTING

I break this food sourcing down into two categories: active and passive.

- active food sourcing: pursuing prey on foot; baiting/calling prey into range to employ a weapons system to harvest the animal
- passive food sourcing: fishing and trapping

Passive hunting may be a bit of a misnomer. You still have to perform a number of tasks in order to catch fish or trap animals. The reason I say that it is passive is because you can build a fish trap, a fish basket, a trotline, or any other kind of fishing tool, then place it in action, leave it in that location, and return later to find out the results. That's not the case with active hunting. You are present during the entirety of the experience that makes up a successful kill or an unsuccessful no kill.

Keep in mind, that while engaged in either active or passive hunting, you should also be on the alert for scavenging opportunities.

FISHING

I'm fortunate that I've been able to spend years perfecting the art of hand fishing. Without any gear at all, I can find the right spot in a stream and grab ahold of fish heading downstream. To me, that's the ideal. I also realize that it's not a practical approach many of my students can take. So, with that in mind, here are some other techniques, tips, and tricks that you can employ.

Funnel trap. This requires nothing but material you have on hand. First, select a site on the stream where natural barriers to a fish's progress already exist: large rocks, fallen trees, etc. Then, using those natural obstacles as a starting point, build an additional obstruction that will prevent fish from moving downstream. Place a log or a series of rocks that will block them and also divert the water toward one bank of the stream or the other. Along the bank, and in the middle of the stream, use rocks and sticks to form a kind of corral from which the fish cannot escape.

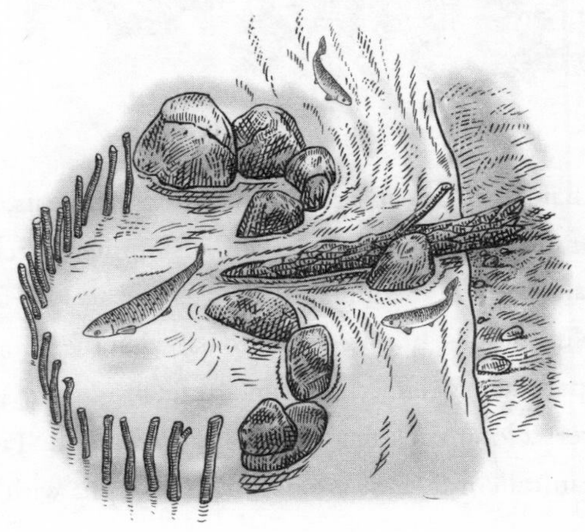

A variation on this is the M funnel fish trap. Using long sticks that you press firmly into the stream's bottom, form the letter *M*. Place them as close together as possible while still allowing the water to flow through it. Leave a gap at the bottom junction where the two diagonal "legs" of the M would come together. That gap should roughly correspond to the size of the fish you believe is in that stream. That gapped portion of the M should be facing upstream.

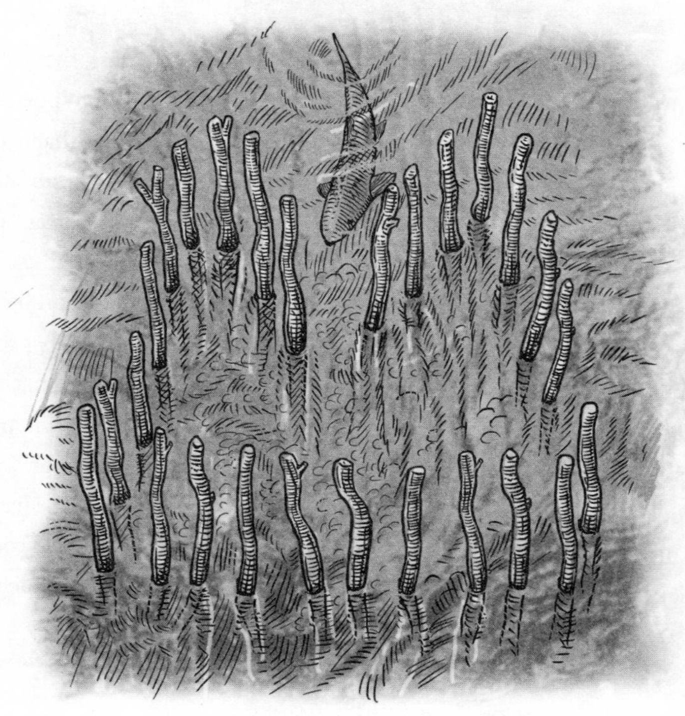

You can add bait—any meat scraps from previous meals, for example. The beauty of the fish trap is that it is self-sustaining. Catch one fish, clean and gut it, and use the inedible portions as bait to lure in the next fish. When possible, animals, like us, prefer to eat what they normally do, so those guts are particularly effective as an attractant.

Trotline. Insert a long stick firmly into the streambed. Tie a line to that stick using natural cordage or what you've brought with you. Pull that line taut as you move away from the first bank toward the second bank. Either secure the line to another stake, to a good-sized branch, or around a rock. Take short lengths of line and attach baited hooks at approximately one-foot intervals along the length of the main line you have laid out.

Basket trap. If you're going to be in one location for a while, you can make this two-piece basket trap while you are sitting in camp. The finished product will look like the image below. Basically, it consists of an outer woven basket and a smaller one that fits inside it. I like to think of this two-part assemblage as a basket and a funnel.

Here are the materials you will need . . .

For the frame:

- five one-inch-thick-by-five-foot lengths of vine, approximately one-half inch to one inch thick
- five sticks a little less than one inch in diameter and as long as the distance from your fingertip to your elbow

For the weave: another length of vine. Depending upon the size of the basket you want to make, the amount of vine you'll need will be greater or less. Somewhere between thirty and sixty feet of vine may be needed.

If you can't source vine, you can use other kinds of cordage: rope or other long, flexible material.

Here's how to assemble the basket:

1. Lay the five sticks on the ground so that they all cross a midpoint and form ten spokes.

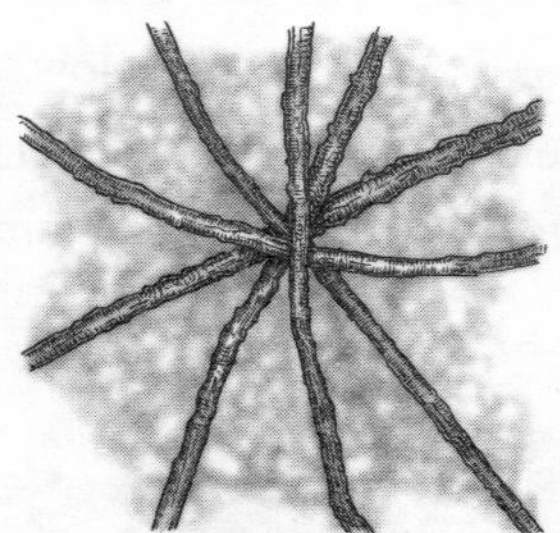

2. Using whatever cordage you have, secure that center by weaving vine, root, or rope around and between each of the spokes.

   Raise each of the ten spokes so they are perpendicular to the ground and the bound bottom rests flat.

   In order to get a proper weave, cut one of the sticks at the "hub" where they all intersect.

In the illustration above, note how there are now nine full spokes and one stub. Also note how the weave goes over and under the sticks.

3. With the bottom of the basket now consisting of those nine full spokes and the one stub, lift and gather each of the full spokes up and secure them temporarily with the vine, root, or cordage material you are using. (For the remainder of this, I will use the term "flexible material" in place of vine, root, or cordage.) To make the frame larger, press down with your hand on the gathering point and tighten the flexible material to the now upright frame. It will look like this:

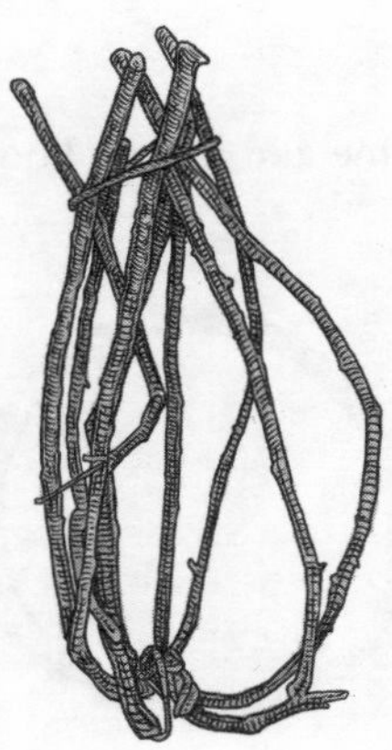

4. Starting at the bottom, weave your flexible material over and under the nine full spokes that form the frame. Continue this weaving process until the basket retains its shape. Untie the top of the basket and finish up the weaving until you have a full cone shape. Below is a partially completed view. Allow six or so inches of the frame spokes to be exposed.

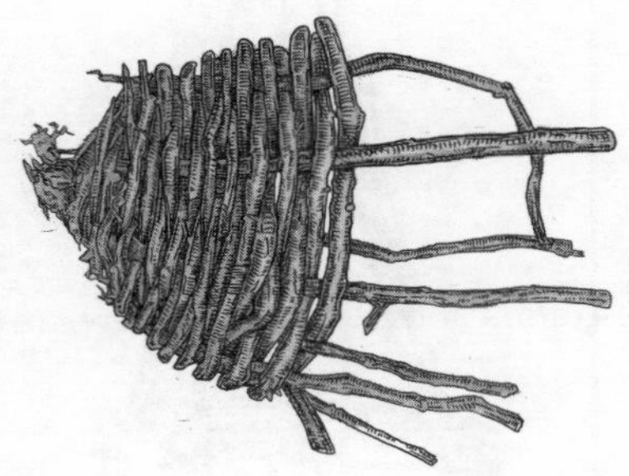

Once the basket is complete, turn your attention to the funnel portion. The funnel fits inside the larger basket, so it has to be smaller: between one-third and one-half the size of the basket. To make the funnel, you will need:

- five short sticks of a length suitable to the above proportions
- approximately one foot of one-inch or narrower vine
- additional flexible material that you used to weave the basket

To create the funnel:

1. Take the section of vine and form a hoop. Use flexible material to secure the ends of it.

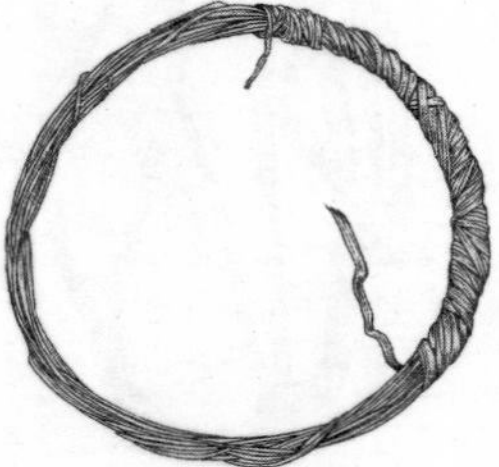

2. Attach the five short sticks to the hoop, securing it with flexible material. With the funnel's wide end now secured, tie the other ends of the sticks together. At this stage, the funnel will look like this:

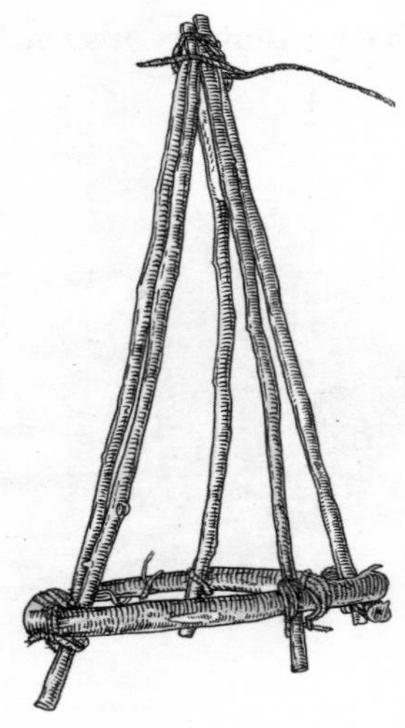

3. Proceed as you did with the basket, using over and under weaving to produce what will look like a smaller version of the basket.

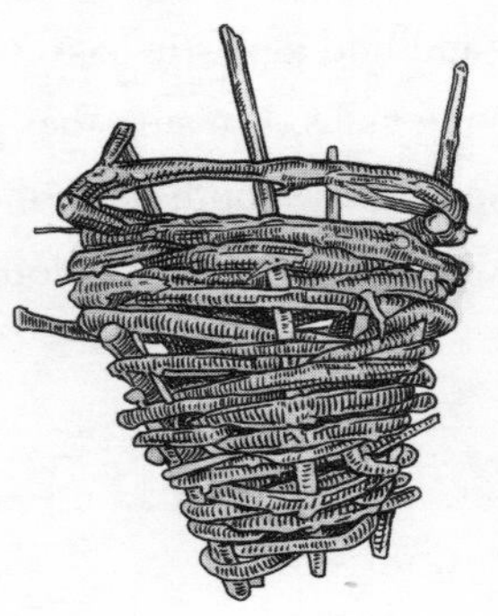

4. Once you have the funnel complete, place it inside the basket. It should fit snugly so that the two pieces won't separate. The objective is to place the basket trap in the water. A fish will swim into it, but it won't be able to turn around and exit it. You will leave the trap in place for a number of days and remove only the funnel portion that contains the trapped fish. You want to avoid having to lift out and re-secure the outer basket. Why is that? The basket trap will be naturally buoyant. You don't want all your efforts to float away, so you have to overcome that buoyancy issue.
5. After you've baited the trap with worm, scraps of meat, or other attractants, use rocks to weight the rear of the trap. Take two sticks and form an X with them through the top of the trap. Once you place the trap in the water, drive those two sticks into the streambed or lake bottom.

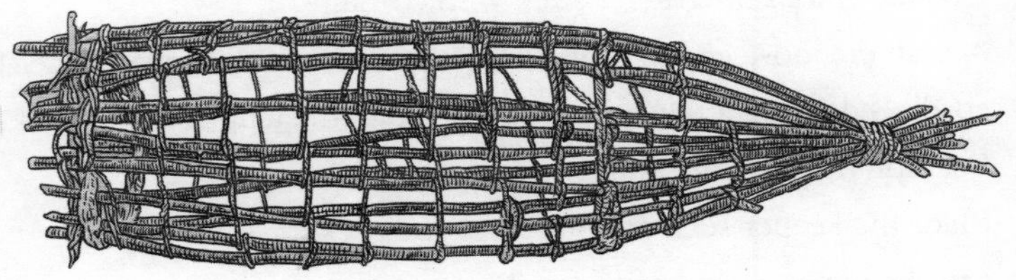

Fish traps are commercially available, of course, but they are cumbersome to carry with you out on a trek. Also, you can make them at home using a plastic basket, but, again, taking one with you is not really ideal. You may be lucky and find a plastic basket while out in the wild. Using your problem-solving skills, I'm sure that you can come up with an improvised basket trap that uses both natural materials like the one I've described here and found materials like a clothes basket.

LAND TRAPS AND SNARES

Capturing and killing small game can provide you with a sufficient amount of meat to keep you going. Two of my favorite methods are low-tech and possibly no-tech (depending upon whether or not you use natural cordage you made or synthetic that you purchased).

THE PEBBLE DEADFALL TRAP

This is about the simplest trap I know of. You will need:

- a large, heavy rock with a flat surface
- one fingertip-to-elbow-length trigger stick
- one three-to-four-inch keeper stick
- a round pebble or stone large enough to support the stick
- bait

To assemble the trap:

1. Tie one end of the trigger stick with cordage.
2. Attach the loose end of that cordage to the shorter keeper stick. The cord needs to be a few inches shorter than the length of the rock.
3. Position the rock on a flat area.
4. Place the keeper stick at one end of the rock.
5. Lift the opposite end of the rock.

6. Pull the cordage and trigger stick toward the lifted end of the rock.
7. Lower the rock onto the untied end of the trigger stick. It may take some time and adjustments to get it to balance.
8. Lift the rock and the trigger stick up and place the pebble underneath the round pebble or stone.
9. Place the bait at the lower end of the rock where the smallest gap is located.

The trap works when a critter comes along to get the bait and trips the cordage so that the trigger stick falls off the pebble and crushes the unsuspecting food source.

THE THREE-STICK SAM SEA TRAP

I learned how to make this one while in Thailand and it remains one of my go-to traps. Like the one above, it requires a minimal number of pieces. This time, instead of using one trigger stick and one keeper, it involves the use of three sticks that form a triangle.

Notch the sticks so that they fit together. Place the bait as you would with the Pebble Deadfall Trap. Instead of tripping the cordage, the animal will displace the bottom leg of the triangle and bring the rock down on itself. Keep in mind that the length of the sticks will determine the angle of the rock and the amount of falling force that will be produced. A shallow angle means less falling force. A steep angle means greater falling force.

THE PAIUTE DEADFALL

Named for a Native American tribe, this one combines some of the elements from the two previous traps: sticks and cordage, along with a falling rock.

As you can see, the cordage is tied at one point and wrapped around a channel carved into the other stick. Also, instead of balancing the rock on the lone upright stick, another stick angles downward from the rock and rests in the crook of the Y at the top of the vertical stick. Just like with the others, the bait is the attractant, and when the animal disturbs the delicate balance of the structure, it causes the rock to fall.

Location, location, location. Siting your traps and snares is essential to your success in low-tech and no-tech hunting. The same is true, really, for high-tech hunting, where even the most powerful weaponry won't be of any use unless you can find game. Larger game tends to follow certain tracks, especially in wooded areas. It's not always possible to spot these game trails easily.

When walking upright, we may miss what an animal moving lower to the ground will see as an open avenue through the trees, for example. If you get down on all fours and look at the scene from that lower perspective, a game trail may reveal itself to you. Place your snares and traps along this route to greatly enhance your chances of success.

Along with game trails, the following will help you determine the best places to set your traps. Anytime you are out in the wild, be on the lookout for:

- water holes and feeding sites
- animal tracks and droppings
- chewed vegetation
- nesting sites
- den holes

Also, always be aware of local, state, and federal guidelines regarding trapping and snaring. When moving to new locations, disarm any traps or snares. Be vigilant about checking your snares and traps regularly. They will often not kill your prey immediately. That raises an ethical issue: you don't want your prey to suffer needlessly. Also, in areas that are somewhat heavily trafficked with hikers and others, a snare or trap may get triggered by someone's dog. I'm frequently out in the bush with my dogs, and their curiosity and seeking needs shouldn't count against them.

SNARE TRAPS

Nearly every snare trap operates on the same basic principle. An animal places its body inside a loop of wire or cordage. Upon doing so, it triggers a release mechanism that frees up cordage that is under tension due to being tied to an engine that will spring back to its upright position. That springing action will pull the cordage tight, drawing the loop around the animal and lifting it off the ground or keeping it trapped.

Rule number one of snare trapping: Don't build the trap in the location where you want to employ it. Why? It will take a bit of time to build the snare, and you don't want to leave your scent where you hope to spring that snare.

The process works like this:

1. Select a site from a distance. Choose a location along a game trail that has young, springy saplings that are about head height.
2. Return to your base camp or move off to a different location far from the snare site. Check your windage and note the direction it is coming from and move upwind.
3. Assemble the trap.
4. Return to the snare site to finalize the trap and put it into action.
5. Retreat to a neutral location (i.e., your base camp or somewhere out of scent range).

GROUND SNARE

I don't have a super-technical name for this one, but I've used it with great success. It is relatively simple to source the three parts for the trap:

- a flexible young branch about two feet in length that can be bent into a U
- a toggle stick approximately six inches in length with one end flattened

- a trigger stick approximately six inches in length sharpened to a kind of flat chisel point

With those pieces prepared and a short length of cordage in your possession, move to the snare location you've previously selected. Be sure to avoid as much as possible brushing against any leaves or other vegetation to prevent leaving your scent behind.

Setting the snare in position:

1. Once you are on-site, select a small sapling and strip the lower branches from it. This sapling will become your spring stick.
2. Toss the branches to the side and then later collect and remove them from that location to avoid contaminating the site with your scent.
3. Bend the spring stick and note where it will come in contact with the ground when bent.
4. Take your U-shaped stake branch and insert it approximately at the point where the sapling made contact with the ground.
5. Make sure the two ends of the U are securely in the ground. Depending upon the type of terrain and the condition of the dirt, three to four inches of buried U stake end should be sufficient.
6. Secure one end of a four-foot length of cordage to the top of the sapling.
7. Approximately six to ten inches from that knot, tie a loop around the center of your toggle stick.
8. Form a loop using approximately one foot from the bottom end of the cordage and tie it off.
9. Insert the trigger stick into the ground centered under the U stake.
10. Place the toggle stick onto the top of the trigger stick as in the image on the next page.
11. Place the looped cordage so that it rests against the U stake.
12. Place bait near the trigger stick.
13. Move away.

When an animal investigates the bait, it will knock the toggle off the top of the toggle stick. Once that is dislodged, it frees the spring stick to

return to its upright position. That, in turn, pulls the cordage up, tightens the loop, and ensnares the animal. It won't die immediately. It's up to you to be vigilant about checking your snares and dispatching the animal to end its suffering.

Most snares employ similar techniques. The mechanical principles are also essentially the same. A sapling for a tree branch must whip up quickly to pull the cordage noose tightly to secure the animal. Snare wire can be used in place of cordage. This may be necessary when going after larger rabbits or snowshoe hares, for instance. In my experience, cordage has worked for most squirrels.

Here is another type of snare you can build:

And here is a hook trigger that you can carve in place of the trigger/toggle stick that I used above:

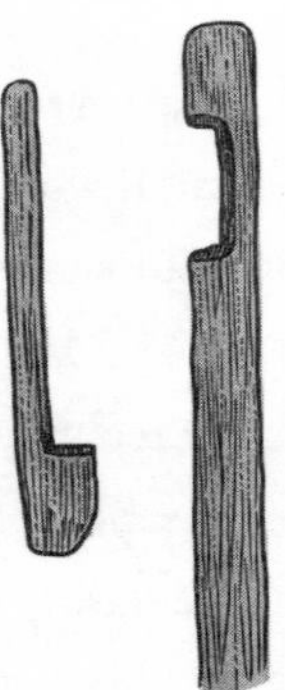

And here it is when in use; the animal will dislodge the hook end from the notch and set the spring engine in motion to tighten the noose:

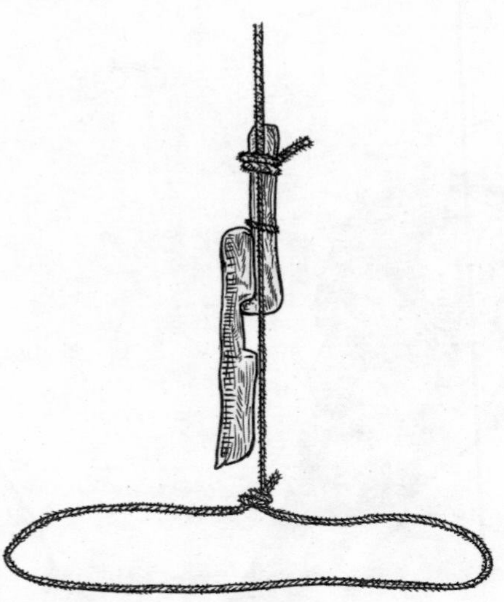

There are a multitude of guidebooks out there that only cover snares and traps. If this brief overview has captured your curiosity, then you've got plenty of other resources to turn to. My advice is to master at least one trap and one snare to add to your collection of skills, knowledge, and abilities.

SCAVENGING

Yes, in that story I told earlier about taking the chunk of meat from that deer, I was scavenging. Scavengers tend to be looked down on in human society. The same is true in the wild: we tend to be in awe of apex predators and denigrate scavengers. It's likely that our primitive ancestors were scavengers before they gathered and hunted, so I don't hold a dim view of scavengers or scavenging. When I scavenged that deer meat, the mountain lion did the hard work. I respected its skills and took only what I really needed, leaving the rest for it and, eventually, other animals to consume. Scavenging is like sharing the wealth. It also allows for very little to go to waste and perpetuates the processes of nature. Technically, a scavenger is an organism that feeds on refuse or carrion: dead and decaying flesh. I don't limit scavenging to consuming carrion. To me, anything that has been discarded or abandoned—even temporarily, as in the case of the mountain lion and its mule deer—qualifies as something to be scavenged. So that means that bird's eggs, beehives with honey, and mounds of insect larvae or eggs are also fair game for me to discover and utilize. This is all about resources and using as many of them as you can to maintain your energy and, therefore, your life.

Compared to hunting and gathering, scavenging is a more passive activity. You often come across something that you can utilize as a food source when you are more actively engaged in gathering or hunting. Coming across an ant mound with delicious larvae to consume is based on chance more than skill. Scavenging also relies more on your knowledge and experience, since toxins can be produced when flesh decays, rendering it harmful when ingested. Since starvation in the wild is an unlikely outcome, the general rule of thumb should be that when in doubt about the safety of what you want to digest, err on the side of caution.

INSECTS AND WORMS

In many parts of the world, insects and worms are consumed regularly. In fact, insects are the most readily available source of protein on earth. They also provide us with healthy concentrations of other life-sustaining nutrients: fat, calcium, phosphorous, omega-3 fatty acids, fiber, iron, zinc, carbohydrates, B vitamins (especially riboflavin), chitin (prebiotic fiber that helps provide nutrients for our gut bacteria), and antioxidants.

The list goes on, but, bottom line, worms and insects are more healthful and provide some nutritional benefits that exceed those in the meats we typically consume.

A Note on Cooking

When out in the field, you're really limited to how you can cook insects and worms. Here are a few safety tips to keep in mind:

- You can certainly eat them raw, but as is true with other foods, they can contain things that are potentially harmful, like bacteria.
- As with water in the wild, the general rule of thumb is to boil insects and worms before consuming them. That way you are reducing the risk of ingesting harmful bacteria.
- After that, heating them in a pan over an open fire is the most likely way you'd cook them. Whatever else you have at hand that you can use—oils, spices, seasonings—will add to that simple cooking method. Essentially, what I can say is that you'll be cooking at its most basic level: adding heat.

SAFELY ENJOYING WHAT NATURE PROVIDES

GRASSHOPPERS AND CRICKETS

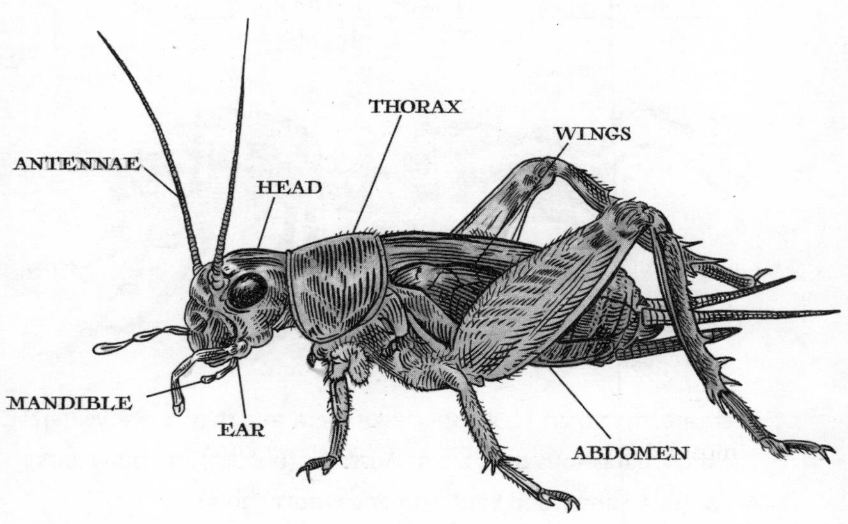

- Many are edible and protein rich. (General rule: the more brightly colored they are, the more likely they may be inedible/unsafe.)
- Some individual grasshoppers and crickets may have worms in their systems that could cause physical distress, so it's best to cook them before eating to destroy the worms.
- They're cold-blooded, so they're at their slowest in the morning, and you can catch them by hand or set down a piece of fabric with a heavy knap. They'll get their legs tangled up a bit in the fibers, and that, too, will slow them down.
- Create a cricket trap by taking a water bottle and placing an attractant inside it: a light source, rotten fruit, etc. Bury the bottle, leaving the top exposed. Leave it for a few hours and you'll discover your catch inside.

- Prepare them by plucking the antennae, legs, and wings (optional) and then cooking the head, thorax, and abdomen.

ANTS

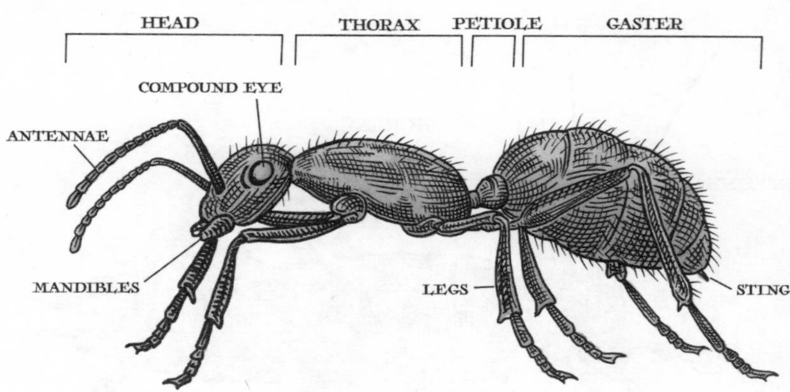

- There are more than 12,500 species of them, and they're everywhere!
- The most dangerous ones are in Australia (bulldog and pony ants), Africa (safari ants), and South America (bullet ants).
- Fire ants in the United States have a very painful sting. They are easily avoidable due to their red color. Here is their range:

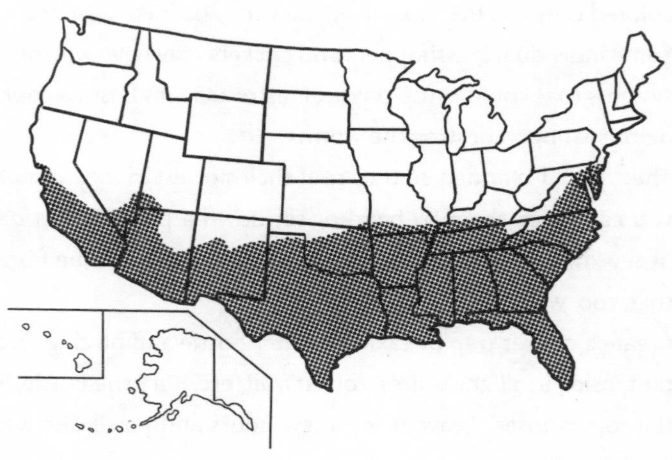

- You can easily gather ants in your hands by poking a stick into their hill: they will crawl up the stick.
- Avoid eating them live, as they can sting you.
- Boil for five to six minutes to neutralize the acid in them.

TERMITES

- Mature adult termites can fly, so they're more difficult to harvest. Other life stages of termites can't fly and are easily found in punky/rotting wood.
- Because they spend most of their time in wood, termites don't pick up as many parasites that they can pass along to you.
- They are best roasted in a dry pan until very crispy.

GRUBS

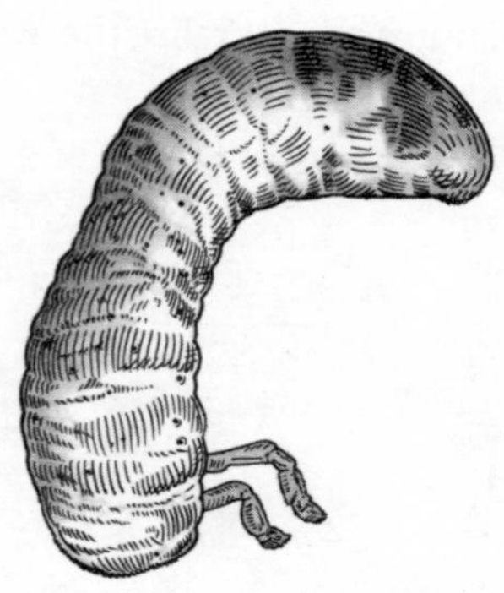

- While you're poking around in a stump, you may come across grubs.
- You can also strip bark from a live tree or look under a rock and beneath leaf piles and harvest grubs from there.
- They're big enough to be skewered and spit roasted over an open flame.

OTHER EDIBLES

- earthworms (Squeeze out their poop before ingesting.)
- scorpions (Cut off the stingers before eating and be sure to cook them to neutralize the venom. Exercise caution in harvesting.)
- aphids (These little guys attach themselves to leaves and are therefore easily sourced. They are best boiled.)

EDIBLE BUT POTENTIALLY DANGEROUS

- slugs and snails (They're served in restaurants, but those are raised under controlled conditions. Slugs and snails are tasty, but they may have eaten things that can harm you. If you must eat them, cook them thoroughly.)

How to Test for Safety

It makes sense to field-test these scavenged goodies before you find yourself in a survival scenario or on a longer outing when you want to go primitive. Just as new gear should be tried out in advance, the same is true for what you put in your body—solid or liquid.

- Cook the food source.
- Eat a tiny sample.
- Wait several hours.
- If there are no issues, then proceed with a larger sample.
- Wait several hours. If there are still no issues, then consume with confidence.

GATHER

By now you can probably predict what I'm about to say. Nature provides all, and in the case of gathering food, you can find an astounding abundance of wild greens, flowers, tubers, barks, fungi, seeds, stems, berries, and fruits to consume. I've seen more than a few survival instructors narrate enormously long lists of medicinal and edible plants that they think their students can retain in their memory. I've also seen students' memory banks fail, at which point they suffered meltdowns when confusion and stress overwhelmed them. All that information flooded out of their brains and did them no real good.

For that reason, I recommend that my students commit to memory, at minimum, eight different plants for the region and the season in which they will be out in the wild. I call these the "straight eight." (If you haven't noticed by now, rhyming makes it easier to memorize lists of things.) So your region and the season and the straight eight will get you started. And those eight plants are just a starting point.

The reason I have you starting with just eight over the course of a full calendar year is because it's important to observe these plants for their full seasonal life cycles. You need to know what a dandelion, for example, looks like early in the season, when a shoot is just coming up and developing, as well as when it begins to grow leaves, flowers, goes to seed, and then dies. In the case of a dandelion, even when it appears desiccated, its roots are edible. Seeing plants as they go through their entire life spans is a must.

Once you've gone out and foraged for those straight eight based on memory during a full cycle of seasons, you can try incorporating a few more, possibly discard others, and develop a second set of straight eights that will be equally great for that region throughout the year.

I always aim to have a straight eight that runs the gamut from plants that you can eat, plants you can use to treat, and plants that can't be beat:

- eat = edible
- treat = medicinal (can combat infections and relieve headaches, diarrhea, vomiting, indigestion, etc.)
- can't be beat = can be used as tools (cordage, sap, resins, tinder)

I usually select my straight eight in a 3:3:2 ratio in the order presented above. That's me. You need to do you, and, as a result, your ratios may look different. You may not want to utilize plants for anything other than food, and that's a fine approach.

So is utilizing field guides that are region-specific or more focused on foraging. I either own or have consulted dozens of field guides that others have written as a way to school myself on what plant life is available where. I scan them in anticipation of my outings and commit to memory the straight eight.

I highly recommend that you do the same, but to give you a leg up on your studies, here are ten plants that can be of nutritional or other value to you in the different regions of the United States:

- **Northwest:** dandelion, seaweed, mustard, stinging nettle, wild rose, burdock, cattail, chickweed, lamb's-quarter, miner's lettuce, mountain sorrel, pineapple weed, sheep sorrel, watercress, bracken, bulrush, wild asparagus
- **Northeast:** dandelion, mustard, wild onion, stinging nettle, purslane, lamb's-quarter, sheep sorrel, acorn, wild lettuce, blueberry, wintergreen, honeysuckle, wood sorrel, chokecherry, Labrador tea, currant
- **Southwest:** agave, prickly pear, mesquite, Mormon tea, dandelion, watercress, dock, miner's lettuce, cattail, cholla bud, sego lily, piñon pine nut, wild onion, purslane, yucca, acorn, sotol
- **Southeast:** dandelion, wild onion, persimmon, arrowhead plant, wild strawberry, Jerusalem artichoke, milkweed, sorrel, pawpaw, blackberry, wild pecan, muscadine, stinging nettle, purslane, pineapple weed, cattail, bulrush
- **Most common across the United States:** dandelion, common burdock, lamb's-quarter, sorrel (various types), plantain, purslane, cattail, bulrush, brambleberry, blueberry, cranberry, chickweed, red clover, garlic mustard, miner's lettuce, stinging nettle

As you can see, there's a lot of regional overlap. I'll begin with a sample straight eight that are the most common across all regions. Again, many fine foraging guidebooks or even experienced individuals can be of great assistance as you familiarize yourself with edible plants to gather.

Dandelion. One of the most recognizable edible plants, ounce for ounce they pack a bunch of nutrients in a small package. They're a better source of nutrients than kale and spinach. You can eat the leaves—a little bitter; the blossoms—much sweeter; and even the roots—roast them and then boil them in water and you've got a natural coffee substitute. They also have medicinal value because of their anti-inflammatory properties.

Common burdock. Notable due to their pink and purple (and sometimes white) disklike florets, they can grow to be three to six feet high. In that way they're like the eager kid in class extending his arm and waving his hand in the air saying, "Pick me!" Sometimes *they* will pick *you*: they have small burrs that will catch on your clothing. They bloom from midsummer to early fall. The tender, lighter-colored parts of the root are best to eat. Discard the darker portion at the bottom. What's left must be boiled for twenty minutes before pan-frying or roasting them. They're a member of the same family as dandelions and have medicinal value as well—as an antibacterial—and also contain many important antioxidants.

Purslane. Many gardeners know this as a weed, but it is a green, leafy vegetable that contains 93 percent water, making it an excellent way to get nutrition and hydration in a two-for-one deal. It grows close to the ground and in dense, spreading patches. The leaves are green and oar-shaped, with small yellow flowers dotting the leaf clusters. Like dandelions, purslane is nutrient dense and can and probably should be eaten raw. Some say that the cooked leaves can have a slimy mouthfeel. Your mileage may vary.

When I'm on a low-tech or no-tech jaunt, I sometimes use purslane to flavor one of my favorite soups. With this basic jerky broth, you can create your own soup from whatever is at hand from the plants listed above and the mushrooms you will learn about below. Remember, be creative! What you will need:

- gear: a small pot or other cooking vessel (lid preferable but optional)
- a heat source: a fire or cookstove

Ingredients:

- jerky
- preprepared rice (or you can make this ahead in the field)
- purslane stems
- water (amount varies with size of your pot)
- juniper berries or other edibles for additional flavor and nutritional value

Preparation:

1. Bring a pot of water to a boil.
2. Cut jerky into bite-size sections.
3. Once water is boiling, add jerky to the pot to rehydrate it. Return water to a boil. Cook until your desired jerky tenderness is reached.
4. Add in the purslane stems. Return water to a boil.
5. Once re-boil is achieved, add in the rice and bring to a boil again.
6. Remove from heat and allow to cool to desired temperature before consuming.

Stinging nettle. These perennial plants grow to three to seven feet tall. As their name implies, five of the six species of this plant have tiny needles on their stems and leaves. When touched, it releases a chemical that produces a stinging sensation. Care should be taken in harvesting them, but once the young plants are soaked or boiled, they can be used for cooking because that irritating chemical is removed. They can also be used to make an herbal tea. If the plants have entered their flowering stage and are either yellow or purple, they should not be ingested. You will also know if they have entered this stage if the leaves have developed gritty particles called cystoliths. Consuming them can cause irritation to the kidneys and the urinary tract.

Brambleberry: A bramble is a shrub-like plant in the rose family of plants. It has thorns and produces fruits like raspberries, blackberries, dewberries, boysenberries, and loganberries. The fruit ripens in late summer, but the stems, shoots, and leaves can also be eaten in the spring.

Chickweed. You may have found that some of these plants have invaded the sanctity of your lawn. They're notable for their stringy stems and small white flowers, which are present throughout the growing season. Chickweed doesn't have a milky sap; it runs clear. It also has hairs growing along the stem, which has an elastic inner section. Chickweed can be consumed raw.

Sorrel. A number of varieties exist and produce flowers of different colors. Their leaves resemble clover, and it's easy to confuse them. (That's okay, really, since clover is also edible.) Wood sorrel is the easiest of the species to identify because the leaves are heart-shaped. It likes shade and can most often be found beneath other plants. It produces a yellow or purple flower and has a lemon-like citrus flavor—whether you consume the flowers or the leaves. They're good to eat raw or cooked.

Lamb's-quarter. This is often found with a white dust-like powder coating the leaves. When moisture is present on the leaves, beads form and run off. The leaves themselves look like the footprints of a goose. Their flowers are very small and green and cluster along the stem and upper branches. They can often be found near water sources such as streams and rivers. When eaten raw, they should be consumed in small quantities, since an acid in them can be toxic. However, cooking rids the plant of this acid.

Mix and match your straight eight, or if you're good to go with the ones listed here, you'll find an abundant food source that nature has provided you free of charge.

MUSHROOMS

As with plants, mushrooms can be bountiful, depending upon the region and the season. Because of the possible toxicity of some species, a thorough study of guidebooks and/or a trusted teacher is a must. What I present here is by no means a comprehensive look at fungi. The seasonal, regional, and geographical variations on what species can be found when and where is so great that I can't provide you with all the information that you will need. Many foraging guidebooks that I have consulted are for a particular region. I choose to consult them because their level of specificity and applicability is the best.

I've seen estimates of more than five thousand wild mushroom species in North America. A little more than a dozen can kill you if ingested. Another approximately five dozen are toxic and can make you sick. When you look at those numbers, it's tempting to think that eating any of them is a relatively low-risk proposition. But all it takes is ingesting one of those seventy or so to ruin your day or end your life.

It is best to stick with the tried-and-true. I've heard some wilderness instructors refer to the "foolproof four." The list of the most common ones in North America includes all of those plus another half dozen. I've placed an asterisk after the foolproof fungi:

- morel*
- oyster
- lion's mane
- chanterelle*
- black trumpet
- giant puffball*
- fairy ring mushroom
- chicken of the woods*
- maitake
- hedgehog mushroom

MUSHROOM STRUCTURE

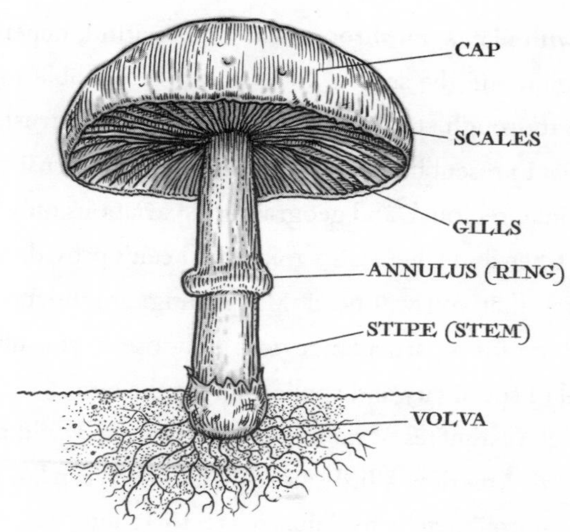

There are four main parts of a mushroom.

The cap sits atop the stalk, and the mycelium are the roots that enable a mushroom to push its way from underground or out of a stump or deadwood. The underside of the cap is important for identification purposes because many caps can look alike; however, depending upon the gills, tubes, spines, or ridges, you will be dealing with very different species with various degrees of edibility/safety.

The gills are lines radiating out from the stem to the end of the cap. The spores look like beard stubble in a sink.

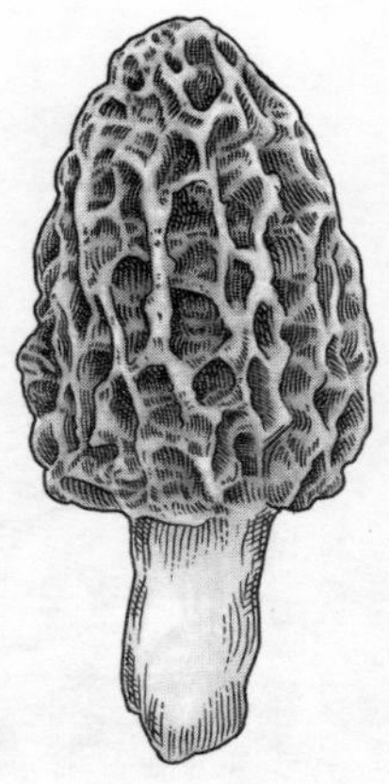

Morel. Among mushroom foragers, morels are one of the real prizes they seek because these mushrooms are so delicious! Their conical shape and honeycomb-like structure makes them easy to identify. They typically grow in wet or damp places among dead leaves in forests. Because of their brown color, however, they can be difficult to spot in their dark haunts among rotting foliage of a similar color. They typically can be found in late spring at most latitudes.

What separates the beginner mushroom harvesters from the veterans is that the latter know to look for other signs of a particular variety of mushroom besides the mushroom itself. These signs are known as "indicator species." Many mushrooms feed on decaying wood, and different tree species alert you that a particular type of mushroom may be growing nearby. Additionally, the presence of certain plants and wildflowers will sometimes indicate that the soil conditions and temperature are prime for a particular mushroom species to pop up.

Oyster mushroom. The oyster mushroom is so named because of its oyster-shell-shaped cap. The mushrooms are white, gray, or tan and have very closely spaced gills running along the undersides of the caps. They grow on or near trees and logs. Because of this, they have very short stems. They appear most often in summer and fall.

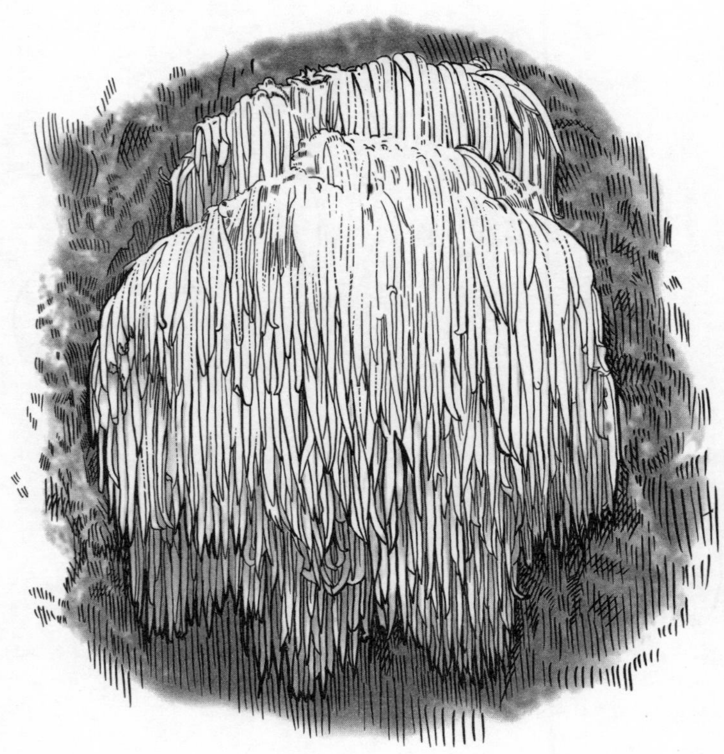

Lion's mane. Its long spine looks like a lion's mane. It grows on hardwood trees and in clumps that add to the mane-like appearance. Many say that it tastes much like lobster. It is also sometimes called the mountain priest mushroom, the bearded tooth mushroom, or the bearded hedgehog mushroom.

Chanterelle. When fully mature, the chanterelle's fluted shape and yellow or white flesh differs from younger ones, whose caps have fewer curls and are flat. Rather than growing out of wood, it springs out of open ground or in forests, often at the bases of trees. It is found mostly in the West and Alaska.

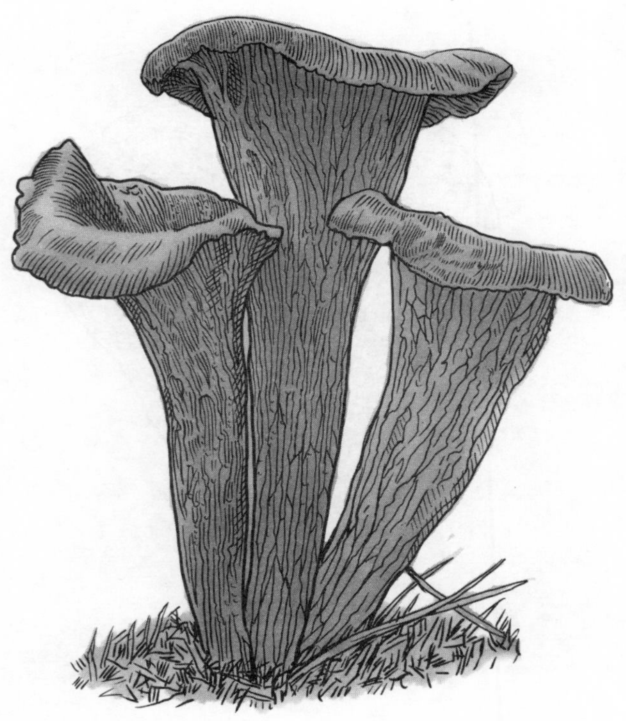

Black trumpet. Also known as the horn of plenty or the horn of death mushroom, the black trumpet does have a horn-shaped cap, and its black color is often associated with death. Most black trumpets are grown in areas populated with hardwood trees. One species grows near pines, but it is far rarer. Like most mushrooms, they grow in moist, shady areas with decay and dead wood. They are also often close to chantarelles. The black trumpet does not have gills; instead, it has fine veins on the underside of the cap and down the shaft.

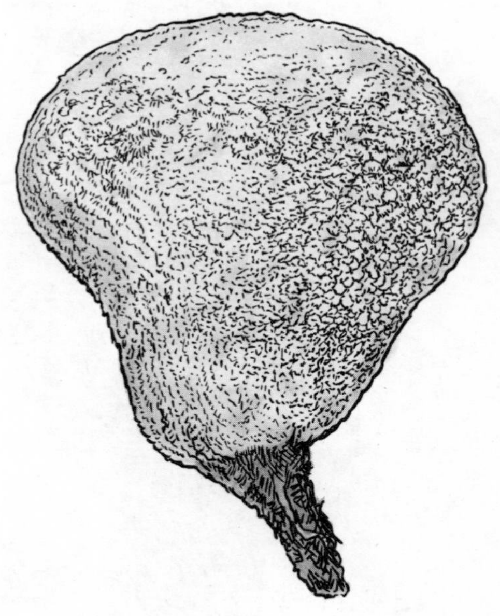

Giant puffball. This large, round mushroom seems to be an exception to the rules. It doesn't have the usual gills, cap, or stem that most mushrooms have. It is white in color and can be as small as a table tennis ball or as large as a volleyball. The largest ones can be nearly as tall as a typical car tire. Some have a smooth appearance, and others have a cracked, almost pineapple-like surface. Though large and easy to spot, the giant puffball is not very flavorful. When fully mature, it emits a cloud of spores when stepped on or kicked.

Fairy ring mushroom. This species has a cap with a knob-like protrusion. It ranges from tan to red-brown and often grows in a rough, circular pattern in grassy areas. It has dirty-white gills and a straight, tough-skinned stem. It is available widely from the start of summer to autumn.

Chicken of the woods. In some places in the country, chicken and waffles is on the breakfast menu; this mushroom resembles pancakes or waffles more than it does chicken. Regardless, this large species and its orange-yellow color makes it easy to spot. (Thus, it's one of the foolproof four.) Whether its meaty, citrusy taste resembles chicken is up for debate, but it is considered a delicacy in many cultures. The caps grow like overlapping shelves, and the bright yellow underside has pores (tiny holes) rather than gills.

Maitake. This species is also known as the hen of the woods. Maitake mushrooms grow at the bases of hardwood trees in late summer through November. They have traditional medicinal uses in Japan and China, where they are used to treat diabetes and hypertension. The maitake is a bracket fungus with a shelf-like growth pattern similar to chicken of the woods. The undersurface of the cap is not gilled but has pores. They also grow from trunks of standing trees and felled ones.

Hedgehog mushroom. Hedgehog mushrooms look much like chanterelles, but turn them over to examine the undersides of the caps, and you will see the feature that distinguishes them. The small spikes are referred to as "teeth." The yellow color of the caps helps them stand out in shady, wooded areas. They grow singly or in pairs, and have a smokier flavor than the chanterelles and their fruity, apricot-like flavor.

Here are a few more recipes you can enjoy using items you've managed to trap and gather.

SQUIRREL TACOS AT HOME

- 4 whole squirrels (feeds 3), gutted, skinned, and with paws removed (To remove paws, pop the joints and cut the tendons. Do not cut the bone or it can wind up in taco meat.)
- 2 cans (12 ounces each) cheap Mexican beer (Only 1½ cans are needed. Drink the rest.)
- 3 garlic cloves, minced
- ½ tablespoon salt
- 3 jalapeño peppers, shredded on cheese grater
- 1 tablespoon ground cumin
- 1 tablespoon paprika
- 1 tablespoon chili powder
- 1 tablespoon cayenne pepper

- corn tortillas, for serving
- shredded cheese, avocado, fresh cilantro, pickled onions, sour cream, and lime juice, for serving

1. Place all ingredients except for the tortillas and serving ingredients in a pot.
2. Place over heat, bring to a low simmer, and cook for 5 to 6 hours.
3. Carefully remove the bones from the squirrels.
4. Return the squirrel meat to the pot and mix with spoon.
5. To serve, use tongs to place the meat on corn tortillas. Add cheese, avocado, cilantro, pickled onions, sour cream, and lime juice to taste.

TROUT IN THE BUSH

Use bark from an old tree as a serving platter and dandelion root as a crunchy side. Pull the roots, wash in water, and start munching.

- 1 trout cleaned with head on (feeds 1 person)
- 1 cup wood sorrel
- ¼ cup wild garlic, crushed between your fingers to expose oils—the more the better
- 1 stick, 2–3 feet long, with a sharpened end (must be green so it doesn't burn)

1. Prepare a coal fire.
2. Stuff the body cavity and mouth of the trout with wood sorrel and crushed garlic.
3. Skewer the trout with the stick through mouth into the meat of the tail.
4. Set the trout 10 to 12 inches over the coals with the trout's dorsal side (back) facing the flames. Feed the flames with small sticks to maintain the heat (no pine or resin-based trees, since they add a nasty taste of turpentine to fish).
5. The trout's skin will darken and the juices will run from it. The trout is ready when the skin slides off or when you peel it off to reveal the clean meat that has been cooked in the juices of the sorrel and garlic.

SMALL-GAME SOUP AT HOME OR IN THE BUSH

Mix and match meats if needed. Marmot is the best-tasting. One marmot feeds three people. Two rabbits feed three people. Three squirrels feed three people. One raccoon feeds three people. Tear and cut the meat into pieces. I like big chunks. You'll need a large pot to hold all the ingredients. If mushrooms are available (lion's mane, oyster, or morel), clean, chop them big, and add to the pot, too.

- 3–4 pounds small-game meat (deboned)
- 1½ cups dandelion tubers/roots or diced carrots
- 2 cans (12 ounces each) beer or stream water (24 ounces)
- 2 cups cubed burdock roots or potatoes
- 1 cup spruce tips

- 1 cup diced wild garlic (This may sound like a lot, but the wild version is very mildly flavored compared to the kind commonly available in grocery stores.)
- 1 tablespoon salt
- 1 tablespoon black pepper (You can substitute 1 cup watercress or pennycress, which will result in milder flavor but is available in the wild.)

1. Prepare a coal fire or other heat source.
2. Combine all the ingredients in a large pot.
3. Set the pot over the heat and simmer until the burdock root is soft, about 90 minutes, stirring occasionally so nothing sticks to the pot. Add water as needed to keep everything covered.
4. Serve and enjoy. (The juice is good!)

CHAPTER 10

THRIVING IN THE OUTDOORS

As important as it is to meet all your physical needs, most of us will never face a situation in which our survival is imminently at risk, and I hope that's the case for you. What I've shared so far will help if you do face those dire circumstances. Even if you never do, I believe that being prepared and able to source shelter, fire, water, and food will greatly enhance your experiences in nature. Many of my most satisfying moments as a human inhabiting this planet have come from mastering skills to help meet my most basic needs while in the wild. I've been to lots of places and have done a lot of things in my life. Even when I leave my Colorado home and go out into a local field or wildlife area and source food or other materials I can use to make tools or other items, I feel a sense of satisfaction that goes beyond anything else I've experienced.

As I've evolved from avid outdoorsman to survival teacher, I've developed a deeper and deeper appreciation for what our ancient hominid ancestors did. Excuse the pun, but they brought so much more to the table than the food that sustained their lives. We may think of them as brutish, animalistic, and primarily driven by an instinctual desire to survive, but that sells them short. They were far more capable than most of us have been taught, and their problem-solving ability, creativity, and curiosity enabled them to become apex predators who thrived in the wild. We have a lot to learn from them.

Today, as a result of all my experiences in the wild, I have a deeper appreciation for and understanding of how they lived. In fact, as much as possible, I try to emulate what it is like to live wild and to possess wild wisdom. My wild wisdom isn't solely the result of my experiences. I've had the pleasure of meeting others who have studied so-called primitive ways, and I've learned a lot from those exchanges. What I love most about what I do out in the wild and as a teacher is that I'm engaged in a lifelong learning process. We really don't "know" all that much about our ancestors and how they survived. We surmise a lot, and that's true even of those who make their living studying ancient peoples.

Along with spending time in the bush and talking with others who have a similar interest to mine, I've been asked to work with members of the departments of anthropology and archaeology at the University of Colorado (CU) Boulder. One of my passions is making primitive tools. Some of what I make are weapons, like the atlatl. It is a premodern tool that assists in spear throwing by extending the length of the lever that is the human arm. I was asked by some folks at CU Boulder to assist them in an experiment to determine the terminal ballistics of Stone Age projectiles. I've been throwing atlatls I've made for more than twenty years. There aren't many of us around who know how to do so effectively. So I guess you could say that I'm really into how primitive people survived and thrived.

The primal urge that I have and that I think on some level most of us have—to be self-reliant and to rise to challenges—is a strong and central psychological need that draws us out into nature. For the most part, in the rest of our daily lives, we don't have to fend for ourselves. Often, rising to the challenge of meeting our basic needs requires little more than just purchasing something. As an advocate for a low-tech means of living in the wild, I'm not one to go out and source the items I need to survive from a store. I frequently engage in forays outdoors to find materials to make the tools and other gear I need. By satisfying that need to count on ourselves—our knowledge, skills, and abilities—we become happier and healthier people.

Along with being able to meet our basic physical needs, it's important to consider other ways that nature can provide for each of us. Thriving in the natural world brings out the best, most authentic self that I can be. It does that by forcing me to be creative and to solve problems using primarily what nature has gifted me.

The level of comfort I experience while out roaming in the wild exceeds any other comfort I've experienced in my life. It's there that I'm in my element, so to speak. In the wild, I do more than just what comes naturally to me—or is instinctual? Over the years, I've continued to master skills and overcome challenges. Now, as a result of refining and adding to my knowledge, skills, and abilities, my way of living primally has become second nature. What I once had to think about, I now frequently do without having to search my internal memory banks or data storage systems. I rely on my wild wisdom and feel a kind of gratification and thrill from employing skills that our ancient ancestors used to survive. It sounds like I've taken a step back, but in ways large and small I feel like I've taken a giant leap forward. I'm healthier physically, mentally, emotionally, and spiritually than I've ever been in my life. Mother Nature provides all, and I've benefited greatly from her generosity. So can you.

CAMPCRAFT

Many of the how-to techniques I've covered in this book fall under the very large heading of "Campcraft." Although I fully advocate for a minimal/primal approach, that doesn't mean I encourage you to go out and be as miserable as you possibly can be—quite the opposite, in fact. Making your stay in the wild more comfortable is why you will employ most of the creativity I encourage you to use outdoors. Instead of merely surviving, I believe that it is possible to thrive and actively enjoy making your experience more pleasant. That's what "thrival" is all about.

Also, consider this. When you're out in the wild, you'll experience quite a bit of downtime. You won't be able to fill those idle hours using electronic devices. So, for me, I can't think of a better way to be engaged in the outdoor experience than practicing various types of campcraft to increase your level of comfort and enjoyment.

Again, you likely don't think about our human ancestors "enjoying" their lives. You may think that it was a 24/7 battle for survival. That wasn't the case, and more and more we're coming to understand their desire to express themselves creatively and produce creature comforts.

Neanderthal artists likely engaged in other artistic endeavors than the cave paintings that date back to twenty thousand years before human arrival in Europe. It makes sense that we are reconnecting with a primal urge to make by engaging in campcraft.

While the main focus of this book has been on sharing my wild wisdom, much of it can extend into the rest of your life. I've developed such an appreciation for ancient ways of living that I incorporate some of these activities into my daily routine when at home between forays into the wild. That's particularly true of flint knapping. Many of the campcraft products you create in the wild can also be done at home once you source the materials. (Be sure to check on the regulations in the areas you explore with respect to taking natural resources.) While a dose of the great outdoors every once in a while is beneficial, bringing the wild indoors and into as many aspects of your life as possible has even greater benefits. By practicing campcraft at home, you don't have to travel far to get away and experience a different way of being.

If I haven't been out in the wild for a while, I start to feel edgy and restless. Shaping a stone cutting tool out in the workshop helps take the edge off. Yes, most campcraft activities are practical, but being in a good state of mind and maintaining it is necessary both in the wild and at home. Surviving is just as much a mental practice as it is a physical one. Conserving your mental and physical energy will greatly enhance your chances of survival and enrich your experience in the wild. You want to make it out of the wilderness and back to safety as well as succeed while out in the wild. The more you can do to ease your burden and occupy your mind, the better off you will be.

I've talked with many people who have wound up lost in the wild or who chose to go deep into it. For them, nighttime was the most difficult, especially if they weren't able to start a fire. Negative thoughts and critters and insects tend to creep in when the sun goes down. Having something to do in the long hours until sunrise, in addition to sleeping, can ease some of those worries as well as make it easier to perform your survival tasks: sourcing food, water, and shelter-making materials.

For me, one of the simplest-to-make but most useful camp-craft items is cordage. I've spent hundreds and hundreds of hours sitting around a fire or in a cave, making cordage out of plant fibers. I've gotten to the point where I can do it with my eyes closed or otherwise in complete darkness. You should aim to be able to do the same and maintain a similar level of competence and dexterity in low or no light.

When I instruct students in how to make cordage, I stress that they learn the technique first and then experiment using different fibrous materials: method first and material later. Depending on the area you live in, you'll have access to different materials you can use, but the same technique should work with just about anything.

1. Gather fibrous material. Vines, roots, bark are the most common.
2. Straighten the length of material and hold a short section (three to four inches) between the thumb and forefinger of each hand.
3. Use your nondominant hand to hold the cordage securely.
4. With your dominant hand, twist the piece of cordage using your thumb in the direction of your body—to the left. (Imagine the gesture that people make with their forefinger and thumb to signify cash.)

5. Once the material rolls over and forms a tight loop, stop. You've now created the top of your cordage, which consists of the loop and two strands coming off it.
6. Grasp the loop between the thumb and forefinger of your nondominant hand.
7. With your dominant hand, repeat the twisting motion from step 4 to tighten the fibers.
8. Roll the other strand over the top of the one you've just twisted.
9. Alternate using the dominant hand and then the nondominant hand, twisting each strand and rolling it over the other strand. (If you are right-handed, that means alternating the left twist and the right twist. If you are left-handed, that means alternating the right twist and then the left twist.)
10. Repeat the process until you've used up the remainder of the material.
11. The final product should resemble the twists that you are familiar with seeing in ropes or twine.

Again, this is a skill that you can easily practice at home and get to the point where this becomes a part of your KSA toolkit, which you can take with you out in the wild every time.

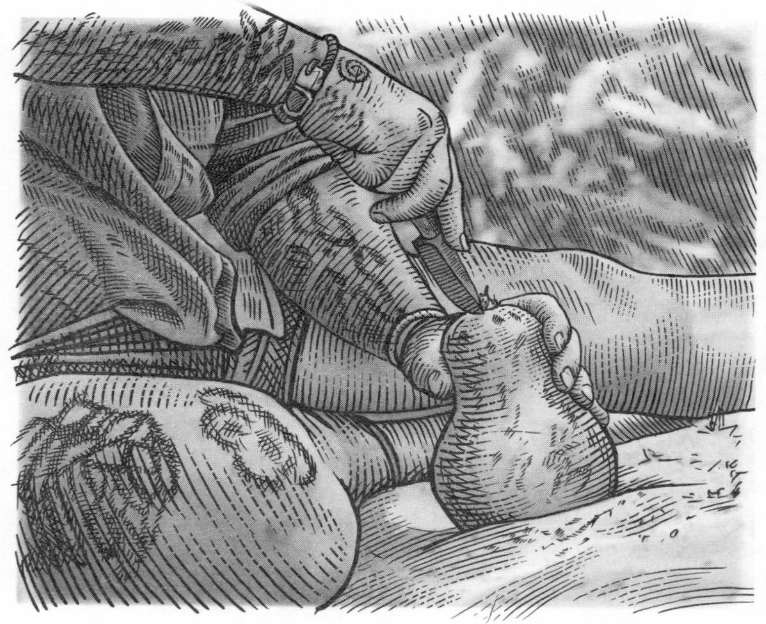

Out in nature, you'll frequently need containers to hold things. When foraging for mushrooms, insects, worms, or even water, those vessels will be invaluable. You can gather more and carry more if you have some kind of container to carry what you find. Vessels also offer you an opportunity to get creative and make them more decorative if you so desire.

Among the types of vessels I've made or adapted for use are:

- bush buckets
- pack baskets
- storage baskets
- skulls
- shells
- bowls
- wooden bottles
- horns
- bark containers
- pots

Carrying things is essential when you are mobile in the wild. Along with vessels, I've made packs, pack frames, storage bags, waist wraps, and carry slings. Easing your carry burden will make moving along less of a pain. So will being as well fed as possible and preparing your food efficiently and well.

Along with crafting items to help make you more easily mobile, other items can help you gather, hunt, or consume food. I break these items down into the following groups:

- weapons: rabbit sticks, spears, atlatl, stone sling, archery set
- traps: deadfall traps, spring pole traps, swinging traps, pit traps
- nets: fish netting, trap netting, storage netting
- "kitchen" gadgets: pot hangers, skewers, spoons, forks, ovens, meat smokers

Your quality of wildlife will also improve if you don't have to hunt as frequently. That means preserving the food items you've gathered or hunted for as long as possible:

- food preservation: hot smoker, cold smoker, bush refrigerator, quick root cellar.

An open fire doesn't have to be your only source of light or heat or protection. I've made the following to provide me with those three comforts:

- light: torches, beeswax candles, rendered-fat lanterns, fat candles, oil lanterns
- heat for cooking as well as warmth: hot smokers
- protection: clothing: sandals, buckskin clothes, breechcloths, shirts, ponchos, hats

As much as I advocate for grounding to the earth, spending all your time in contact with the ground can be painful. For that reason, during my camp-crafting time, I've made:

- bedding: mats, blankets, pillows, nests
- lounging: beds, chairs, stools

While in the bush, I carry a minimum number of tools and supplies to utilize raw materials fashioned from what's at hand. That means that I make my own:

- cordage: reverse-wrapped two-ply cordage, sinew process, bark cordage, roots, vines
- adhesives: pine pitch glue, hide glue, sap stickers

- tools: made from stone, bone, or wood
- cleaning supplies: soaps, brushes, washes, combs, sanitizers, cleansers

I normally go out in the bush on my own or with my dog, but as long as his keen sense of smell isn't offended by my stink, I'm usually okay with a suspension of hygiene protocols—to a point. I am capable of, and have made—and have put to good use—soap from rainwater, the silty, fully burned ash from my fire, and animal fat rendered from my cooked meat. The ash is actually lye. It is a metal-based compound that is a natural antibacterial. I pour boiling water into a vessel I've made that contains ash to make a thick slurry. I allow that to rest overnight and add melted animal fat poured through fabric and only allow the liquid into the mix. Add just enough fat to thicken the mixture, then allow it to set for a few days, and you've got soap.

IT'S NOT JUST ABOUT ELEMENTAL SURVIVAL

I mentioned earlier that not every bit of campcraft you engage in needs to have a practical benefit. As our early human ancestors did, I like to engage my creative side while out in the wild. I produce and use paints, dyes, and brushes to decorate some of the things I make or otherwise express my creativity. The same is true for fashioning musical instruments. I may not be the best musician, but I'm an enthusiastic one, and I enjoy making and playing drums, flutes, and whistles much like our so-called caveman predecessors did. We don't have any record of who the Mozart of the early humans was, but I'm sure talent levels varied then just as they do today.

STONES AREN'T JUST FOR ROLLING

I spend many hours engaged in the lithic arts. The word "lithic" comes from the Greek word *líthos*, or stone. I engage primarily in flint knapping, which is the process of taking stone cobble or antler billet and striking a piece of high-silicate stone to create a conchoidal fracture. Remember shooting a window with a BB gun when you were young and getting grounded for a month? The ninety-degree cone that's produced when the BB strikes the glass is the same ninety-degree cone a flintknapper will produce when striking the stone.

I use repetitive strikes with hard hammer stones or soft antler billets to perform lithic reduction—the removal of stone material—to systematically reduce the target stone's thickness and establish a desired shape. The end shape can be anything from a small arrow point to a stone knife, a stone scraper, a burin, a spear point, an adze, an axe head, or even a stone drill.

A general rule of thumb to determine the suitability of stone for knapping is that, when tapped lightly with a smaller rock, the material produces a higher-pitched tone or ring. Additionally, the stone's interior will have a waxy, glassy, smooth finish that's free from inclusions; for the most part, it will break like glass.

The tools one needs to flint knap are simple. I use items sourced from the land: antlers for soft hammer percussion and river cobbles ranging from golf ball to softball size for harder strikes. These basic tools are abundant and easily sourced from nature, and are the same tools our ancestors have used for nearly three million years.

A FINAL REMINDER

I began by stating that curiosity is your exploratory guiding principle. I wonder. I wander. And as you do your own roaming, you need to employ your essential critical thinking skills—observing, comparing/contrasting, classifying and dividing, and analyzing—to experience and use to your advantage the various phenomena around you. To meet your four basic needs—shelter, fire, water, and food—you're going to have to do a lot of problem-solving and rely on your creativity to find solutions.

Because I believe in the know-more-and-carry-less approach, I encourage you to place more in your brain and your mind than in your pack. As you move from a high-tech to a low-tech to a no-tech methodology, you're going to find that your problem-solving ability and creativity will be exercised and refined to a greater and greater degree each time you go out in the wild. Nature will provide you with all the basic resources you will need to survive and to thrive. How you choose to use those resources is another function of your curiosity and creativity. If you let those two forces loose in your outdoor life—and hopefully in the other areas of your life as well—you will thrive. As a species and as individuals, we wouldn't have advanced as far as we have if we hadn't asked over and over in one form or another this basic question: *I wonder if*. . . I've seen lots of depictions of early humans and, rather than reading a mute, unthinking approach in their facial expression, what I see is an active intelligence speculating, wondering, and working out solutions. They left behind a legacy that we can tap into, and I believe that we can add to that legacy by literally and figuratively relying on our own devices: our problem-solving capacity and the tools we make.

JUST DO IT

I went out into the wild well before I had gained much knowledge about survival. I know the slogan "Just do it" is from an old campaign that an athletic footwear giant made famous, but it also describes some of the ways I have been able to thrive in nature. Early on in my explorations, I just did what felt right. I didn't always have names for the things I tried. I didn't examine case studies of those who had gone out into the wild before me. I just did it. I make no claim that I pioneered some of these concepts and practices. My ignorance and not my innovativeness were primarily responsible for me learning the names of things I'd done after I'd done them.

When it comes to forest bathing, I later learned that others had done it long before me and given those actions a name.

Long after I'd just done it, I read a post describing the forest-bathing concept. I learned that in Japanese it is known as *shinrin-yoku* or "taking in the forest atmosphere." *Shinrin-yoku* is a traditional form of healing and preventive health care for many people in Japan. Many city dwellers and those who live in the woods spend time in the forest. I employed this concept unintentionally at first, since I was always outside and felt inspired to take certain actions and behave in certain ways when there. I later adopted *shinrin-yoku* practices and modified them to suit my own circumstances and needs. Call it scavenging or taking advantage of what Mother Nature has to offer, but making forest bathing my own felt deeply satisfying.

The basic concepts of forest bathing are pretty simple. Find and visit a forest or natural area. Slowly move among the trees, breathing in the air, listening to the sounds, feeling the elements, and achieving a relaxed state. Another way to forest bathe (and my preference) is to simply find a spot in the forest, sit, stand, or lie on the ground, have some parts of your skin touch the natural environment, and ground yourself to the earth. Breathe slowly, eliminate movement, listen to the sounds around you, feel the natural occurrences (air, rain, sun, wind, etc.), and relax. Don't impose a time limit on yourself. This isn't like an exercise routine in the gym where you have a certain number of sets and repetitions to do. You aren't going to be scored on your performance. Letting go of as many thoughts as possible is an essential element of the practice. The idea is to establish as direct a connection as possible with the forest as you can.

You also don't need any specialized gear. You don't have to perform a prescribed set of movements. You empty your mind as much as possible and simply exist in the woods and become a part of the natural environment. As far as we know, trees, plants, flowers, and most everything in the natural world doesn't consciously consider past and future. I much admire my dogs, as do many owners admire theirs, for their ability to exist in the moment. That's the kind of state you hope to achieve while in the forest.

I experienced firsthand the healing benefits of forest bathing after I had my heart attack. Among them were:

- a sense of happiness
- fulfillment
- increased energy
- improved mood
- reduction of stress
- an overall feeling of connection to the land

I engaged in forest bathing routinely, but with a twist: I would add the naturally occurring conditions of the time to my forest bath, if you will. If it was raining, I forest bathed in the rain, or even the snow. Whatever the weather and environmental factors were that day, I embraced it as the natural state of existence. Routinely, I found myself lying on the ground on my back, half-naked, eyes closed, just taking it all in—the sights, smells, sounds, and touch of everything around me.

I would sit high above on a cliff, inside a cave, covered in mud, sunburned, dehydrated, and even in an ice-cold stream. Yes, my method was different from traditional forest bathing, but it was my way, and I felt better every time I did a version of it. Forest bathing, whether in the more traditional sense or my personal version of it, is the first step some people can take to invoke their primal past and rejoin the natural world.

I recommend that people go out in the natural world and just be. Be there for yourself and nobody else. Spend time connecting to the world around you, and you may discover a side of you that has been long lost or find new aspects of yourself. Embrace that new or long-lost side of you and your world could change entirely.

STAY GROUNDED

Like forest bathing, grounding (sometimes called earthing) is a way to establish or reinforce our physical connection to the earth. In this case, grounding creates an electrical connection. The earth is like a giant battery and has some natural electrical elements that our body can benefit from. I'm not a scientist and can't give you all the technical concepts behind grounding, but I can tell you what it did for me during my recovery from my heart attack and what it does for me today.

I'm not one to wear shoes if I don't have to. When I do, I prefer moccasins, leather sandals, or a hiking-type shoe. Social protocol dictates that I must wear footwear at certain times—attending my kids' fifth-grade spelling bees, in airports, at jury duty and local establishments—but when I'm in the mountains, woods, jungles, or any part of this wild world, no shoes. I have been doing this for some time now and can tell you that when I'm "free-toeing," I feel awesome, energized, and focused. I run barefoot, I go out into the wilderness barefoot, I hunt barefoot, and I do pretty much everything barefoot.

Grounding for me during my heart attack recovery restored my physical balance, helped me sleep deeper, gave me more energy, and helped me make a more substantial spiritual connection to our ancient past. Grounding in all actuality is a catchy and hip name for something we have always done. We are not born with shoes on, so why do we wear them? Our ancestors in harsher climates needed foot protection from extreme exposure and developed footwear but still walked barefoot as much as possible. From a protection standpoint, footwear is beneficial, but it can also limit mobility and the wearer's connection to the earth.

At first, I didn't know how grounding worked. But after spending a lot of time barefoot or with minimal footwear that promoted greater contact with the ground, I felt better. I slept better. I gained strength. My stress level fell, and I was centered. It could be that most of my grounding takes place in the woods, but even at home I had the same results. Give it a shot! All you have to do is pop those shoes off, walk barefoot across the earth, and see what happens.

My intent has been to provide you with many answers to your questions about how to survive and thrive in the wild. I also hope that I'll spark many other questions and you'll go out into the wild to find your own answers and devise solutions that work best for you and how your brain works. My wish for you is that you'll take the opportunity to refine my tips and techniques with your own unique approaches to creatively solve the problems you encounter. Your curiosity and creativity will greatly enhance your experience in the wild. And whether through word of mouth or otherwise, I hope you'll add your own tips, tricks, and techniques to the body of wild wisdom that I'm just one contributor to.

That sense of being part of a larger group of people who appreciate our shared ancient and contemporary methods of survival is one of the great joys I experience in my life. As I've said many times to many people, I have my way, but that is not *the* way. More than anything, in sharing my wild wisdom, I believe I've set you on a path that will allow you to find your own way.

INDEX

Note: Italic page numbers refer to illustrations and tables.

R

U

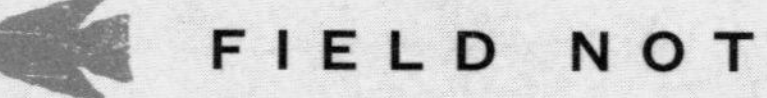

FIELD NOTES